Cultures of the Curatorial

Hospitality

Hosting Relations in Exhibitions

Beatrice von Bismarck, Benjamin Meyer-Krahmer (eds.)

Sternberg Press

7 Introduction

Beatrice von Bismarck, Benjamin Meyer-Krahmer

I. Hospitable Ethics / Ethics of Hospitality

19 Curatorial Hospitality?

Ruth Sonderegger

27 Remarks on the End of Hostilities

Dieter Roelstraete

37 "As If" We Came Together to Care

Andrea Fraser

II. Hosting and Guest-ing

51 Hospitality: What Kind of Support Do Curators Require from the Institutions Who Hire Them?

Alice Creischer, Andreas Siekmann

59 A Toast

Anthony Huberman

63 Art, Exhibition, and Hospitality

Thomas Locher in Conversation with Beatrice von Bismarck

79 Competing Agencies: From Host to Guest to Parasite; A Case Study of unitednationsplaza

Wiebke Gronemeyer

III. Gift and Visibility / The Gift of Visibility

101 Showing Showing: Louise Lawler and the Art of Curatorial Hospitality

Beatrice von Bismarck

117 It's The End Of Hospitality As We Know It (And I Feel Fine)

Lorenzo Fusi

123 Hosting Significant Others: Autobiographies as Exhibitions of Co-Authority

Nanne Buurman

151 Hospitality Exhibited: Rirkrit Tiravanija's *untitled 1994 (meet tim & burkhard)*

Jörn Schafaff

IV. Asymmetrical Gatherings / Encounters and Asymmetries

169 Pertaining Asymmetry

Erik Hagoort

187 Invitation to my ~~Studio~~ *in* the Libertarian Inter-esse

Stefan Römer

203 The (Un)spoken Abuse: Curatorial Hospitality through the Lens of Criticality

Maja Ćirić

Beatrice von Bismarck, Benjamin Meyer-Krahmer

Introduction

A curatorial situation is always one of hospitality. It implies invitations—to artists, artworks, curators, audiences, and institutions; it receives, welcomes, and temporarily brings people and objects together, some of which have left their habitual surroundings and find themselves in the process of relocation in the sense of being a guest. Thus the curatorial situation provides both the time and the space for encounter between entities unfamiliar with one another. It offers resources to satisfy very different kinds of needs, gives material and physical support but also responds to a need for recognition, respect, or attention. Finally, and very importantly, it operates with the aporia between unconditionality and regulated conditionality that is inherent to all thinking around hospitality: between an unconditional welcoming and acceptance of the other on the one hand (accommodating anything and everything that is on the move and interested in accepting hospitality) and, on the other, the marginalizations and exclusions legitimized through various rules and regulations in the field.[1]

Viewed from the perspective of hospitality, the curatorial can be discussed in analogy to the current socio-political situation. It reflects key topics evoked in discussions concerning the current migrant situation: the conditions along the borders and accommodations for refugees, including issues of de-contextualization, displacement, and rootlessness, encounters with the foreign and foreign people, the satisfaction of basic human needs, and processes of access restriction, inclusion, and exclusion. The goal of this publication is to shed light on the socio-political relevance of curatorial hospitality within this analogous relationship. Drawing first on the eponymous conference held at the Hochschule für Grafik und Buchkunst (HGB) / Academy of Fine Arts Leipzig,[2] the publication is composed of contributions exploring the question of how the curatorial can contribute to the urgent discussion surrounding hospitality in the face of the current refugee crisis.

The discussion within the curatorial field can begin with what have until now been rather scattered arts initiatives at the level of art institutions. On the one hand, we find hospitality used in the context of marketing-strategic welcoming practices, the primary purpose of which is to secure both broader and more diverse audiences and the tourism-promotion opportunities they present. Yet the concept of hospitable reception is also finding its way into institutional practices, even beyond its commercial usefulness. Charles Esche's commitment to a migration-sensitive museum practice—which he has emphasized in a number of different contexts—stresses hospitality as a guiding principle and is a tried-and-true example of a long-term strategy for enabling hospitable situations beyond the ad hoc reflex that guarantees refugees free admission to museums and exhibition spaces.[3] Part of this is an understanding of the exhibition as a site of participatory encounter as practiced and defined by curators Maria Lind, the collective What How & For Whom, or (in the theater context) Matthias Lilienthal. What's more, food and eating—the "materialization of 'being a guest'"[4]—are often used as a hook in artworks exploring the notion of hospitality, and such works have featured prominently in exhibition programs in recent years.[5] Within this context not only the ambivalence of the gift with its associated social demand for reciprocity, but also the consumerist perception of hospitality are made subjects of critical discussions, however, not infrequently they are also being used in affirmative ways.

Until now, neither artistic nor institutional practice has considered the unique potentialities that the curatorial, with its hospitable structure, could bring to the discourse and the socio-political practice of hospitality. This is where *Hospitality—Hosting Relations in Exhibitions* comes in. How can thinking of the curatorial in terms of hospitality be used to critically analyze the parameters of curatorial practice, and thus lend insight into its socio-political relevance in particular? From this perspective, and besides the aforementioned art institutional and artistic approaches, the question of the curatorial-hospitality relationship is expanded in three different ways: as an immanent ethical question, the task is first to take up and further develop the set of questions surrounding curatorial ethics, as has recently been discussed, and to develop it further from the perspective of hospitality.[6] Second, sociological, anthropological, and philosophical discourse surrounding gifts and giving offers points of reference for an analysis of what the curatorial offers to create hospitableness in the first place. Third, and finally, no discussion of the specific characteristics of curatorial hospitality would be complete without the question of the inherent responsibility attributed to it, and that it accepts.

The at first fundamentally positive connotations that hospitality conjures—also in the curatorial field (where it appears to stand mostly for a position of generosity that takes the interests of audiences, artists, and works as guests into consideration, and dissolves in these same interests)—stem from an idea of unconditional hospitality of the kind Jacques Derrida calls for in *Of Hospitality*. Here, we find an update of the open concept of accommodating all those who travel. Understood as an anthropological, fundamental right, this concept persisted into the Middle Ages, although laws redefining hospitality in the sense of alien's or foreigner's law emerged as early as antiquity.[7] This increasingly restrictive, nation-regulated right to hospitality led to the "birth of the foreigner" and, at the same time, to the "dismissal/deportation" of the guest.[8] This negatively connoted understanding of a legally mandated hospitality (in terms of "exclusion") draws its legitimacy mostly from the guest's intangibility. This touches on the temporary circumstances of the guest, who, in order to be a guest, is only present and allowed to be present for a limited time. The temporariness, transience, and fleetingness that characterize hospitality designate the guest as something unfixable in time and space. It is this moment of the ungraspable that makes the encounter with the guest uncanny, and triggers the impulse for regulation and control.[9]

Consequently, power effects have pervaded hospitality since no later than the dawn of modernity. They are largely aimed at the allocation of resources to, or defining the identity and status of, those considered to be "guests." In the curatorial field, intangibility and the control efforts it triggers—from restriction to assimilation—apply not only to people, but also to objects. Understood as a practice that brings people, things, spaces, and discourses together and into the public,[10] the curatorial accommodates and hosts not only human actors but also artworks, artifacts, and display objects. In the expanded environment, these "guests" might also include objects that are only temporarily incorporated into the curatorial situation, having been introduced by other participants such as visitors, for example, or through another kind of interim use set-up, such as meals or an accompanying program of events. The means and processes of allocation and defining used to encounter the intangibility of the mobile and transitory cast activities traditionally associated with the curatorial in a different light: viewed in the context of hospitality, the acts of selecting, collecting, organizing, preserving, and mediating more manifestly reveal their ambivalence between care and custody on the one hand and classification into existing value systems (and thus alienation) on the other. Analogous to the socio-political context, acts of naming and identifying, categorization, ordering, and assessment exemplify forms of subjugation to existing criteria and standards, and thus form the basis for both hierarchization and exclusion.

Accordingly, these acts also form the basis for allocating space—the key resource for hospitality.[11] Having space, or the opportunity to take up space, refers in the first instance to a physical place that, in the context of the curatorial, can mean public space as much as art institutional space. But beyond that, and far more comprehensively, "space" in the context of hospitality refers to an openness towards the guest that includes the social, physical, and political areas of action and, quite fundamentally, the realm of thinking.[12] Giving the guest "space" is a determinant for the qualitative and quantitative allocation of those other resources (time, finances, or materials) that are required for a temporary stay and allow the guests to appear, with the resultant forms of encounter, communication, exchange, and mediation between all participants in the curatorial situation.

The particular position of making these allocations—who they accept or how they can reject, who they benefit and which benefits are at stake for each individual involved in the curatorial-hospitality situation—is best understood in terms of the paradoxical logic of giving. To the extent that the thinking around giving is tied to reciprocity in the anthropological and sociological tradition, hospitable openness toward the guest is also in a compensatory relationship.[13] In this sense, the giving of space creates a social obligation or commitment, which is manifested in a mutual exchange defined by rules.[14] For the curatorial field, this functionalization of giving as part of an exchange economy points to the fact that hospitality also entails opportunities for hosts, not only in terms of guaranteeing the existence and survival, respect and appreciation of the guest, but also of stabilizing the host socially and financially, of gaining prestige and status. Both curators and art institutions find that extending invitations and making one's own house available for the encounter is an effective means of boosting personal or institutional prestige. Vice versa, the acceptance or rejection of an invitation and the particular formulation of one's own guest-status can also mean that artists, freelance curators, representatives of cultural institutions and cultural communities, but also various audiences, acquire social, economic, cultural and—quite significantly—symbolic capital, and experience their mutual revaluation. What is revealed here is the specific feature of curatorial giving: it consists in creating relationships with the goal of public perceptibility. The gift that comes to bear in curatorial hospitality is the facilitation of relations in the public between the various participants, individuals, and objects involved in the curatorial situation.

Preconditions for the public perceptibility of curatorial constellations are the collective structure of the curatorial and its participation in shaping the appearance and pictoriality of those involved. It is, in other words, a special kind of "giving of perception" (*Wahrgebung*), to borrow Kathrin Busch's term coined for the concept of the gift in the register of the visual,[15] a term which is here expressly used to describe the relationships between participating individuals and objects, and the fabric these create. Artists, curators, and visitors, but also gallerists, funders, critics, and scholars appear together with the exhibits, display objects, spaces, and discourses, creating relations that constitute the curatorial situation.

The codifying power effects are clearly visible in the relationships curatorial hospitality enables. The gift can be reduced to an economized reciprocity tailored to usability and calculated purpose,[16] and analogous to the various resource allocations, it can be subjected to criteria brought into force by naming, ordering, and evaluation. This process establishes the prerequisites and conditions of the curatorial situation, the hierarchies and dependencies between those involved, the limits of the (guest) space, and the roles: as guest or host, artist or curator, subject or object, local or foreigner. Attribution and acceptance of responsibility are key to curatorial hospitality in these processes—which ultimately follow the strategy of appropriating the intangible, of making the intangible familiar with one's own norms and rules. Taking curatorial responsibility for exhibits and collection objects invokes the Latin word *curare*, "to take care of," where the profession has its historical genesis. Responsibility grounds, if you will, the curatorial profession's traditional service orientation; it does so first and foremost in the interest of art objects and artifacts, then in the expanded sense for artists, institutions, and the public, and not least in terms of thematic content. To claim responsibility in recourse to the term curare, reconfirms an authority that offers protection, respect, and recognition on the one hand, but at the same time also determines the status and say or lack of say given to those taken responsibility for.[17]

Just as (to follow Pierre Bourdieu's argument) an invitation can never be turned down completely, because even rejection is still an answer within the logic of giving,[18] attempts to ignore, blank out, or neutralize the paradoxes and aporias moored in hospitality also fall short. In terms of a critical analysis of hospitality in the context of the curatorial, it appears to be more promising to take its specific possibilities seriously, which consist in mapping and carrying out the contradictory nature of hospitality relations on a meta-level. What is in focus here is less identities than practices—the way in which someone or something becomes a host or a guest, operates as host or guest, the acts by and within which the hospitable relationship is in progress and being continuously (re)performed. With this praxeological perspective, the space of hospitality constitutes itself through active references and temporary relations between participating actors and actants, and can be understood in terms of a continuation of the post-colonial concept of a "contact zone" of people and things.[19] Roles and positions appear expressly as the result of power and conflict-determined attributions that are mutually interchangeable (between host and guest, curator, artist, visitor, or even exhibited object), and especially in opposition to prevailing traditions or rules.[20] This consequently releases tasks from a fixed connection to roles and positions, so that acts of inviting and hosting, resource allocation or designation can be repeated and assumed in many ways from various sides. Authority, authorial power, or the concession to subjectivization are explicitly temporarily defined; the attribution, assumption, or concession of these powers are part of the practices within which the conflicts and negotiations at play in the curatorial-enabled encounters get reflected.

With this understanding, hospitality appears temporalized, in the sense of a hosting. Processed, complexified, and multiplied, it is, in the words of Mireille Rosello, "played and replayed at many different levels, among a multitude of actors whose position of power and powerlessness is not only relative but also disconnected from their identity."[21] The relations which format the curatorial constellation are accordingly dynamic. The unique potential of curatorial hospitality lies in the ability to both make operative and portray these relations in all their conflicts, ambivalences, and paradoxes. Their political relevance consists in the performativity of their analogous relationship to existing social conditions.

1 This also touches on Jacques Derrida's fundamental distinction between absolute, unconditional hospitality and legally mandated hospitality, which is key to any critical look at hospitality. Cf. Jacques Derrida and Anne Dufourmantelle, *Of Hospitality: Anne Dufourmantelle Invites Jacques Derrida to Respond*, trans. Rachel Bowlby (Stanford, CA: Stanford University Press, 2000).

2 "Hospitality—Hosting Relations in Exhibitions," International Conference: Cultures of the Curatorial, Hochschule für Grafik und Buchkunst (HGB) / Academy of Fine Arts Leipzig, December 13–14, 2012.

3 For more on Charles Esche's hospitality-oriented museum practice in terms of New Institutionalism, see for example "Charles Esche: Temporariness, Possibility and Institutional Change," in *In the Place of the Public Sphere?*, ed. Simon Sheikh (Berlin: b_books, 2005), 122–41, esp. 124–25; and Alex Farquharson, "Institutional Mores," *ONCURATING.org* 21 (December 2013): 55–59, here 57.

4 See Irmtraud Hnilica, "Von Mäusen und Männern: Prolegomena zu einer Narratologie der Gastlichkeit," http://www.iaslonline.de/index php?vorgang_id=3053, a review of *Gastlichkeit: Erkundungen einer Schwellensituation*, ed. Peter Friedrich and Rolf Parr (Heidelberg: Synchron, 2009), in particular her view on the contribution by Wolfgang Braungart and Sascha Monhoff, "'Wir sind nur Gast auf Erden': Symbolon, Symbol und die Theo-Poetik der Gastlichkeit," 89–102.

5 Here we mention only the most recent of such exhibitions: "Arts and Foods: Rituals Since 1851," Triennale di Milano, Milan, April 9–November 1, 2015, curated by Germano Celant as part of the Expo Milano 2015, held under the motto "Feeding the Planet, Energy for Life." See *Arts and Foods: Rituals Since 1851*, ed. Germano Celant (Milan: Electa, 2015). For more exhibitions that use food as a metonym for hospitality, see the contribution by Beatrice von Bismarck in this publication, "Showing Showing: Louise Lawler and the Art of Curatorial Hospitality," 101–16.

6 For more on the current debate surrounding curatorial ethics, see *MJ Manifesta Journal*, no. 12 (2012), and also the conference "Curatorial Ethics," Kunsthalle Wien, April 9–11, 2015, http://www.kunsthallewien.at/#/en/events/curatorial-ethics.

7 Evi Fountoulakis and Boris Previsic, "Gesetz, Politik und Erzählung der Gastlichkeit: Einleitung," in *Der Gast als Fremder: Narrative Alterität in der Literatur,* ed. Evi Fountoulakis and Boris Previsic (Bielefeld: transcript, 2011), 7–27, here 9.

8 Hans-Dieter Bahr, *Die Sprache des Gastes: Eine Metaethik* (Leipzig: Reclam, 1994), 236, quoted in Fountoulakis and Previsic, *Der Gast als Fremder*, 9.

9 Cf. Fountoulakis and Previsic, *Der Gast als Fremder*, 12.

10 Cf. Beatrice von Bismarck, "Kulturen des Kuratorischen," in *Handbuch Ausstellungstheorie und -praxis*, ed. ARGE schnittpunkt (Stuttgart: UTB, 2012), 166.

11 Cf. Derrida and Dufourmantelle, *Of Hospitality*, 25.

12 Cf. for example *Vom Geben und Nehmen: Zur Soziologie der Reziprozität*, ed. Frank Adloff and Steffen Mau (Frankfurt: Campus, 2005); Anne Dufourmantelle, "Hospitality—Under Compassion and Violence," in *The Conditions of Hospitality: Ethics, Politics, and Aesthetics on the Threshold of the Possible*, ed. Thomas Claviez (New York: Fordham University Press, 2013), 13–23.

13 Cf. Marcel Mauss, *The Gift: Forms and Functions of Exchange in Archaic Societies* (New York: Norton, 1967).

14 For more on this interpretation of the concept of "giving" in a sociological context, see the introduction in Adloff and Mau, *Vom Geben und Nehmen*, 9–59.

15 Cf. Kathrin Busch, *Geschicktes Geben: Aporien der Gabe bei Jacques Derrida* (Munich: Fink, 2004), 10.

16 Kathrin Busch argues against a reduction of giving in the field of contemporary visual art in her essay "'Dass Gut Schenken Eine Kunst Ist': Für eine Ästhetik der Gabe," *Zeitschrift für Ästhetik und Allgemeine Kunstwissenschaft* 50, no. 1 (2005): 25–55.

17 Gayatri Chakravorty Spivak addresses the aporetic character of responsibilities when she begins her text with the words: "Responsibility annuls the call to which it seeks to respond." Gayatri Chakravorty Spivak, "Responsibility," *Boundary* 2, vol. 21, no. 3 (1994): 19–64, here 19. For more on the understanding of responsibility in the area of the curatorial invoked by the Latin term *curare* without reflecting on its own subject and object-ascriptions, see Miguel A. Hernández-Navarro, "The Curator's Demands: Towards an Ethics of Commitment," *MJ Manifesta Journal* 12 (2012): 5–12, here 7: "The only mandate and principle the curator has, which he shouldn't betray, is that of fidelity and respect towards the other. Curatorial ethics therefore comes from an ethical experience of the subject, which is that of responsibility. In a world where responsibility is questioned and has disappeared from the individual sphere, curators have the single duty of being responsible individuals. That is why curating is an ethical profession, because, from the very etymology of the term, its task is to take care and be in charge of things, 'to be responsible for' things."

18 Cf. Pierre Bourdieu, "Marginalia: Some Additional Notes on the Gift," in *The Logic of the Gift: Toward an Ethic of Generosity*, ed. Alan D. Schrift (New York: Routledge, 1997), 231–44, esp. 238.

19 The term was coined by Mary Louise Pratt in "Arts of the Contact Zone," *Profession* (1991): 33–40.

20 According to Derrida, responsibility is inconceivable "without a dissident and inventive rupture with respect to tradition, authority, orthodoxy, rule, and doctrine." Jacques Derrida, *The Gift of Death* (Chicago: University of Chicago Press, 1995), 27.

21 Mireille Rosello, "Conviviality and Pilgrimage: Hospitality as Interruptive Practice," in Claviez, *The Conditions of Hospitality*, 127–44, here 132–33.

I

–

Hospitable Ethics / Ethics of Hospitality

Ruth Sonderegger

19

Curatorial Hospitality?

20

Why do I find it so maddeningly difficult to write about hospitality? (I took refuge in Mireille Rosello's book *Postcolonial Hospitality* again and again during the time I tried to fathom this difficulty; especially in a quote from René Schérer in the introduction to Rosello's book: "Isn't hospitality the madness of our contemporary world? To praise hospitality just when, in France and almost everywhere else in the world, the main concern is to restrict it, from the right to asylum to the code of nationality! Disturbing, excessive, like madness, it resists all forms of reason, including *raison d'état*."[1])

To what degree are my attempts to approach hospitality thwarted by the current deportation (these very days and hours) of some of the refugees that were and will remain crucial for both the European refugees' protests and Europe in general? Is it anything but cynical to speculate about hospitality in a geopolitical context where not only hospitality but also basic human rights are trampled underfoot? In a context where several persons are deported to countries where their lives are at risk? What is so disturbing about the current deportations of asylum seekers when one knows that such actions are already an everyday occurrence? Does it make a difference that those who are being deported right now have played a tremendous role in reminding Europeans, indeed anyone, of the gaps, yawning abysses, and paradoxes of Western constitutions and democracies? Should the activist refugees be treated differently, more hospitably, because they have helped (some of) those who profit from such constitutions and democracies to become more reflective and self-critical regarding human rights and questions of trans/national citizenship? Should they be treated differently because they have revealed (to us) how poor and possessive our understanding of human rights has become; how intricate the relation between the right to stay and hospitality is? Because they not only challenged but re-invented our understanding of citizenship?[2] Because they re-educated complacent citizens like me? Doesn't such a hierarchy between activist refugees, on the one hand, and those refugees and asylum seekers who don't have the opportunity or enough energy to speak up, on the other, go against the grain of hospitality's universal if not infinite claim?

Why do I find it even harder (at this moment) to think about curatorial hospitality than about hospitality tout court? Is it because I assume we should not spend our time reflecting on the luxury of curatorial hospitality before we have realized the most elementary forms of hospitality? Is elementary hospitality, a hospitality that might consist in providing and sharing shelter, food, and friends in order for all to have a dignified life, more important than curatorial hosting? Isn't one on a par with the other? What speaks against reflecting upon hospitality and trying to act hospitably in distinct contexts at the same time? In contexts that might, after all, turn out to be not so different? Is the conjecture that curatorial hospitality is impossible unless it goes hand in hand with hospitality in a much broader sense convincing? (Rosello seems to pose a similar question when she asks: "Wouldn't respect for the guest also entail that each of the subjects that (s)he encounters, inside the foreign house (neighborhood, nation), be shown the same consideration as him- or herself? Can a slave owner be hospitable at all?"[3]) Wouldn't this, if applied to a curatorial context, imply that respect for the guest in an exhibition entails that all beings inside (if not also outside) the respective exhibition be shown the same consideration as the guest?

Should one suspect that we distract ourselves from current violations of the most basic rights and customs of hospitality by concentrating on hospitality in curatorial practices? Is such a shift in concentration displacement activity? Although, isn't hospitality more than a basic right, namely a gift that we cannot offer everybody? Is it perhaps not even fully realizable in relation to one single being?

Is it pure coincidence or backwardness that it is mainly churches or monasteries that give shelter to refugees in so-called secularized (Western) countries—even shelter that goes beyond and against the law? Why have exhibition rooms and institutions rarely, if ever, opened their doors to refugees and asylum seekers, despite the widespread belief that in Europe belief in God has been replaced by art-religion?[4]

How on earth could one be inclined to think that curatorial hospitality is easier to achieve than hospitality toward refugees? Are the stakes not similarly high? Isn't it obvious that inhospitable relations of exploitation and power structure curatorial practices from the very beginning? Are we able to imagine, if only briefly, what the world of exhibitions would look like if all the actors involved were paid decently; if payment was not restricted to the duration of an exhibition and hospitality was not restricted to the opening event (when sponsors are present); if contracts with cultural producers took the living expenses between exhibitions into account? What could hospitality in the context of exhibition-making amount to in light of the tremendous gap between practices of curating and practices of mediating?[5] How could a curator take notice of secretaries, cleaners, interns, in a hospitable way? Does the curator cross paths with these people? How could hospitality have an effect on those who do not come into contact with institutions and people that host exhibitions? How could the institution invite them in? And how could their possible disinterest be respected? Isn't it rather cynical, or idealistic at best, to reflect upon or even claim curatorial hospitality in times that are as precarious for curators as they are for artists, cultural producers, and mediators?

Doesn't my emphasis on various powerful asymmetries and axis of violence in the curatorial field make things worse? Doesn't it reiterate and reinforce them? Or could it be legitimate to underline these asymmetries in order to point out, *ex negativo*, that relations of hospitality require a certain degree of reciprocity—not symmetry—between the host and the guest? In order to emphasize that hospitality requires both parties to be in a position to adopt both the role of the host and that of the guest—even if we admit that every act of hospitality falls short of its own infinite aspirations? Is hospitality turned into paternalism if it is clear from the outset, or assumed at least, that one party is always and exclusively the host while the other is always a guest? How humiliating is it, or can it become, if one is always invited without ever having the material means to invite back? Is hospitality under such circumstances turned into a privilege that is condescendingly granted despite all good intentions? Does hospitality imply the ability to accept invitations where and when they are least expected, that is, that the host opens herself up to the most infinitesimal invitations of the guest?

Might the Dutch artist Matthijs de Bruijne's acceptance of a job offer from the Dutch union of domestic workers be a good case in point?[6] (His explanation of his decision to accept reads as follows: "They want to hear stories, want to think. Their work is dull and the conditions numbing, revival only comes through new experiences and perspectives. While they are considered to be conservative, they have asked me to work for them, to join their fight and to invent a new imagery, a new language to talk about their reality in order to change it. And they will pay for that. This was a simple choice: do you want to continue to do low paid work for a group of people that is betraying you time after time?"[7] Earlier in the same article, De Bruijne described such betrayal by asking: "Is it possible to find worse conditions of labor in the Netherlands, than those of the cleaners? Yes, it is. One example: Dutch art institutions these days more and more often decide to hire their assistants as interns. Interns, who often will be doing the work of a departed, paid employee. The only difference is one of income: the intern will be unpaid.")

Why is it almost unbelievable that an artist was offered a long-term contract by a domestic workers' union in times when the curatorial world can hardly even think of something similar for artists and cultural workers? Is it really unbelievable? Furthermore, doesn't this job offer and its acceptance remind us that hospitality should not be seen and practiced as a state of exception? That hospitality rather requires long-term practices that allow for an alternating give-and-take? Would this imply that we should work towards conditions that allow our guests to be able to invite us (back)? And what if the guests want to stay?

1 Mireille Rosello, *Postcolonial Hospitality: The Immigrant as Guest* (Stanford, CA: Stanford University Press, 2001). The quote from Scherer's *Zeus hospitalier: Eloge de l'hospitalité* (Arman Colin: Paris, 1993) is on page 7.

2 Ljubomir Bratić, "Der Alptraum der verwalteten Ordnung. Die Überzähligen haben schon gewonnen!" no-racism.net, January 1, 2013, http://no-racism.net/article/4351/.

3 Rosello, *Postcolonial Hospitality*, 16.

4 When refugees from the *Refugee Protest Camp Vienna* came to the Academy of Fine Arts Vienna on October 29, 2014 their wish to (temporarily) stay was not granted, on the contrary. For more information about the Vienna refugee camp protests see *Refugee Protest Camp Vienna* (blog), accessed January 29, 2015, http://refugeecampvienna.noblogs.org and "free erase territorialize," special issue, *transversal*, accessed January 29, 2015, http://eipcp.net/transversal/0313.

5 See Nora Sternfeld, "What Can the Curatorial Learn from the Educational?," in *Cultures of the Curatorial*, ed. Beatrice von Bismarck, Jörn Schafaff, Thomas Weski (Sternberg Press: Berlin, 2012), 333–43.

6 For two of De Bruijne's shadow play videos that were commissioned by the cleaners' union see Vimeo, http://vimeo.com/32666644 and http://vimeo.com/49909059. The videos can also be found on the union's homepage: http://www.schoongenoeg.nu/afdeling/domestic-workers/. Both sites accessed January 29, 2015.

7 Matthijs de Bruijne, "Ideology and Labour Conditions," in *Art and Ideology Critique After 1989*, ed. Eva Birkenstock et al. (Cologne: Kunsthaus Bregenz / Verlag der Buchhandlung Walther König, 2013), 344–47.

Dieter Roelstraete

Remarks on the End of Hostilities

1.

How did a relatively obscure legal scholar, a specialist in the Byzantine business of constitutional theory who decided to throw in his academic lot with the ascendant Nazi Party in 1930s Germany, become such a revered point of reference for a wide range of left-leaning thinkers in postwar critical discourse? Giorgio Agamben, Hannah Arendt (primarily through the legacy of Walter Benjamin, the aforementioned jurist's contemporary), Alain Badiou, Simon Critchley, Jacques Derrida, Chantal Mouffe, Antonio Negri, Slavoj Žižek … all have, at one point or other in their well-publicized intellectual trajectories, entered into a dialogue with the work of Carl Schmitt, the lodestar of a prominent philosophical strand within the neoconservative movement and author of such unlikely latter-day classics of twentieth-century political theory as *Political Theology and The Concept of the Political*. The core distinction that, according to Schmitt, defines the latter, "the specific political distinction to which political actions and motives can be reduced is that *between friend and enemy*," helps to explain (in my opinion) the controversial appeal his writings hold for a broad swathe of theorists peopling the opposing half of the political spectrum. This distinction, Schmitt continues, "denotes the utmost degree of intensity of a union or separation, of an association or dissociation."[1] Clearly, it must be the clipped, economic clarity of Schmitt's precepts, his confrontational style and insistence on decisions, divisions, distinctions—between something so arch-sounding as "friend or foe," no less—that explains his popularity among the lonely paladins of a disillusioned, thoroughly gutted and rudderless Left. His is the spirit of defiant, self-assured *antagonism* that is so palpably present in nostalgia-infused contemporary theories of *agonism* (agonistic pluralism, agonistic models of democracy etc.).[2] Schmitt's thoughts and theories are of course inextricably linked with the terminal crisis of a certain liberal tradition whose death throes shaped the political drama at the heart of the Weimar experience, and the return to political currency of Schmitt's thoughts and theories likewise points to a deep crisis (again, in my opinion) in the current (neo)liberal consensus. It is the realization that nothing better symbolizes certain key aspects of that consensus culture than the global economic phenomenon that is the contemporary art world, that may lend some validity to the introduction of Schmitt's stark triangular paradigm of decisions–distinctions–divisions into art-theoretical debate.

With this introduction, I want to argue that Schmitt's concept of the political in particular may have some unexpected critical relevance for the contemporary art world; in that world, too, a case could be made for the legitimacy of the signature Schmittian distinction between friend and enemy. And in the context of the ongoing debate concerning hospitality ("hosting relations") in artistic and curatorial practice, this distinction, or rather tangle of distinctions, could be rephrased as that between the good host and the bad host, between the good guest and the bad guest (also: between the good host and the bad guest, between the good guest and the bad host), between the hospitable and the inhospitable. These are useful distinctions to make, I believe, at a time when the specter of hospitality can be seen to haunt the entire contemporary art world.

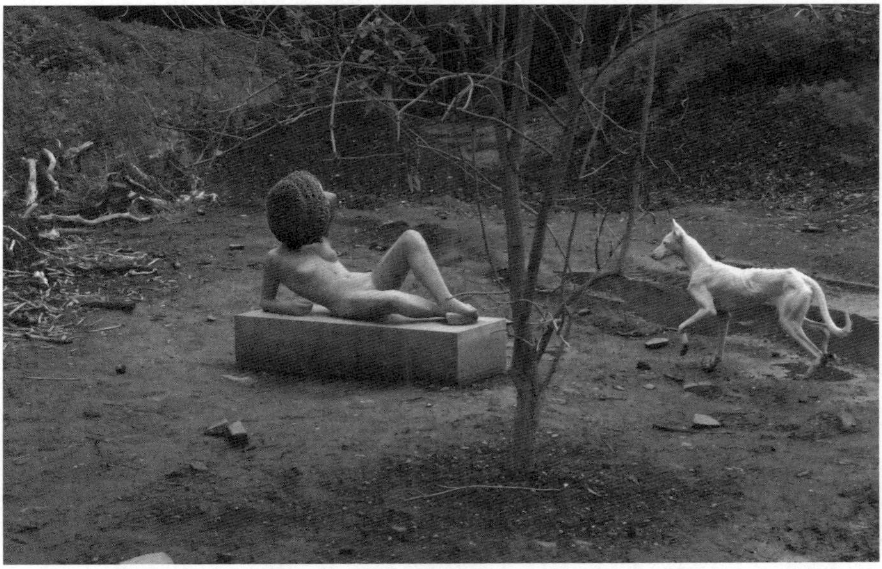

Pierre Huyghe, *Untilled*, 2011–12. dOCUMENTA (13), 2012

2.

It hardly bears repeating here that the art of hosting and the ethos of hospitality are absolutely central to the business of curating. Hosting is in essence what a curator does: he or she "hosts" artists, artworks, and artistic relations (between artists, between artworks, between artists and artworks) inside his or her curatorial constructs—which are of course made possible, explicitly or implicitly, by wider *institutional* constructs—and a deep spirit of hospitality should rightfully be expected to imbue all aspects of (institutional) curatorial culture. (Hospitality is a key component, obviously, of institutional culture's *mental architecture*—if not of its actual space: hosting is of course first and foremost a material act and physical fact, the work and wear of bodies in space and time.) Needless to add that many of these relations are also profoundly reciprocal: the curator is always also a *guest*, most notably of the artist—in his or her studio, among his or her artworks. (No one has said it better than Anthony Huberman in his essay "A Toast."[3]) The workings of the global art world are governed by and large by a politics of friendship articulated in the language of caring and sharing, of contributing and participating, of shelter and tending; one does not even have to be reminded of the etymology of curating to appreciate that the psychodynamics of contemporary art does not, as a rule, foster "trouble with strangers"—nothing quite so confrontational.[4] Although it is of course very important that conduct and interactions within the contemporary art world be governed by certain implicit codes and unspoken rules ("good manners"), it is equally important that this laudable ethos of *dialogue* and mutual understanding does not compromise the *dialectical* life force that is so crucial to our modern conception of art—that art can continue its fundamental work of negating and negativity. (Provided, of course, that we agree upon the continued relevance of this modern conception of art—art as critique, as cipher of otherness. I assume we do.) The real challenge for the modern "curatoriat" may well be this then: how to construct and cultivate an artistic environment in which antagonism is not merely respected or tolerated, but is actively guaranteed and safeguarded; in which there is room (though not necessarily "tolerance") for bad hosts and bad guests alike; in which a vital measure of art's fundamental *inhospitality*, its hostility to many things (among them, people), is maintained—an art world of friends and foes, of friendship and enmity and sound reasons for distinguishing between both. "Hospitality, hostility, *hostpitality*."[5]

3.

An anecdotal interlude: whenever talk of bad hosts and bad guests arises, I cannot help but think of the "work" of the Berlin-based Russian performance artist Aleksander Brener—known for spray-painting a dollar sign on a painting by Kasimir Malevich and naming it a "dialogue with Malevich" after the fact—who I once half-witnessed defecating in a small room in Berlin's Kunst-Werke where the Danish film artist Joachim Koester was giving a talk. (Koester is about the friendliest person you're ever likely to meet in the art world: incongruously, he had been the subject of Brener's taunting once before.) Not surprisingly, everyone present failed to appreciate the oppositional charge of Brener's deed—he had done something similar before, in the Pushkin Museum of Fine Arts in Moscow, in front of a Van Gogh painting—and we all sympathized with the Kunst-Werke staff member who had to clean up Brener's mess after he had been hounded out of the Berlin art center known for its cutting-edge, politically adventurous

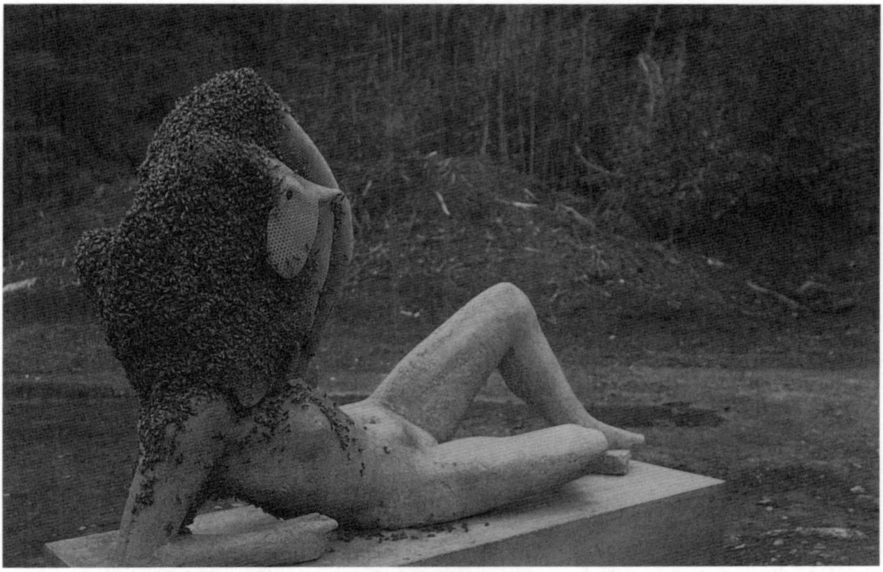

Pierre Huyghe, *Untilled*, 2011–12 (detail). dOCUMENTA (13), 2012

programming and its widely documented openness to spirited debate. I remember still occasionally shivering with rage just thinking back over the incident the next day (Joachim Koester is a friend of mine, and I had been one of Brener's more vocal opponents during said altercation) while I was biking down one of Prenzlauer Berg's leafy streets, only to be stopped in my tracks by the unlikely sight of Aleksander Brener and his partner in crime Barbara Schurz sipping from a couple of Milchkaffees on a terrace while contently perusing the day's newspapers. I saw them, but they did not see me, and much of my pent-up anger was thereby somehow silently defused. Some weeks later, I learned of the rumor that something similar had taken place at the opening of Andrea Fraser (indeed, the *grande dame* of institutional critique) at Galerie Christian Nagel in Berlin; there too, Brener had relieved himself inside a packed art space, leaving behind the foul-smelling brown imprint of "protest." It is worth keeping these images and memories in mind when pondering both the conundrum of "radical" hospitality in art (how far do you, the host, let the guest go?) and the virtues of distinguishing friendly enemies from plain enemies, and hostile friends from friends proper.[6]

4.

One of the more important discoveries I have made during my first year as a curator working in the American institutional art field concerns the notion of what is within this field commonly referred to as "social practice." This paradigm, roughly equivalent to what Europeans habitually identify as "relational aesthetics," has now become so widespread that even the *New York Times*, not usually known for its forward-looking or wide-ranging taste in art, dedicated an in-depth feature to the phenomenon in question, noting how "its practitioners freely blur the lines among object making, performance, political activism, community organizing, environmentalism and investigative journalism, creating a deeply participatory art that often flourishes outside the gallery and museum system."[7] Not surprisingly for an art "movement" that involves lots of cooking and talking, alternative economies and lifestyles, sleepovers and workshops, education and exchange, hospitality features as one of its cardinal virtues: in many cases, social practice is effectively a hosting (caring, healing, nourishing, sheltering) practice. It is of course notoriously difficult to assess or even discuss the merits of many social-practice projects as art, and it is equally difficult to assess or even discuss their value as, well, "social" practice, that is, *outside* the context of art. The point, in part, of many of these projects is to question the very nature of art's separation from society, as well as the techniques of estimation and valuation that are part of this separation. These challenges and interrogations are obviously especially topical in the context of the American art system, where the market quite simply wields much more power. From the perspective of my previous curatorial experience at a public art institution in Europe, it is perhaps inevitable that I should question the soundness of social practice's (obviously well-intended) therapeutic impulses: I see artists propose and do things that I rather expect (or want) others to do and propose. Is it really art's role (*or* the art world's) to care, heal, nourish, and shelter—to *host*? And is it, in turn, the curator or the institution's role to host these artistic positions, so enmeshed in the corrupting language of civic duty? Should art's relationship to the social fabric be such an affirmative one, that is, one of reform and support? If the social fabric is as broken and battered as it so often appears to be today, the answer to that last question should probably be yes. Indeed, under the current circumstances of an unrepentant, suicidal neoliberalism—one that truly did not fail to "let a serious crisis go to waste"[8]—it may seem positively preposterous to argue for a return to art's essence as (*pace* Adorno) *asocial* practice. A certain type of asocial practice, or a certain interpretation of asociality, may well be what got us, in an art world that is part and parcel of the neoliberal world order, in this inhospitable mess in the first place, and it is only laudable that a growing number of artists once again feel called upon to make a difference (of sorts) by showing us one potential way out ("hospitality"). Such a difference, however, can only truly be made when art (in this case, social practice) once again clarifies its object, that is to say, specifies who deserves or needs caring for, healing, nourishing, and sheltering, and who does not: a process which the curator inevitably forms a part of—and it is only logical, *and* ethical, that the curator should openly assume this responsibility. The language of hospitality that the art world has adopted with such vigorous, inspiring enthusiasm only becomes meaningful in its self-imposed limitations, in deciding and defining who should be treated as a guest and who should not. Social practice, yes—but only up to a point, and beyond this point art should probably revert to the tried and tested formula of an asocial practice, one that can tell friend and foe apart. Only thus—to return to Carl Schmitt's precept—can art become political *again*.

1 Carl Schmitt, *The Concept of the Political*, trans. George Schwab (Chicago: University of Chicago Press, 1996), 26–27. The best English-language biography of Carl Schmitt currently available is by Gopal Balakrishnan and is simply titled *The Enemy: An Intellectual Portrait of Carl Schmitt* (London: Verso, 2002).

2 See Chantal Mouffe, *The Democratic Paradox* (London: Verso, 2000), 103: "from the perspective of 'agonistic pluralism' the aim of democratic politics is to transform *antagonism* into *agonism*." Mouffe defines antagonism as the struggle between enemies, and agonism as the struggle between adversaries, thereby complicating Schmitt's assertion that "the enemy is not merely any competitor or just any partner of a conflict in general. He is also not the private adversary whom one hates." Carl Schmitt, *The Concept of the Political* (Chicago: University of Chicago Press, 1996), 28.

3 See Anthony Huberman's contribution to this publication, 58–61.

4 *Trouble with Strangers* is the title of Terry Eagleton's book-length "study of ethics" (Oxford: Wiley-Blackwell, 2008); it is also, as far as I know, the best three-word definition of the problem of ethics as such. Eagleton's primer, although heavily indebted to the theories of Jacques Lacan, has not been translated into French; its title would sound something like "difficultés avec les étrangers," which could then be translated back into English as "trouble with foreigners." The defining ambiguity of the "étranger" as both stranger and foreigner is predictably central to French theories of hospitality, most notably Jacques Derrida's *De l'hospitalité* (1997). In this short text, Derrida suggests: "That is where the question of hospitality begins: must we ask the foreigner to understand us, to speak our language, in all the senses of this term, in all its possible extensions, before being able and so as to be able to welcome him into our country?" An extensive answer to this question follows: "Let us say yes *to who or what turns up*, before any determination, before any anticipation, before any *identification*, whether or not it has to do with a foreigner, an immigrant, an invited guest, or an unexpected visitor, whether or not the new arrival is the citizen of another country, a human, animal, or divine creature, a living or dead thing, male or female." Jacques Derrida, *Of Hospitality* (Stanford, CA: Stanford University Press, 2000), 15, 77.

5 Ibid., 45. Consider this alongside the following excerpt from another book by Derrida that I have already alluded to: "*the very work of the political* […] the *properly* political act or operation amounts to creating (to producing, to making, etc.) the most friendship possible." Jacques Derrida, *The Politics of Friendship* (London: Verso, 1994), 8. In short, Derrida is the Anti-Schmitt.

6 One of the puzzles that circulate around such exhibition projects as "Feast: Radical Hospitality in Contemporary Art" (organized at the Smart Museum of Art in Chicago in the spring of 2012) concerns the exact use of the word "radical" in its title—it primarily invites testing the *limits* of hospitality, which is of course precisely what someone like Aleksander Brener, well aware of the art world's institutionalized commitment to the *rhetoric* (if not the *practice*) of hospitality, does. I borrow the term "friendly enemies" from my colleague Charles Esche, who has used it to describe certain key aspects of the working relationship between artist and curator. Esche, an important point of reference for the aforementioned "Feast" (curated by Stephanie Smith), is among the few in the contemporary art world who consistently speak of the importance of the friend/enemy distinction—not merely of drawing that proverbial line in the sand, but also of naming names, of identifying friend and enemy alike.

7 Randy Kennedy, "Outside the Citadel, Social Practice Art Is Intended to Nurture," *New York Times*, March 20, 2013.

8 See Philip Mirowski, *Never Let a Serious Crisis Go to Waste: How Neoliberalism Survived the Financial Meltdown* (London: Verso, 2013).

Andrea Fraser

“As If” We Came Together to Care

When I was invited to contribute to this book on the topic of "Hospitality — Hosting Relations in Exhibitions," I admit that I felt, at first, rather doubtful of the theme.[1] I interpreted this framing of curatorial relations, like the fascination with gift economies in some sectors of the art field, in terms of hospitality as motivated by a desire to escape contemporary, capitalist relations of labor and exchange. Like gift economies, however, relations of hospitality would seem to represent neither a resolution of the problems of capitalist relations, nor a development beyond them, but rather a regression to pre-market relations as they survive in customs, rituals, and other practices seen as more cultural than economic. The characterization of hospitality (according to the concept of the conference out of which this book developed) as constituting "*a specific aesthetic, social, political, and economic constellation*" seemed at first contradictory: how specific can hospitality be across these radically different dimensions of activity and existence? Does it function to elide those differences? Or does it serve as a meta-relation that traverses these four spheres? And what about that fifth sphere that seems so notably absent from this list: the *ethical* dimension of relations that rules of hospitality prescribe. Indeed, the question of hospitality in exhibitions may be, above all, a question of the ethics of curatorial relations.

However, despite my doubts about the term, with just a little bit of reflection I have to admit that "hospitality" does indeed resonate with a significant aspect of my experience of working with curators and art organizations. With that admission, I have to wonder whether it is a repressed element and, if so, why and through what mechanisms. While the relationship of host and guest seems to call for a sociological or anthropological perspective, what the term hospitality evokes for me is rather the psychological dimension of curatorial relations, particularly in terms of the affective investments and unconscious aims that may be operative in those relations. These investments and aims may be activated, organized, satisfied, frustrated, furthered, or fended off by field-specific practices and may be regulated by implicit or explicit field-specific ethics, but they are not themselves field specific. Indeed, what "hospitality" may frame are the investments and aims central to our most fundamental relational template — which may also be our most ambivalently inflected and readily repressed: that of parental care and infantile dependency.

From the perspective of psychoanalytic object-relations theory, all our relations — internal and external, psychological and social — are affectively invested. They are not only sustained but produced as relations by a cathexis of energy that may be considered sexual, aggressive or, more broadly, emotional. What this energy is directed toward, whether person, thing, idea, representation, narrative, or any other entity, is constituted as an object by this investment of energy itself. Such affective investment not only produces objects and relations in a psychoanalytic sense but also constitutes the psychological dimension of all objects and relations.

Pierre Bourdieu offers one account of how "original libido" (that is, for him, "the socialized affects constituted in the domestic field") transforms into "specific libido" through "the transference of this libido onto agents or institutions belonging to [a specific] field."[2] "Impulses that push toward a self-investment in the object" are determined by "a particular universe of objects offered socially for investment." Through this process, as he notes elsewhere, "the social order collects, channels, reinforces or counteracts psychological processes depending on whether there is a homology, redundancy, and reinforcement between the two systems or, to the contrary, contradiction and tension."[3]

Psychoanalysts, and particularly analysts influenced by Melanie Klein, have developed and extensively elaborated a parallel account of how groups, institutions, and the roles within them both activate and contain unconscious processes, phantasies, and affects. A fundamental premise of psychoanalytic perspectives on institutions and group relations—most notably those developed by Wilfred Bion in the 1940s and '50s, and others who followed him[4]—is that operating alongside the most specifically defined social tasks, relations, and aims are a full spectrum of psychological relations and aims that remain largely unconscious. In a formulation that seems to mirror Bourdieu's, Bion sees these unconscious aims as having the potential to reinforce or contradict conscious social aims both at a micro and macro level, in small groups as well as major social institutions that serve to collect, channel, and contain unconscious forces within individuals, larger groups, or society at large. Groups, institutions, and institutionally sanctioned social relations may serve as defenses against anxiety and aggression or as opportunities for sublimation, and also as structures that process and metabolize raw and potentially toxic internal or external stimuli into thought, representation, and meaning.

While Bourdieu developed a theory of institutions as social fields, psychoanalysts have considered institutions, groups, and dyads as intersubjective fields in which relations and roles are produced and reproduced through shared unconscious structures and dynamics.[5] These structures include not only unidirectional but bi- and multi-directional vectors in which various positions, roles, attributes, affects, and phantasies are not only ascribed to others but also enacted intersubjectively. Among the primary mechanisms identified by Bion as operating within—and perhaps even constitutive of— groups as intersubjective fields is projective identification. Klein introduced the term to describe a phantasy through which parts of the self are split off and attributed to an external object (people, things, ideas, representations, etc.).[6] Bion developed the concept of projective identification from a unidirectional, *intra*subjective, or "one-body" phenomenon of attribution to a process that unfolds intersubjectively when projections are unconsciously taken up by others, in whom they activate corresponding phantasies. In his later work focusing on analyst-analysand and mother-infant dyads, Bion expands the concept further, identifying projective identification as *the* primary form of emotional contact: the mechanism through which infants relate to caregivers at stages that Bion understands not only as pre-linguistic but also as pre-thought. At these stages, the caregiver functions as a "container" for overwhelming stimuli (internal and external). The infant projects unthought and unthinkable stimuli into caregiving containers by acting "in a way that engenders in the mother feelings that he does not want, or which he wants the mother to have."[7] The mother thus is made conscious of and able to speak about and act on this stimuli even before the infant is able to form this stimuli into thought. Through this process the caregiver not only modifies the overwhelming feeling so it can be safely taken back by the infant but also transforms raw emotional experience into thought. By internalizing this function the infant also develops the capacity for thought.[8] Bion designated this process (which he also characterized variously as a function, an apparatus, and a configuration) with the "abstract representation" of "container-contained."[9]

Bion analysed groups as a kind of shared unconscious phantasy that activates a "massive regression to mechanisms described by Melanie Klein as typical of the earliest phases of mental life."[10] While Freud viewed groups in terms of Oedipal family patterns, Bion viewed groups through the lens of pre-Oedipal object-relations that release psychotic anxieties of persecution and annihilation as well as depressive anxieties of loss and guilt. He analysed this group-induced regression in terms of its "basic assumptions": that is, the unconscious aims on which a group may be acting at any given time, alongside or instead of its conscious aims or tasks. The basic assumptions elaborated by Bion include "fight-flight,' when a group behaves "as if" its purpose is to preserve itself against a threat; the basic assumption "pairing," when a group behaves "as if" its purpose (or that of a couple of its members) is to give birth to a bright future and a solution to all of its problems; and the basic assumption "dependency," when a group behaves "as if" its purpose is to be sustained, nourished, protected, and cared for by an individual, an idea, an object, an organization, or some other entity invested with the capacity to satisfy its needs.[11] And, of course, these same unconscious aims can also be found in an individual's relations to groups, organizations, or other individuals in specific institutional roles.

All three of Bion's "basic assumptions" correspond to early phases described by Klein. Fight-flight corresponds to the persecutory anxieties and defenses of what she calls the "paranoid-schizoid position"; dependency corresponds to the ambivalence, anxiety of loss, and guilt felt in relation to attachment figures in the "depressive position"; and pairing corresponds to the sexual energies of Oedipal configurations when the group becomes a kind of primal scene that promises to give birth to an ideal future or self. Both Klein and Bion see these positions not as stages to be moved through and left behind but as continuously active, constituting our basic psychic structures with, in particular, a constant interplay between persecutory and depressive configurations. Similarly, while only one basic assumption predominates in a group at any given moment, there may be a rapid turnover of basic assumptions. Nevertheless, particular organizations, groups, and tasks often foster particular basic assumptions through the definition of tasks and the roles and attributes of people authorized in relation to tasks. Bion noted that fight-flight assumptions are particularly active in military and political institutions, while dependency assumptions predominate in religious, educational, and medical institutions. His British heritage may have influenced his focus on the aristocracy as a primary institution of pairing. I would suggest that institutions of celebrity (including artistic celebrity) have replaced (or augmented) the aristocracy in that role.

One need not think too deeply to associate different curatorial scenarios with Bion's basic assumptions. Fight-flight can be identified in the curatorial project that mobilizes artists, audiences, and organizations to attack internal or external problems, whether institutional, social, economic, or artistic. Pairing corresponds to the curatorial project that aims to create a new work, exhibition, practice, solution to society's problems, among other aims, and often unfolds through a close collaboration between curator and artist. But the most traditional role for curators—a word with roots in "care"—would seem to encompass dependency quite directly, even explicitly: the curatorial project that nurtures, cares for, and protects artists, artworks, culture, or heritage. And when that role is performed in the intersubjective field constituted by artists, audiences, curators, and other institutional staff, it is likely to activate unconscious aims and investments well beyond those of caring for objects or works.

Certainly, the curatorial functions of temporarily taking in and taking care of artists and artworks that enter an organization or the field of a specific curatorial project can be considered in terms of hospitality. Nevertheless, from a Bionian perspective, "hospitality" as a representation of curatorial functions, and "host-guest" as a representation of a curator's relations to artists and other groups, suggests a kind of shadow aim and shadow relations that appear alongside more specifically artistically and organizationally defined curatorial tasks. It suggests the operation of unconscious aims in something like a "basic-assumption hospitality," which would be active when a group behaves "as if" its purpose is to take in or be taken in, shelter(ed), entertain(ed), and otherwise provide(d) for. Even while such a purpose may indeed be identified in aspects of the tasks consciously taken by curators—or consciously given curators by institutions, artists, and others—and may directly further those tasks, in Bion's terms it would be understood, nevertheless, as a form of the basic assumption dependency.[12]

Unpacking the implications of curatorial hospitality as a form of the basic assumption dependency would require a long detour into an account of the depressive position analysed by Klein and of the mechanisms of dependency analysed by Bion, as well as the forms of "leadership" those mechanisms produce. It will have to suffice to say that experience with psychoanalytic group relations demonstrates the depth and durability not only of the desire to be cared for and protected but also of its associated anxiety and ambivalence.[13] The persecutory anxiety of being attacked, starved, and abandoned that helps sustain dependency contends with the anxiety and shame associated with the loss of control and autonomy and, above all, the loss of that front-line of defense against the most acute anxiety, omnipotence—which, if lost to the (dependent) self, is then projected into a person, idea, or other object so it can be re-introjected as some form of sustaining power. Greed for care that represents more than the satisfaction of needs can underlie competition for scarce resources, including curatorial attention. Frustration can turn greed into envy and produce a hatred of the object of dependency. Dependency thus tends to continuously produce (through projection) and simultaneously undermine (and when frustration activates fight-flight, attack) authority, often putting those it attaches to in a difficult bind. Most importantly, where fight-flight gives free rein to aggression, and pairing admits only the most optimistic outcome of joining, dependency conjoins to care a broad range of object-relations, including destructiveness. This is not destructiveness projected onto others with persecutory anxiety, but the destructiveness of the self or group, especially as manifest in greed for and envy of care. Dependency is thus associated with the anxiety of loss and guilt due to destructiveness, which also characterize the depressive position analysed by Klein. If a group can tolerate the frustration of wanting and not having, the anxiety of not knowing and not controlling, the ambivalence of wanting and hating the same object, and if projection also gives rise to empathy, this guilt may result in efforts to repair the damage done (or imagined). And it is this urge to make reparation, to turn greed into generosity and envy into gratitude, that Klein identifies as the foundation of culture.[14]

In a "Postscript" to a paper written as a lecture for a group of social scientists, Klein describes a discussion with an anthropologist who questions her theories by noting a culture in which it is considered admirable to cheat and a weakness to show mercy. When further discussion reveals that this culture nevertheless observes "rules of hospitality," Klein finds acceptance for her theories by arguing that "hospitality links with family life, with the relation of children to one another," and to the mother as protector even of "a hated sibling."[15] Evoked by mercy, hospitality is linked to the transformation of hatred and aggression in the sheltering, not of friends, but of enemies.

One wonders if Klein was aware of the etymological development of "hospitality" from "host," or *hospes* in Latin, which in turn probably derived from *hostis*, which means enemy, the word from which hostility also derives. The transformation of hostility into hospitality could not be a better outcome from a Kleinian perspective. However, it is always an unstable outcome. To the extent that the generosity and gratitude that ideally characterize relations of hospitality are motivated by the urge to make reparation, the link between hospitality and hostility can never be severed completely.

What is it that the curatorial field seeks to repair with hospitality? Relations of hospitality tend to be represented as immanently unobjectionable, if sometimes vulnerable to contextual evils. In Klein's story, hospitality appears as a last refuge of empathy in a culture without mercy. In art, hospitality seems to figure as a last refuge of generosity and gratitude in a culture of exploitation, but is at constant risk of being ruined by asymmetries, dependencies, exclusions, and strategic motives, or devolving to greed and envy—or is it to economic exchange? Rather than resolving the problems of capitalist relations, or moving beyond them, reframing them in terms of hospitality may only exacerbate them. The dependency of artists on "host" curators and organizations is not lessened by the forms of support often encompassed by "hospitality" but may be increased by them, especially if such hospitality is offered in lieu of sustaining levels of direct compensation. When artists are not compensated for their work on curatorial projects at economically sustaining levels but only in the form of per diems, travel expenses, temporary accommodations, and free meals, these can become a poor substitute for financial compensation that tethers artists to curators and organizations in ways that can feel limiting of autonomy and even infantilizing, generating both more dependency and resentment.

Of course, framing curatorial relations in terms of hospitality does not in itself change their social and economic conditions, with all its asymmetries, exclusions, and strategic motives. It may, however, represent an effort to deal with these conditions, or the anxieties they provoke, through the mobilization of particular psychological and intersubjective structures. Framing curatorial relations as hospitality may be a way of working with and through the guilt and reparative impulses attendant to the "basic assumption" dependency. The empathy of care and anxiety of harm may motivate the formulation of ethical principles that distinguish hostile relations of economic exploitation from hospitable relations of care and strengthen the latter. If this work is to succeed, however—if the regression to basic-assumptions is to promote the development of the field—it must do more than serve the repression of relations of economic exchange. It must be recognized that those relations, including relations of economic exploitation, are not replaced by but only refigured by being framed as relations of care; that these relations of exploitation are not only a bad outcome of hospitality, but are also the source of the need that occasions it and contains it, from which hospitality can never completely free itself.

1 This first sentence is a welcome opportunity to thank Beatrice von Bismarck for, once again, with her invitations, patience, and perseverance, providing me with the occasion and the encouragement to address issues I have been preoccupied with for some time, but without the proper motivation to overcome my anxiety about developing them.

2 Pierre Bourdieu, *Pascalian Meditations*, trans. Richard Nice (Stanford: Stanford University Press, 1997), 164.

3 Pierre Bourdieu et al., *The Weight of the World: Social Suffering in Contemporary Society*, trans. Priscilla Parkhurst Ferguson et al. (Stanford: Stanford University Press, 1999), 512.

4 Wilfred R. Bion, *Experiences in Groups* (London: Tavistock Publications, 1961). For another early effort to apply Kleinian theory to institutions, see Elliott Jacques, "Social Systems as a Defense Against Persecutory and Depressive Anxiety," in *New Directions in Psychoanalysis*, ed. Melanie Klein, Paula Heimann, R. E. Money-Kyrle (London: Tavistock, 1955).

5 While Bion uses the term "emotional field," it should be noted that the term "intersubjective field" was not developed by Bion but by other analysts with and without reference to his work, most notably in this context by the French-Argentine analyst Madeleine Baranger. See Madeleine Baranger and Willy Baranger, *The Work of Confluence: Listening and Interpreting in the Psychoanalytic Field* (London: Karnac, 2009).

6 See Melanie Klein, "Notes on Some Schizoid Mechanisms" [1946], in *The Writings of Melanie Klein*, vol. 3, *Envy and Gratitude and Other Works* (New York: The Free Press, 1975), 1–24.

7 Wilfred R. Bion, *Learning from Experience* (London: Heinemann, 1962), 31.

8 Ibid., 34–37.

9 Ibid., 90–91. The model of container-contained was applied by Bion himself to a wide range of phenomena, from verbal expression to the institution of psychoanalysis, and by those who followed him to groups and organizations of all shapes, sizes, and functions. Container-contained also seems apt for application to artworks, museums, exhibitions, and curatorial functions, as containers that hold artworks and our raw experiences with them and metabolize these into thought and meaning. This may be the subject of another essay. However, I would caution against our own over-developed capacity, in the art field, to rapidly digest and metabolize insights from other fields in ways that, rather than producing meaning or enabling us to think previously unthinkable experience, may reduce those insights to no more than fuel for the production of discourse that only recapitulates what we think we already know. "Thus one gets not development but division and multiplication—cancerous, not qualitative increase. There appears to be a great increase in ideation, but ... all ideas turn out, on inspection, to be the same one." Wilfred R. Bion, *Attention and Interpretation* (London: Karnac, 1970), 127.

10 Bion, *Experiences in Groups*, 141.

11 Although Bion himself did not seem particularly satisfied with his formulation of basic assumptions, they seem to have withstood the test of thousands of applications in organizations and study groups over the past five decades without significant modification. To my knowledge only two additional basic assumptions have been proposed during that time: the basic assumption "oneness," proposed by Pierre Turquet, when a group behaves "as if" it is in a state of unity and complete homogeneity; and the basic assumption "me-ness," proposed by W. Gordon Lawrence, Alastair Bain, and Laurence Gould, when a group behaves "as if" there is no group at all. The basic assumption "incohesion: aggregation/massification" has been proposed by Earl Hopper as an alternative formulation inclusive of both "oneness" and "me-ness." See Pierre Turquet, "Leadership: The Individual and the Group," in *Analysis of Groups: Contributions to Theory, Research, and Practice*, ed. Graham S. Gibbard, John J. Hartman, Richard D. Mann (San Francisco: Jossey-Bass, 1974), 349–71; W. Gordon Lawrence, Alastair Bain, and Laurence Gould, "The Fifth Basic Assumption," *Free Associations*, vol. 6, part 1, no. 37 (1996): 28–55; Earl Hopper, "Incohesion: Aggregation/

Massificiation: The Fourth Basic Assumption in the Unconscious Life of Groups and Group-like Social Systems," in *Building on Bion: Roots*, ed. Robert M. Lipgar and Malcolm Pines (London: Jessica Kingsley Publishers, 2003), 198–225.

12 — While the concept for the conference occasioning this book seems to evoke hospitality as a form of reciprocity that only *may* turn into dependency, I would argue that in fact the reverse is true: hospitality is a form of dependency that only *may* turn into reciprocity at some future point when that hospitality is returned. However, in most cases the relatively fixed roles of curator and artists would preclude such reciprocity.

13 — It should be noted that what Bion developed was not only a theory of group relations but above all a practice of experiential learning about unconscious dynamics in groups, uniquely applying not only psychoanalytic theory but psychoanalytic technique to social institutions and processes.

14 — Melanie Klein, "Envy and Gratitude," in *Envy and Gratitude*, 188–89, 220. Other Kleinians have identified reparation with creative impulses, most notably Hanna Segal in "A Psycho-Analytical Approach to Aesthetics," *International Journal of Psychoanalaysis*, no. 33 (1952): 196–207.

15 — Melanie Klein, "Our Adult World and Its Roots in Infancy," in *Envy and Gratitude*, 263.

II

—

Hosting and Guest-ing

Alice Creischer, Andreas Siekmann

51

Hospitality

What Kind of Support Do Curators Require from the Institutions Who Hire Them?

I will read you a few things from an "etiquette manual for art institutions" that we have put together based on our experiences with both large and small institutions in recent years.

These experiences can be summarized as a situation in which institutions are increasingly confronted with the threat of budget cuts or increasing costs, or with requests to prove increased economic efficiency or to rationalize. We believe that this call for efficiency is no longer imposed on institutions from the outside, but has instead been transformed into an internalized obedience that, under the guise of neoliberal principles, affects the nature of collaboration and the sense of justice for each participant.

Such calls for efficiency may appear especially arrogant to younger generations of curators and artists. By this I mean younger people who have in recent years effectively become cultural managers, who must take unpaid internships, who are academics and teach without pay as they need to keep teaching in order to retain the possibility of earning a professorship, and so on... The arrogant viewpoint of "re-educated" Germans of the second postwar generation. We assume that this generation are the product of a historically exceptional time of political ethics (due to the pressure of competition between ideological blocs) that younger generations—who are under pressure from the neoliberal deconstruction of democracy—simply do not know or understand.

1. If You Begin a Project with (Visiting, Freelance, Independent) Curators Who Are Employed Outside the Institution in Which the Project Is Based:

Invite the visiting curators to visit the institution in advance of the project, or in its early development, and explain the specific institutional difficulties. Invite the visiting curators to take part in finding solutions. Introduce the visiting curators to as many of the people who work at the institution as possible, not only to the chief administrators. Allow time for the visiting curators to thoroughly explain and discuss their concepts with the staff. Invite the staff to be engaged in a discussion about the project, and to bring their own ideas into the discussion.

All the institution's departments should be in contact as early as possible with the visiting curators, and should trust the curators' experience. If they do so, the people who work in each department will gain great experience and knowledge from the visiting curators. Don't be afraid to lose control. The visiting curators are not crazy; they want the project to take place.

Make sure that people working in all departments know one another as colleagues and are able to work together. Often we have had the impression that institutions consist of completely isolated cells that don't communicate with one another.

Find a way to continue the internal discussions generated by the curators —for example, with newsletters. If there is an assistant for the project, he or she should meet regularly with the curators at the institution, and should take part in all events that accompany the project.

2. Create Public Interest and Discussion Early; From the Beginning of the Project

The "public" does not simply exist; it has to be constantly created through discussions and working processes. Introduce the visiting curators to local people and institutions who might be interesting for, or interested in, the project. All of this will create a discursive field for the project.

Find synergistic connections to seminars at universities, institutions, self-organized spaces, etcetera, very early in the project's development, and try to create a continuous process of discussion and exchange. Foreign curators will be particularly grateful for this. Don't centralize the discussion via the institution, and don't "trademark" it. This would create a closed and hierarchical atmosphere. Try to integrate newspapers and other media into the project at an early stage. Invite the curators and the artists to publish in these newspapers. Artists are not dumb. They are able to write. They often want to articulate themselves directly without the buffer of an institutional interpretation. Make sure that the articulation of the artist always has priority in institutional or art historical mediations.

3. Money

Most institutions are not flexible with their budgets, and are very short of money. But often the distribution of funding is a power play and an attempt to force certain decisions. Don't try to conceal the simple truth that the one who distributes the money has the power—in spite of all talk about collaboration. Be aware of this reality, and be as transparent about it as possible.

Try to explain any funding difficulties as early and as clearly as possible. Be patient if the curators don't immediately understand everything. Try to find solutions together with artists and curators. Trust the artists, they are not all simply "demanding machines." Trust the experiences of the artists and the curators.

Try to get project funding from the state, so the internal distribution of funds can be much more flexible. In this way, one can also distribute money from these internal funding sources to the artists much more quickly, if needed. Put aside a specific amount of money for installation costs, as it will be needed during the time of installation.

Be clear in your decisions and try to explain precarious situations to the artists and curators as openly and politely as possible.

4. Artists' Research Projects

... are currently very fashionable, but are often not understood or supported by institutions. In particular, the financial structure of museum exhibitions is not created to manage projects that require more than six months' time for research. Artistic research projects need financial support for much longer than the time required to produce an exhibition. So they often lead to exhibition institutions feeling overly strained. Time pressure also usually results in foolish, hasty (and, in the worst-case scenario, ignorant) work.

5. Decision-Making

The most traumatic moments for curators are when they are told about decisions in an abrupt and irreversible manner. In these moments the institution becomes a machine of power, and its members turn into arrogant and brainless fulfillers of this power.

Problems should be made transparent to the curators or artists as soon as they appear. Decisions cannot be taken without consulting the curators or the artists as early as possible. Curators are not narcissistic tyrants; they are capable of finding solutions. Be aware that the institution always has the power to realize or destroy things. It is therefore important to act as sensibly and transparently as possible.

6. Exhibition Installation / IN-Sourcing

Often curators are faced with the most extremely absurd types of outsourcing: tables which cannot be built because of public bidding rules, the impossibility of purchasing just one chair, 4000 euro to rent a container. The inflexibility of exhibition installation is contrary to any artistic experience of making and building things.

This combination of outsourcing and "public bidding procedure" has all the characteristics of neoliberal pressure and repression, from the perspective of the institution as well as the freelancers. It frustrates people who are engaged and qualified. AND it is much more expensive than having a permanent staff. It is necessary to fight for more flexible structures. Institutions should think about "in-sourcing" an exhibition installation team. Arguments for this would be the creation of financial opportunities and the accumulation of knowledge through experience. All institutional knowledge and responsibility is lost through outsourcing.

7. Civility

Most people are overworked and exploited in institutions, but in spite of this, it is important to attempt to find gestures that make guests feel welcome: such as, offering a guided visit of the whole building, providing water and coffee during discussions, inviting guests for lunch or dinner, or picking them up personally at the entrance of the location where the talk is taking place, or (if they are foreigners) giving instructions to help them find their way from the airport to the institution. Remember to write questions instead of imperatives in e-mails.

8. Civil Courage

Often institutions present financial shortages, sponsor coercion, outsourcing, time contraints, and censorship of political content as insurmountable constraints, as if there were no way to protest administrations, sponsors, governmental institutions, or make demands. Often one gets the impression that the directors and heads of institutional departments fear too much for their own careers. The pressures are therefore passed on within the hierarchy as practical constraints or inherent necessities. We spoke at the beginning of this "etiquette manual" about the internalization of neoliberal principles. Perhaps we can also speak of a neoliberal mentality, in which obedience to power is fed by two mental sources: the constant fear of losing one's own position, and the permanent hope of getting another job—as poorly paid as it might be.

Our experience shows that civil courage and an ethos of solidarity within the institution are a possible way to escape these fears and the servant-like dilemma.

9. Autonomy

Institutions, however, have a responsibility to maintain and preserve spaces in which it is possible to think freely, to work, and to act. Institutions should not determine the potential of these spaces, but should keep the spaces' "sense of possibility" (Robert Musil) open. While the concept of autonomy has on the one hand been rightfully deconstructed in the case of work of art, it might on the other hand well take on this institutional political valence. Autonomy, independence, is given to the curator by the institution and manifests itself primarily as an advanced working period that is largely unregulated, with the curator only answering to him- or herself.

10. Filling in Forms

However, curators are often forced to explain their work at the outset, to formalize it, to squeeze it into budget calculations as if each project could be conceived entirely and be ready to be realized without an important period of discussion, experience, reasoning, or reflection, which is independent of the coercion of a result.

Curators, kindergarten workers, teachers, or doctors—they are all subject to the same evaluation and monitoring regime. They spend more time filling in forms that enable them to be evaluated than doing their actual work. This pressure to disclose and predict creative work is a general phenomenon of neoliberal regimes, which measure both creativity and social responsibility as a resource. But this economism is NOT rational; it is part of an ideology, and the ongoing evaluations are useless. Efficiency-spying is absurd. Ultimately, it's not about efficiency, but about the exercise of coercive power and control.

This university has an exhibition space that has been showing a remarkable program for some time. The curator of this space has recently terminated her contract. Perhaps some of the points that we have expressed here relate to the reasons for her taking this step.

Anthony Huberman

59

A Toast*

I was sadly not able to join everyone in Leipzig today but, thankfully, Beatrice and I found a way for me to still give my toast.

I'd like to take this opportunity to ask you to join me in toasting and in thanking the artists. All the artists. To any artist who is in this room right now, or to any artist who is not in this room right now: thank you. I realize this seems like a rather common thing to say, but I think it actually isn't common enough. For me, the theme of hospitality evokes the idea that we usually tend to think of the curator as being the artist's host. The curator invites the artist to the institution, and the artist makes an exhibition as a guest of that institution. I'd like to use this toast to suggest that it's actually the other way around. As curators we are always the guests of the artists we choose to work with. We knock on their doors and ask whether they would be open to having us spend some time in their studio, a place they have so carefully constructed over the course of many years. This is the place of their ideas, their questions, their images, their objects, their convictions, their speculations. As a curator, I am always a guest in this place. It is the artist's territory, the artist's house, and I hope to be able to spend some time there. This doesn't mean that there is no room for my voice to be heard in this place. Like any house guest at any dinner party, I won't sit quietly at the table without saying a word. That would be rude. I have my own opinions and impressions about subjects that might come up, and I will share them with my host. We all know that a dinner party is only any good when there are active and vivid exchanges between those sharing a meal. And since, as a curator, I have knocked on the door of this particular artist for specific reasons, I will have plenty of things to say. And, as at any dinner party, those contributions might lead to a lively conversation, or they might not. My host might find my opinions or impressions really engaging or might find them really boring. In the end, my goal is for an artist to be able to then decide whether or not they want to open their home to me and have me spend more time there. That decision is obviously always theirs to make. The artists I have worked with are the ones who opened their door to me, heard my opinions and impressions, and thought I would be a guest they would enjoy having around for a while. I have been grateful to them for that, and I have learned enormously from my time as their guest. What ultimately comes out of our time spent together—producing a museum exhibition or a catalogue essay or an event or whatever else—is a chance for a curator to represent the experience of having been the artist's guest, a chance to contribute an insight or a perspective that is respectful but hopefully also productive and generative, and is sometimes even provocative. It's a chance for a curator to say thank you. In a way, it's a chance to raise a glass, tell some stories, and give an artist a toast. Too many people think of exhibitions as explanation machines, but maybe we could think of an exhibition as a toast, as a way to thank artists, not dissect them. So once again, to all the artists, thank you for your hospitality. Cheers.

* "A Toast" was delivered at the "Symposium: Of Hospitality," May 4–5, 2012, at the SMART Museum of Art, The University of Chicago, and was subsequently published in *Feast: Radical Hospitality in Contemporary Art*, ed. Stephanie Smith (Chicago: SMART Museum of Art / The University of Chicago, 2013), 348.

Thomas Locher in Conversation with Beatrice von Bismarck

Art, Exhibition, and Hospitality

Beatrice von Bismark: In connection with your exhibition in Stuttgart (Sparda-Kunstpreis at Kunstmuseum Stuttgart, 2013) you took up the theme of hospitality. A curatorial situation always represents, in my view, one that presumes hospitality insofar as it entails various forms of making available and laying claim to, of inviting and accepting, which in turn follow a whole series of rules. These rules are implicit, so that we are dealing with a situation of the governmental, with the acceptance of rules that no longer need to be stated. I have asked myself to what extent art that sees itself as institutional critique has taken up this aspect.

Thomas Locher: The reason why I find your turn to the concept of hospitality so interesting is that I recognize hospitality in certain ways that I approach my work and believe that there is an urgency to address this question in the curatorial field: possibly hospitality in the exhibition world is a somewhat inappropriate term, but perhaps precisely the inappropriate is right.

BvB: What do you mean by "inappropriate"?

TL: Hospitality is an ambitious concept … as it is revealed in a relationship between the art institution, the artists, and the temporary housing of art—whatever it might look like. And this idealistic concept of hospitality distorts the fact that it can be a very ordinary process. And, as you said, as a result of all the rules it is already part or repeatedly part of cultural understandings. The granting of hospitality can, however, under certain political or social conditions be a big risk for the person granting it as well as for the person receiving it.

Hospitality is also understood differently depending on one's cultural background. I believe that the concept possesses a great deal of symbolic capital, and that we should therefore reevaluate it. Hospitality is, after all, a special case of friendship. And through the concept of friendship we can describe concepts such as community, the social, or the relationship to the other, to one's neighbor—and to oneself.

In my early grammatical works, I see it expressed on the level of everyday language, in the ontological models, or in works on questions of human rights, or in the work on the constitution, especially the one on the asylum law. I cannot even say precisely whether hospitality is relevant in older or more recent institutional critique, unless the concept of hospitality should lead us to describe the relationships between the various actors in art in a new or different way. I work on very specific institutions, on human rights, on the constitution, on grammar as representation of rules, as far as speaking, language, writing, and text are concerned.

The question of the museum as a machine for representation is interesting, but there are also other fields in which problematic relationships of representation exist. If we see institutional critique above all as a possibility to accept that which is not a given, if we doubt or criticize its composition, then institutional critique is still a useful method and the field of art is the place where it can happen.

BvB: What I find interesting about the concept of hospitality are the various social levels on which it is applied. If you search the term on Google, right at the top you will find a book of etiquette with very specific rules for how a guest and a host should deal with each other. It is about, on the one hand, making it as easy as possible for the guest to enter and settle in and, on the other hand, about the guest never depriving the host of the feeling that he or she is master in his or her own home. At the same time, just as you said, there are much older approaches to and questions about hospitality, which is never idealized but rather represents a basic rule of society in which, interestingly, the right to hospitality is in a position to violate the otherwise usual rights of a community insofar as it is a higher law. Even if a community were to turn on the person or persons enjoying the right to hospitality, the right to hospitality would still be valid and would have to be applied, even if it contradicted the interests of the community.

TL: Would this be the right to hospitality as, so to speak, a suspension of legality or, let's say, of prevailing laws? Hospitality as the possibility of determining a break with prevailing laws, a repeal of normative attributions and prescriptions for cultural behaviors? An exception in which something new can emerge that does not appear on the level of the expected? That is a powerful potential, and that concept contains possibilities for thinking about the future. These possibilities can open up the relationship to the other, for example, in intercultural societies that bring together people of different origins, states, communities, cities, and neighborhoods that have to come together in different situations. In that context, hospitality would be a rather advanced and emancipatory concept. It has been that, after all, on a number of occasions … Pierre Klossowski reconceived the term in an emphatically erotic sense, in a historical context when the term and the related term of community were being completely discredited by Communism and above all by fascism.

BvB: Some of that has entered the discourse on the exhibition, with Charles Esche, for example, when the term "hospitality" was a way of addressing different cultural communities in the Netherlands as possible audiences for the museum, and was also quite fundamentally about the idea pursued by Jacques Derrida of invalidating the discourse of reciprocity in hospitality. That is to say, it was about the question of the basis on which hospitality or hosting [*Gastgeberschaft*], which also contains the word gift [*Gabe*], can move out of a reciprocal economy so that the gift can also seem like something wasteful.

TL: Waste is an aspect of disposal, when the person giving gives more or uses more than he or she actually has. As with hospitality, it has to hurt in some way when one gives it or gives a gift one doesn't have … when waste and disposal become a risk for one's own economy. The gift is something fleeting, and it hasn't been proven whether it exists at all. Circulation, the cycle of money and goods, is still the dominant image of economic circumstances. And Derrida is concerned precisely with interrupting or breaking through or suspending this cycle.

Suspension is not always a positive concept; depending on the context, it can also be a problematic concept, for example, when under specific political circumstances constitutional or human rights are revoked, when they are suspended. Let's return to art: Beyond a responsibility that art and cultural institutions have as a result of their mission, they have to make a symbolic playing field available in which things can be tried out that perhaps cannot be discussed in society, because the reality of the social is not a playing field. But the symbolic levels of the art and cultural institutions permit such trying out; they allow suspension as a kind of pause or break with what is repeatedly held up to us as a standard or convention.

BvB: What could this aspect of canceling valid laws mean to institutions? Marcel Mauss distinguished between the gift as ritual and the gift as employed in potlatch. As a ritual, it is what makes the exchange of commodities (trade) possible in the first place. The gift produces this situation. In potlatch, by contrast, it is about competition. The one who has the most to offer is the winner. I am interested in the significance this distinction can have for institutions. Is the situation of hosting in art institutions more a ritual that paves the way for other forms of exchange, or are we dealing with a competitive situation? The latter would correspond to current changes in institutions and new economic and social strategies for museums. Hosting is introduced as a value into the competition between institutions because this act reveals the ability to have resources, space, finances, personnel, or symbolic capital. Applying that to your specific situation at the exhibition in Stuttgart, who or what really plays the role of the host?

TL: The situation in Stuttgart was that three artists were invited, one of whom would be the prizewinner in the end. It looked like one of the three people proposed simply received a prize. That is not correct, of course: the prize is not a gift but is rather associated with a counteraction: an exhibition has to be organized, that is, there is a precondition for this prize becoming a prize. And this prize is not something that exists outside the economy. It is preserved in a structure of gift and gift in return, and it is not independent of economic circumstances. Naturally, the question is whether the gift as such exists at all. That is something that is not entirely clear. The interesting thing about a prize is its double meaning in German [Preis = prize/price—Trans.]: a prize is something that is given for something, and price is also a designation of value. What does something cost? Thus Preis has a double function. Naturally, value is attached to the prize as a prize that is given, but every term that has multiple meanings brings the other connotations along; they cannot be repressed but repeatedly come up in the relationship of the giver and the recipient of the prize. And then we have a museum that functions as a link, since it provides the place where the prize is handed over. No one gets a prize simply for existing. Every prize has a social function. It is not without a price.

BvB: If you start at the step before that, then there is this invitation to the exhibition for three artists. This is a kind of generosity that consists of offering space, time, and resources to make this show possible in the first place. Built into this is a quite complex system of give and take. The invitation comes from the museum to the artists, who for their part accept the invitation and specifically in two ways: they accept, first, making the exhibition and, second, competing with the two other exhibitors for the prize. These are the two dimensions of the invitation. At this point one could ask whether the host is the museum or the bank, since both of them are giving something. Moreover, you give something as well, taking on the role of the host, in that you offer something to look at and invite people to view it. At the same time, you play the role of the guest, since by accepting the invitation you make it possible for the offer to be a guest to be transformed into a situation of hospitality.

TL: There are three givers. The bank provides the idea and the means (the money); the museum makes its spaces and its reputation as an art institution available. The bank needs the museum to place its idea for the prize in a cultural framework. The bank needs an institution that occupies a fixed place in art's operating system in order to be able to produce an elaborate form of hospitality at all. It needs the right place with the appropriate furnishings, a collection, specialists, opportunities to produce a public, the opportunity to be able to create a level of appropriateness with an eye on reception, on taking care of the visitors, and so on—everything that institutions have to have in order to do justice to the role of the host, to fulfill their obligation to the public. And it needs the artists with their products. Artists, in turn, need the museum as a machine for recognition, and sometimes they just enjoy exhibiting in great spaces. That is an interesting mix of circumstances—everyone gives and receives something. And we haven't even mentioned yet the critics, gallery owners, and collectors, and, when things go well, the audience, an interested and critical public. Altogether it is a win-win situation with three partners. There are various real and symbolic forms of capital that all three participants have. It isn't as if the artists possess the pure, symbolic capital; it would be too naive to believe that. Nor is the bank's real capital simply evil. Capital and the artist do not stand outside of the economy. Artists are just as much situated in this system of economics and profitability.

They do not find themselves in a privileged situation per se—unless their ideas and products produce an effect in the present or possess an afterlife that goes beyond the relationship of commodity and money. Unfortunately, we cannot predict that. At best, the visitors have an aesthetic experience that cannot be had for free, and hence is not immaterial and noneconomic, but neither is it purely economic. By the way, I too benefit from the museum's reputation; I believe I gain something as well. The bank, which cleverly cooperates with the museum to make these exhibitions possible, also gains something in that it shifts the prize to a cultural field and thus increases the prize's value, since its position means it could not place it there itself. The museum finances an exhibition in economically difficult times. We all take and all give.

The question is: Who gains the most? I don't know whether the artist is the winner of the whole thing. It could also be that the prize as such is "contaminated," because it is a gift—and what we know about the essence of banks as companies is that they don't give anything away. As customers of banks, we know that it is a business. There is no generosity without some calculation behind it. I hope that is true, because I can try to read and assess a calculation. The second "contamination" of the prize is its quality of being a kind of disturbance within a structure of people who are apparently of equal value and have equal rights. The prize shatters this seemingly harmonious structure between givers and takers. It is a prize, and it is only given to one person. Like the gift, the prize is a kind of rift, but we know what a prize is. It is calculated. And we also know that it exists.

BvB: The heart of the question is whether there is, beyond such calculated economics, a symbolic level on which this giving could be a form of giving too much, of wasting, of, as you call it, "altruistic giving," and, if so, from what perspectives this form would be sensible or productive.

TL: I do not stand outside of the economic as an artist. Probably no one does. There is something about the gift or present that does not conform entirely to our understanding of economics. The gift is a special case. There is some suspicion. Why do we feel that? We get gifts on holidays or on a special occasion. The pure gift, the altruistic gift, has something very problematic about it. Because we know that we never really just get something. And that raises the question of generosity and the patronizing. The giving of gifts or alms may be an act of humanity, but it is by no means a form of compensation in the sense of economic justice. There is a difference between the giver and the receiver; they are on different levels socially. In essence, the giver always seems to be in a better position than the recipient. The potential recipient can, of course, reject the gift. And rejection would certainly be an act of self-determination. Like the dichotomy of master and servant … Is the refusal to accept perhaps the only possibility to escape an obligation? But servants are not aware of their true strength, namely, the power of negation. Or perhaps they know it but don't use it. And masters always see themselves in a stronger position, because they know nothing about their own weakness.

BvB: You say there is the possibility of rejecting the gift. But what are the consequences of such a rejection? In your work, you speak of the movement of reversing the law. Can rules that imply an invitation be reversed?

TL: I could also have turned down the invitation, but then there would have been no event. A rejection only makes sense if there is a compelling reason for it and it points out a structure of events that also communicates the rejection and all its reasons to the outside. It has to get fed into the system of communication, otherwise it makes no sense; otherwise it remains in this nonpublic structure of communication and does not contribute as a decision for or against an event. That makes no sense at all.

BvB: Now, in our conversation, you are addressing the acceptance of the invitation …

TL: In the exhibition, I will not address the prize or go into the principles of these reciprocal connections, but this text addresses that question. To the extent that the text is part of an artistic presentation, it is also part of a representation. Our conversation is not just an explanatory addendum but is a fully adequate supplement. My contribution to the exhibition will include works that grapple with social and linguistic relationships—more precisely, with the linguistic character of social relationships, with the obligations of the law, and also with the possibility of suspending it. I will be showing works that describe the relationship to the other in a different way, works that address the different constructions of the subject and its relationships to the object.

BvB: In your work with tables and chairs to which texts are applied you have created, I find, a very concise, ambiguous situation that has to do with hospitality. You invite people to sit down but at the same time offer messages written on the chairs. You play with refusal and withdrawal. The works even refuse in two ways, semantically and functionally. The expectations they can arouse in those who address them remain unsatisfied. For me, this manifests a revealing of the law of invitation.

TL: Few objects embody the human and at the same time the communicative more than the chair and table. A chair is an everyday object and is in use everywhere; it invites and challenges. In the context of art, however, chairs are not just chairs. They are not necessarily chairs to be sat on … I don't sit just anywhere there are chairs. I'm not interested in the real aspect of sitting but rather in the symbolic aspect that lies in the combination of everyday object and language, in the unusual connection of language and object—and in displacement. There are also a few sentences attached to these chairs that are concerned with a certain form of the temporal. Several sentences employ the future perfect tense, which in Jacques Lacan's psychology is conceived as the language of the unconscious, as the moment that points to the future and at the same time goes back to the past—and hence in a sense circles around the future. In the deconstruction of the present that takes place between the viewer, the object, and language here, the present is what cannot be communicated. It can only be communicated through representation, through a spatial and temporal displacement or delay. Hence there has to be a break with the present so that the present can be represented. And it's about that as well; it was conceived as a critique of Minimalism, as an attempt to replace the self-contained identity of Minimalism with the concept of the non-identical.

BvB: I also understand the moment of "interruption" you spoke of in this sense; with the title *Suspended* (2010), in my view, you explicitly make a motivic reference to the chair work. You mark a state of exception that results from the inadequacy of what is offered.

TL: *Suspended* is a navigation system located within a grid, and the grid is also an image of power. But it is more about using a physical localization of texts and signs to reveal the problems of the placelessness of the central subject of human rights: the refugee. An aesthetic form is always a contradictory form as well … in this case, a form where everything seems to be in its place and that uses, in the form of the grid, a system with which every place can be precisely described, in order to—and this is, in my view, the central aspect of the work—formalize the placelessness of the refugee, of "being displaced." "Suspended" means both "hung down from" and "adjourned"—a term with multiple meanings. The big problem with human rights is the inability to honor them. When human rights are needed most urgently they cannot be called upon, because they are suspended, because they no longer have validity … because no one respects human rights anymore in a war situation. That is the principle contradiction: that there have to be constitutional states that guarantee these rights, but precisely where they are needed most urgently they are unavailable and unenforceable.

BvB: The right to hospitality is closely connected with the assumption that one is protected in the place one is a guest, a condition that can be demanded from a society as well as from an art institution.

TL: The term "asylum" comes from a Greek word meaning "inviolable." The institution guarantees the artist a protected space. In the open field, as it were, there is no art. Art needs a localization, a placement; art doesn't just happen. It has to be presented, and this presentation has to fulfill certain conditions. Historically, artists and artists' groups have repeatedly violated these conditions; they have tried to break out of the protected space, which is also delimited and does not offer room for everyone, and to create other spaces with other criteria of assessment. Art institutions create a protected space; they guarantee artists a certain form of appropriateness for their presentation. Things exhibited in art institutions experience a reception that would be difficult or even impossible to experience outside them, because elsewhere art would not even be perceived as art.

BvB: In that case, protection would mean making a time and space available to allow something, whatever it is, to happen. However, that position also runs the risk of paternalism: being the host and lawgiver in one's house means determining what can and does happen there. Here too an aspect of suspension comes into play, insofar as you can permit something within your house that might be criticized and rejected outside your house.

TL: Yes, you don't know how the guest will behave, whether he or she will be a good guest or a bad one …

BvB: What is a bad guest?

TL: A bad guest is, to start with, one who doesn't want to leave. The temporary is something the guest should pay attention to, to the fact that there is a time in which he or she is the guest, and then this time is up.

BvB: So there is a rule that fixes when the time of being a guest is running out?

TL: The duration of the guest as guest is undecided; it isn't clear when it runs out. The question of hospitality is problematic in connection with the issue of asylum because setting a time limit causes a problem. The asylum seeker or the person granted asylum is no guest. The status as guest is inappropriate for the asylum seeker. Asylum cannot be part of thinking about hospitality … unless we remove the temporary, the time limit, from the question of exile and understand asylum as a special case of hospitality. That is the problem of all reflection on issues of migration, asylum, and refugees … Hospitality alone is insufficient to deal with such issues: People come to us from other countries needing protection and then they are supposed to return to the country from which they came. And if they don't do that, they are abusing the right to hospitality. But they aren't guests, since in some cases they cannot ever return. They are immigrants.

BvB: Inherent in the word "hospitality" is that a host makes the other a guest but, in keeping with the Latin meaning of *hospes*, also "foreign." If someone makes someone else foreign, the line between hospitality and asylum becomes fluid. Transferred to the sphere of art, this making foreign indicates the temporary dimension of lingering, such as the limitation of the stay through the duration of the exhibition or its extension through acquisition. How this temporality of hospitality is defined is a matter for negotiation. What guidelines are annulled when a guest stays too long? What possibilities of reversal or suspension exist that would enable the guest to determine the conditions of his or her role as guest? How can you perhaps reverse the law, which has been assigned to you as a result of your having been invited, into something that allows you to determine your role as guest?

TL: The guest may be a foreigner … but isn't every other fundamentally a foreigner? Whether a guest or not? Being foreign can also be something really great, after all, something that enriches my existence … because the foreigner brings something that I am not. Couldn't we embrace, accept, or appreciate the foreignness of the other? Moreover, with the help of deconstruction, you can see yourself as different from yourself, understand yourself as a non-identical subject, and see yourself as a subject that renounces identities … The way I see myself is how I construct the prerequisite for seeing the other. And if I am foreign to myself, then the foreignness of the other is something quite natural.

BvB: How does that apply to exhibition situations? You speak of the idea of temporality in exhibitions. I can't say precisely whether these temporalities correspond to each other.

TL: When guests exceed their time, they violate the convention; they break with the consensus, the unwritten agreement of the exhibition business. The essence of conventions is that they are known to all the actors. So the guests also know that they have exceeded the time allotted to them. And they become bad guests. That stresses the host. I believe, however, that in our field there have to be reasons when such a situation occurs. The bad guest must be able to justify his or her badness; here too there has to be an urgency that can be communicated. In order to resolve this situation, the host has to step out of his or her role.

One could perhaps say that temporal changes in the structure of art are also tied to changes in roles and how the actors see themselves. The actors have to abandon their roles and redefine them. That will not happen painlessly. Rules are not eternally valid; they are negotiable. In the legal sphere, there is always a temporal dimension to validity. New laws replace old laws. And because laws are texts to be interpreted, the laws or rules of the constitution, precisely because they are written to be universal, are reinterpreted again and again. One current example is the debate over equal treatment of adoption by same-sex partners. There has to be pressure in the direction of equality to drive changes toward equal rights. Laws and rules, including those of hospitality, are subject to change.

I would like to return to the question of where the political aspect lies in this. In *The Politics of Friendship*, Jacques Derrida manages to refute the classical distinction of friend and enemy according to Carl Schmitt, who located the political quality precisely in this distinction—as if the subject were only political when summed up in this dialectic. The friend-enemy schema is a radical distinction, as it were, but it always operates only on the level of inclusion and exclusion; it is caught up in thinking about origins, linguistic and cultural identity, gender, and nation. That is what interests me about thinking about friendship or hospitality in connection with questions about the field of art, about changed understandings of the curatorial. And that is the reason why I asked to include a conversation in this publication—

a conversation about a different yet mutual interest in a concept such as hospitality.

BvB: One could say that within the hospitality we are discussing the asymmetries of the situation are clear but the positions are dynamic in terms of how power is assigned.

TL: That would be something … Different positions cannot be smoothed out or balanced in this structure, but they will not always exist everywhere. We do not establish a relationship based on a concept, namely, the relationship of the institution to art or to the public, since the public also appears in the institutions (as guests). The relationship cannot be reduced to one level, but if the differences are not too great, and if the participants have different positions, some stronger than others, then sometimes it can also be reversed or changed. Positions are not fixed for all times.

BvB: Do you understand your art as a gift?

TL: I would despair if I didn't believe there is something beyond that which exists—a beyond, a priceless beyond, so to speak. There has to be something that does not have a price, otherwise there would be no value at all. I believe that if art were a completely normal commodity like any other it would shock me, but I'm not sure. Of course I put myself and my things on the market. The market itself is certainly not a pure market. Some gallery owners who see themselves as part of the system of culture would affirm that: they also produce exhibitions, with their own capital, but with an awareness that they are contributing to something that is called culture. And what we call culture oscillates between "has a price" and "has no price." Now one certainly needs economic conditions in order to take something called culture and bring it into circulation, produce it, show it, sell and buy it, keep it, preserve it, deposit it in structures of memory, describe it, process it discursively … that is to say, everything that happens with works of art cannot happen without an economy. But if there were only economy, it would be awful …

BvB: One of your works is titled *Gift* [2006]. It says: "The gift gives, demands, and takes time," which would bring us back to a different economic logic, one that has to do with the spatial and temporal structure of the exhibition, with granting time but also with taking time, taking time for oneself but also taking someone else's time. The time of attention plays a big role. It is less about a financial logic than about an economy of attention.

TL: Time can be hyper-economic, in the sense of an efficiency of industrial production; the postulate of that logic is "Time is money." Hence other economies of time or other conceptions of time can be productive in a very different sense. On the other hand, wasting time can be a necessary part of artistic production—removing oneself and doing nothing. Although … doing nothing is doing something very important.

BvB: The fact that we meander between different economic logics is ultimately in keeping with the movement of the structural dynamics within the constellation into which you place yourself in your exhibition if one sees it from the perspective of its hospitality.

TL: But it is always also about studying whether there are still spaces or concepts in this field that produce a certain openness; concepts that change and set change in motion, and create new evaluations in a different context. Is there something that is left out in the question of negotiation? A concept that can take on completely different forms and formats in the curatorial and in the exhibition business? The interesting thing is that within the relatively broad field that is the curatorial the concept of hospitality has initiated a search for what this promise of an openness represents.

This conversation was first published in German, in slightly different form, in Ulrike Groos, ed., *Thomas Locher: Kubus; Sparda-Kunstpreis im Kunstmuseum Stuttgart*, exhibition catalogue (Bielefeld: Kerber, 2013), 6–21.

Wiebke Gronemeyer

Competing Agencies

From Host to Guest to Parasite; A Case Study of unitednationsplaza

In the past two decades, the discourse around curatorial practice has lived through different, often simultaneous phases, each marked by diverse patterns of hospitality. From the dominant curator-figure to the artist-curator to collaborative and collective practices, in each scenario the question of authorship weighs differently in relation to the institutional as well as the public sphere.

In a 1996 essay, part of the seminal book *Thinking About Exhibitions*, Bruce W. Ferguson defines the exhibition as a medium of contemporary art "in the sense of being its main agency of communication—the body and voice from which an authoritative character emerges."[1] Therein he refers to so-called standard stories, which for long dominated curatorial, or rather, museological, discourse. In these the host is the institution, instigating and affirming the processes of experience, interpretation, and knowledge production that take place in the exhibition space in the name of the public, which is in the role of the guest. The artist is almost never present in these stories, and if so only as represented by the art object, whose function is reduced to a mere carrier of information with little or no agency. But since the late 1960s, when Conceptual art affirmed the possibility of an art object having agency, the public role of the art institution, that of a host, changed upon the emergence of theories of representation "which situate art and its function in a larger semiotic environment together with strong economic and social demands."[2]

Curatorial practices today are deeply indebted to the changes Conceptual art introduced to the way the exhibition is perceived as a relational space implying complex forms of agencies.[3] The encounter between host and guest in the communicative space of the exhibition is subject to a variety of constellations—aesthetic, economic, social, and political—that condition the patterns of hospitality at stake within the space. These constellations are what artists and curators wrestle with in order to determine possibilities for action in relation to an increasingly compromised public sphere.

Cultural theorist Tony Bennett calls this conditional context of practices the "culture complex," an effective reality in which social and cultural conditions are not abstract domains, but can be described as specific constellations of people and things that are the result of historically specific circumstances.[4] According to Bennett, the notion of culture needs to be interpreted as "a historically fabricated—in the sense of 'materially made' not 'invented'—set of entities [...] paying attention to the processes through which culture was produced as an autonomous realm that was made to

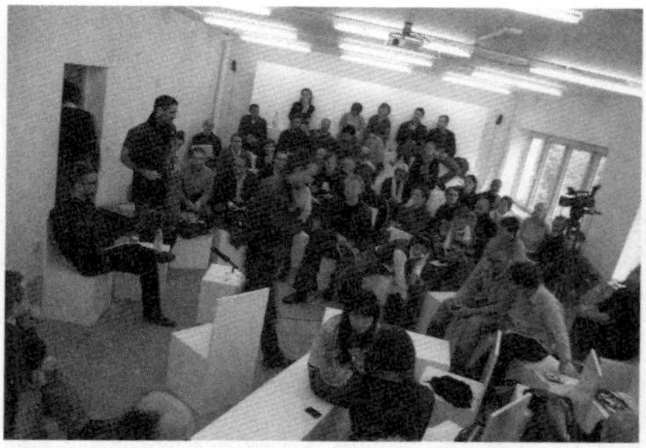

A seminar with Diedrich Diederichsen, October 29, 2006. "Opening weekend: Histories of Productive Failures: From French Revolution to Manifesta 6," unitednationsplaza, Berlin

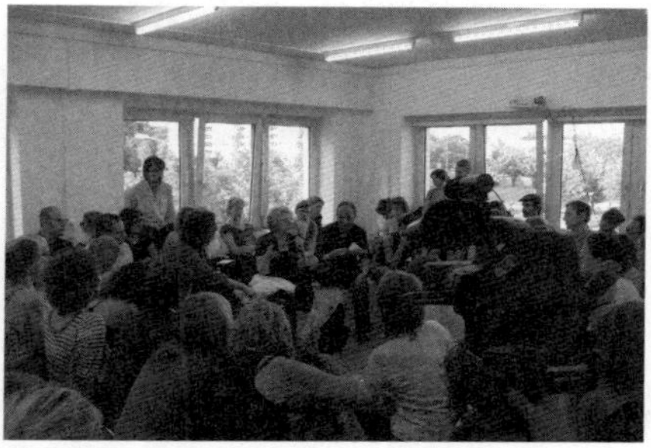

Discussion with Martha Rosler, June 19, 2007. Martha Rosler Library lecture program, unitednationsplaza, Berlin

stand apart from the social in order that it might then act back on it as a moralizing, improving force."[5] Cultural practices, then, emerge from a historically contested ground of the governance of social relations and operate today in a complex of different strategies, knowledge, expertise, technologies, and apparatuses, which are connected to a set of governmental forms of rule-implementing power structures and the specific modes in which power is exercised.[6]

In order to discuss the curated encounter in this context as a situation of hospitality, this essay proposes to look at the complicity of agencies involved in manufacturing a realm for cultural practices to operate in—specifically artistic and curatorial practices. In the culture complex that is the conditional context of such practices, the responsibility a host assumes in any situation of hospitality can be determined by asking how much a host is already, can, or wants to accommodate his or her own dependency on the prevalent socio-economic system.

From Host to Guest to Parasite

Collaborative and collective practices present a particularly interesting perspective for discussing the specific complexities of agencies and responsibilities at stake in the changing landscape of cultural practices today. Oliver Marchart, talking about the role of the curatorial subject between individuality and collectivity, questions whether the collective as a form of sharing responsibility is an answer and alternative to the competitiveness and strive for individualization emerging in what Boltanski and Chiapello call the "project-based polis," a complex form of governmental rule in which the question of authorship is the measure of power and success.[7] Initially Marchart locates a tension between the curator-subject whose "occupational image blends the project organizer and the consultant with the autonomous artist" and examples of collective counter-practices.[8] Even though the latter are considered a result of the project-based polis's imperatives of teamwork and networking, they can productively complicate two things when it comes to breaking through traditional patterns of hospitality in the curated encounter: (1) they result in a demystification of the genius-curator or grand-curator figure; (2) by undercutting authoritarian hierarchies, they effect different forms of subjectivation that serve to question and negotiate the roles and responsibilities of the individual within collective work processes.

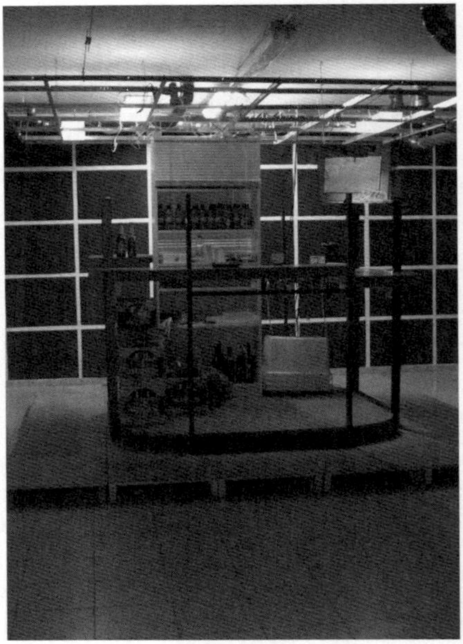

unitednationsplaza bar: Salon Aleman. A project by Ethan Breckenridge, Julieta Aranda, Eduardo Sarabia, Danna Wajda, Willi Brisco. unitednationsplaza, Berlin, October, 2006

A particularly good example of the shifts in roles and responsibilities in collaborative and collective practices with regards to patterns of hospitality in the curated encounter is a discursive project initiated in the fall of 2006 by Anton Vidokle and a group of collaborators.[9] Over the course of a year a self-organized event-based program of talks, lectures, workshops, and screenings, involving around 100 artists, writers, curators, and theorists, took place in a former supermarket office at Berlin's Platz der Vereinten Nationen (United Nations Plaza). The events—during evenings, weekends, and sometimes whole weeks—were free to attend, but the space was quite small. The attendees gave presentations, hosted discussions, or had drinks at the bar. The audiences—at times large, and at times small—were mostly made up of international artists or art affiliates living in Berlin.[10]

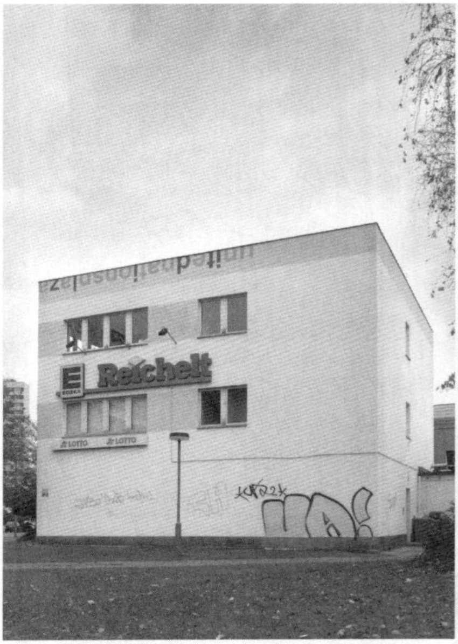

UNP by day. unitednationsplaza, Berlin, October, 2006

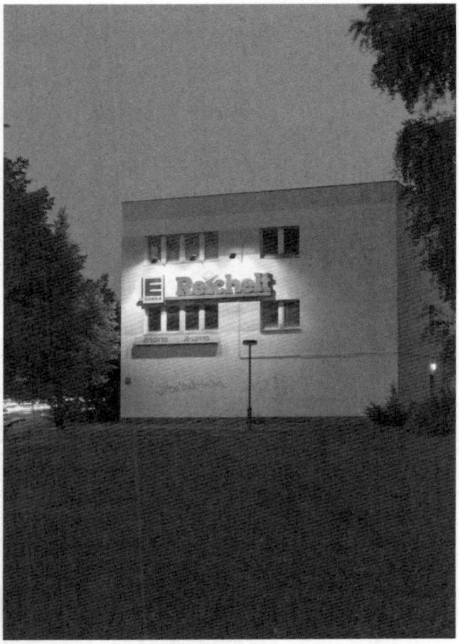

UNP by night. unitednationsplaza, Berlin, October, 2006

Vidokle initiated the project following the cancellation of Manifesta 6, the biennial curated by Mai Abu ElDahab, Anton Vidokle, and Florian Waldvogel that had been scheduled to take place in Cyprus in 2006, eschewing the format of a biennial exhibition for that of a temporary art school, but never happened due to a variety of conceptual and political reasons.[11]

Vidokle's continued interest in experimenting with different discursive formats in the space of the exhibition can be regarded as an attempt to model an alternative pattern of hospitality for the relationship between institution, artist, and public. His writings during and after unitednationsplaza are proof of this,[12] as is the project's spatial setup, its configuration as a gathering space for people. Inside the former supermarket office, different spaces were furnished with a modular system, whose elements could be configured to facilitate all sorts of different activities: speaking, talking, screening, reading, cooking, drinking, dancing, and so on.

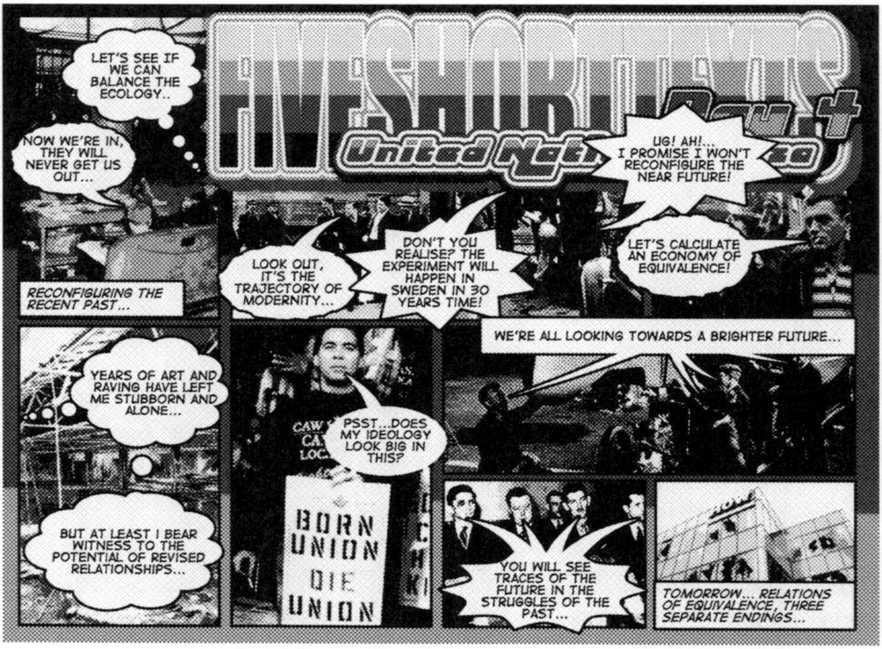

A seminar with Liam Gillick, "Five Short Texts on the Possibility of Creating an Economy of Equivalence," May 7–11, 2007. unitednationsplaza, Berlin

The spatial concept of unitednationsplaza made reference to the ambivalent character of the contemporary art institution, presenting models of institutions, such as galleries, theaters, and schools.

The following analysis looks at the shifts in the roles and responsibilities of all the participants in the project, focusing primarily on Vidokle's role as a host, in order to then consider Marchart's proposition of valuing collective work processes for undercutting traditional patterns of authoritarian hierarchies both in relation to unitednationsplaza and to the cultural field.

Is unitednationsplaza a productive example of such collective work processes? Is autonomy produced by agencies released as a result of processes of subjectivation negotiated within and as part of the collective endeavor? Finally, does this fostering of agency dissolve any distinction between host and guest in the hospitable condition of the curated encounter? If so, how can patterns of hospitality in collective and collaborative practices be described? Answering this question throughout the next paragraphs in

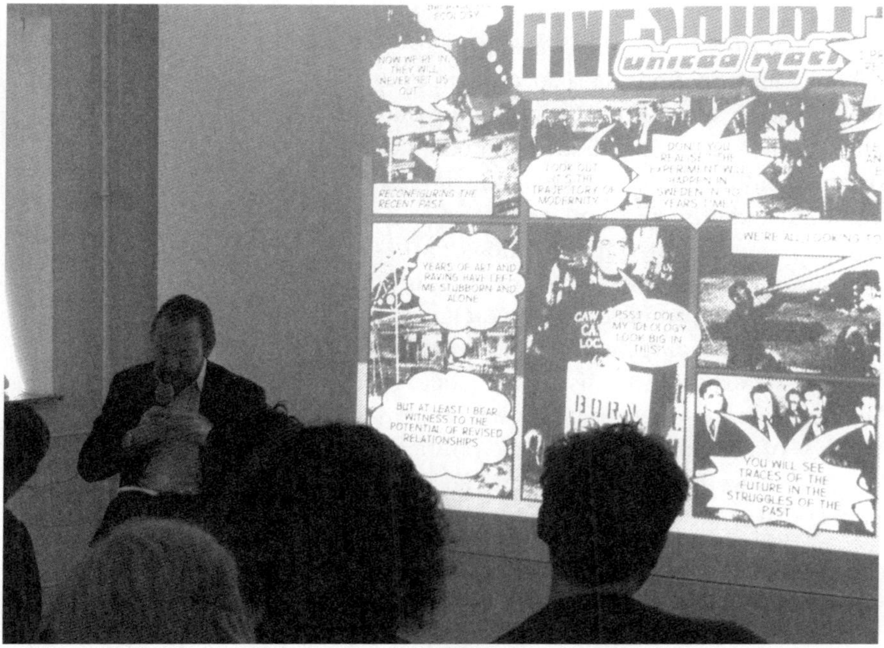

order to consider curatorial agency in the context of an economy of hospitality within contemporary teamwork and network cultures will also address how the complicated social, cultural, political, and economic dependencies resulting from governmental forms of role are wrapped within the collective subjectivities that come to define notions like public authorship or collective autonomy.

unitednationsplaza created a communicative space for relationships to develop over time, with different roles and responsibilities involved in the project all subsumed under the notion of "participants"; it thereby challenged many assumptions that underlie the making and curating of art in contemporary times, such as the clearly defined roles of curators and artists, the space of the exhibition, art as a medium of critique, and the forms in which public engagement is explored in institutional practices. The project was conceived in opposition to what Ferguson calls the "standard story," a straightforward definition of the institution or the curator being the host of an exhibition in which the art object as much as the viewer is a guest with no or only little agency. Referred to by Vidokle as "exhibition as school," unitednationsplaza adopted an exclusively discursive format (with no objects on show) aimed at critiquing the ways in which art practice and education have become modes of production geared towards a consumer-oriented cultural sphere.[13] Resisting an order of things in which artists, curators, and critics assume certain roles and act out certain behavior patterns inherited from the tradition of art as a solitary studio practice and education as a transmission of preordained knowledge from master to disciple, the project instead aimed at an order of things that is not common to the institution, or to the space of the exhibition, or to the realm of academia.

Vidokle explores the discursive model of art practice as an alternative to the framework of the exhibition with regards to how art can function as a catalyst of the cultural, social, and political histories that condition its production, as well as its reception.[14] The ambition and the experimental and self-effacing nature of unitednationsplaza is indebted to the concept of the art school as an alternative model of practice. Vidokle saw the potential of this setup as one that is not simply a process of learning, "but can be and often is a highly active site of cultural production: books and magazines, exhibitions, new *commissioned* works, seminars and symposia, film screenings, concerts, performances, theatre productions, new fashion and product designs [...] these and many other activities and projects can all be triggered in a school."[15] He emphasizes the idea of space triggering processes of transformation rather than being viewed as a secluded and privileged site for knowledge production. Vidokle would want unitednationsplaza to be understood first of all as a transformative project, which prompts the question: How are patterns of hospitality to be configured to allow for such processes of transformation to take place?

Another important part of the narrative framing the unitednationsplaza's constitution of a pattern of hospitality is the role of the public. Here, Vidokle sides with artist Martha Rosler, who in the 1980s observed that "spectators of art have largely lost their political agency as such" and have "no necessary means or particular interest in affecting social change."[16] Vidokle seeks to create a communicative environment in which a kind of active engagement in the sense of a political agency is possible. Therefore he enlists artistic practice to reissue a relationship between art and the public, not only for the sake of the public, but also for the artist to be able to produce the very conditions that enable artistic practice. As a catalyst of society, art's role is to "recuperate the agency of art in the absence of an effective public."[17]

Even though Vidokle would probably not agree,[18] I would preliminarily argue that curators also subscribe to this role as a form of curatorial responsibility—producing a communicative space and thereby *facilitating* a room for arguing, debating, and generating art as a product of the social, political, cultural factors that condition it. From this perspective it seems irrelevant to distinguish between the practice of an artist and that of a curator, or to try to formulate their roles in opposition to each other. Instead, the profile of the curator fulfills equally the demands placed on the figure of the autonomous, innovative, self-organized artist who adopts principles of project-based work and networking. Both artistic and curatorial practices thereby meet the criteria to guide processes of subjectivation.[19] An important characteristic of such practices is the moment of gathering, which Katharina Schlieben describes as integral to social practice as the moment in which processes of subjectivation take place. The patterns of hospitality that devise the curated encounter emerge from a fragmented and incomplete knowledge, which in the process of gathering is ultimately transformed to produce joint social action.[20] The roles of host and guest are dissolved into those of participants in social action.

Vidokle rendered the openness of unitednationsplaza, with its discursive format that facilitated different forms of gathering, by offering everyone who came the possibility to participate to the degree that they wished, thereby allowing "the audience to have an active stake in the situation."[21]

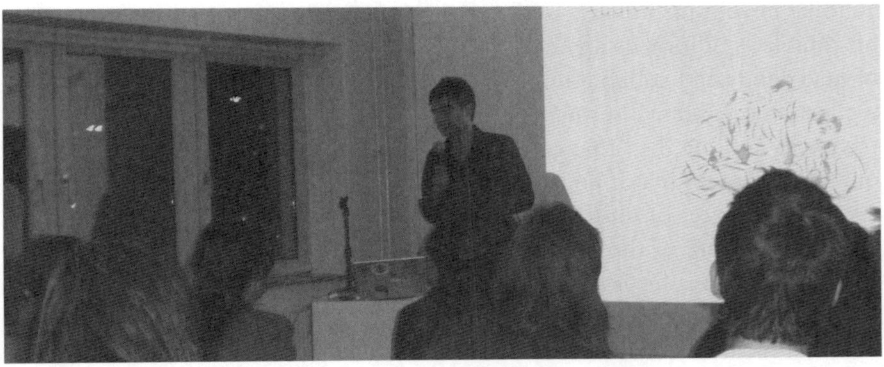

A seminar with Tirdad Zolghadr, "That's Why You Always Find Me in the Kitchen at Parties," March 12–23, 2007, unitednationsplaza, Berlin.

The function of the discursive is not only to provide an open process that offers moments of gathering, but to make sure that the opportunity to gather does not cease, or else the social moment that is being constructed will be lost and the hospitable situation will fall back into certain limitations, those of the exhibition space, for example. In this sense, Liam Gillick describes the discursive as not only what produces the work but also, in the form of critical and impromptu exchanges, as its desired result.[22] The discursive is a mode of construction in the form of a continuous fabrication of speculations over fragments of knowledge waiting to be negotiated through the collective nature of the project. To the same extent, the positionalities displayed in conversations are equally incomplete regarding authorship. Their individuality can only be viewed in the context of their collectivity.

Hosting Relations

Jan Verwoert discusses the authorship of Anton Vidokle in terms of hospitality having a relational quality. "To authorize also means to inhabit the space you open up through your voice, your discourse, to spend time in this space, furnish it and turn it into a place for living."[23] For Verwoert, the kind of authorship that Vidokle assumes is that of a "contemporary host" who is "called forth to conjure up names of saints, seasons or rites of passage to celebrate and themes to interpret in order for guests to be invited, audiences to be invoked, thought to be gathered and works to be created."[24] With other words, Verwoert describes Vidokle as a facilitator, generating the conditions for engagement, functioning as a commissioner, programmer, and editor. Vidolke never puts himself in the chair of the presenter, never discloses the hospitable condition as an authorial gesture. Rather, at most of the events of his friends and collaborators—whether writers, artists, or curators—he is a guest among many. Furnishing the communicative space of the discursive means to assume the "role of being a keeper of the building, as well as one of the voices that it houses."[25] Vidokle's authorial position as the initiator and organizer of unitednationsplaza is somewhat concealed by the collective nature of the project.

However, over the course of unitednationsplaza a series of events challenged the understanding that, as a means of devising a space to let a relation between the host and the guest flourish, the host preliminarily becomes a guest to the discursive condition created. Under the title "That's Why You Always Find Me in the Kitchen at Parties," curator and writer Tirdad

Zolghadr intended to "pursue this possibility of new forms of discussion as rigorously as possible," aiming to "apply the analytical rigor customarily reserved for ideological, infrastructural, or art-critical concerns to the very material format in which these discussions are embedded."[26] In other words, he aimed at testing Vidokle's call for an active, productive engagement, and thereby investigated the discursive as an infrastructure ambivalent towards any form of authorial positioning in relation to the audience's participation. The specific targets of Zolghadr's intervention were the seminar and the lecture, formats that dominated unitednationsplaza. Even when not performed in an academic or otherwise institutional setting, these open spaces for conversation always entail the allocation of roles: speaker versus audience. Zolghadr was interested in pointing to how the audience participation Vidokle was asking for was hindered by the rather conventional academic format. He did this by changing the format every night, inviting other colleagues and artists to devise a program resulting in a variety of performances, a book launch, a scripted discussion, and so on. In particular, an intervention by the artist Chris Evans set off a debate on how strategies of exclusion control the discursive even when the intention is to provide possibilities for inclusion. Evans invited several other participants, including Michael Baers, Natascha Sadr Haghighian, and Zolghadr himself, to sit down at the kitchen table for a discussion that was broadcast via video to the seminar room. The divide between those in the kitchen and those in the seminar room was amplified when the broadcasting didn't work (unintentionally, however). People in the seminar room could not hear anything, which they thought was part of the performance and understood as the intention to alienate the audience from the discussion. In response, some people in the seminar room decided to form their own discussion—buying their own drinks, and eventually using the modular furnishing to barricade the kitchen with the performers inside. Later, the participants in the kitchen asked why nobody had communicated the failing broadcast to them; they questioned how much the other participants' reaction fell prey to reinforcing conventional hierarchies by furthering the agonistic separation with the blockade.[27]

The arguments that resulted from Evans's intervention point to the economies of attention that determine the level of participation and engagement when the discursive is employed as a medium for interaction serving to generate different, predominantly more informal and less didactically governed conditions for knowledge production. Despite its intentions, unitednationsplaza did not articulate precisely the relationship

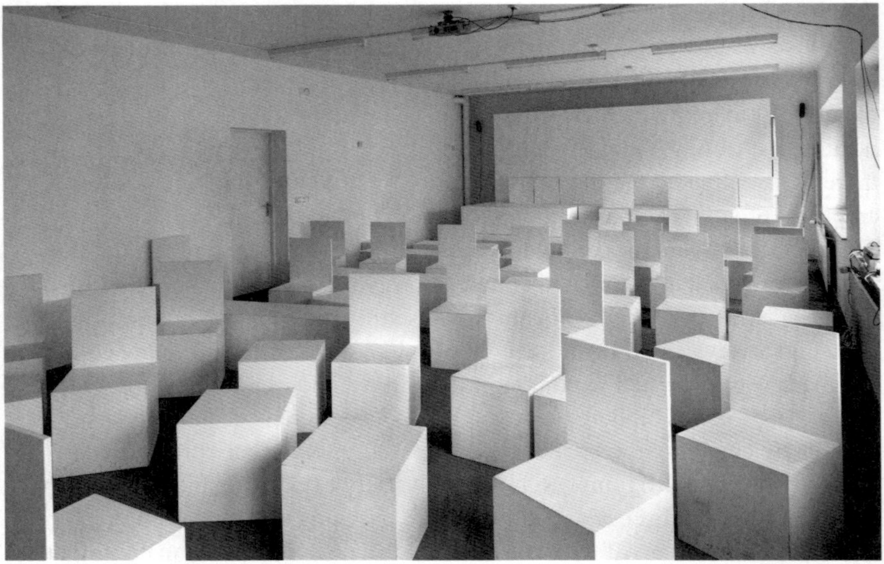

Interior by Nikolaus Hirsch and Michel Müller. unitednationsplaza, Berlin, 2006

between the degrees of freedom provided by means of unconventional formats of presentation and those provided by traditional frameworks (the space of the exhibition, the lecture, the seminar); but rather manifested this relationship in ambivalent, at times paradoxical, and certainly conflictive terms. Rebecca Uchill attests that even though unitednationsplaza points to "limits of open engagement in knowledge production," its various formats, often employing forms of exhibiting, instructing, or governing relations, are indicative of discursive practices that "even at their most experimental, have regulating capacities."[28] The conflictive pattern of hospitality rendered by the project was that in aiming to point to the limits of discursive procedures it in fact acknowledged and accepted them, which for Uchill forces "both producers and produced publics to determine their willingness to operate within them."[29]

unitednationsplaza should not be understood as having produced a limitless space in which authorship was given up entirely. Rather, authorship was collectivized. In this sense, Verwoert describes unitednationsplaza as "a resonating body that makes the voices of many others resound." The collective surrounds the authority of the host. The very format of bringing people together by generating a space for the fathoming of relationships

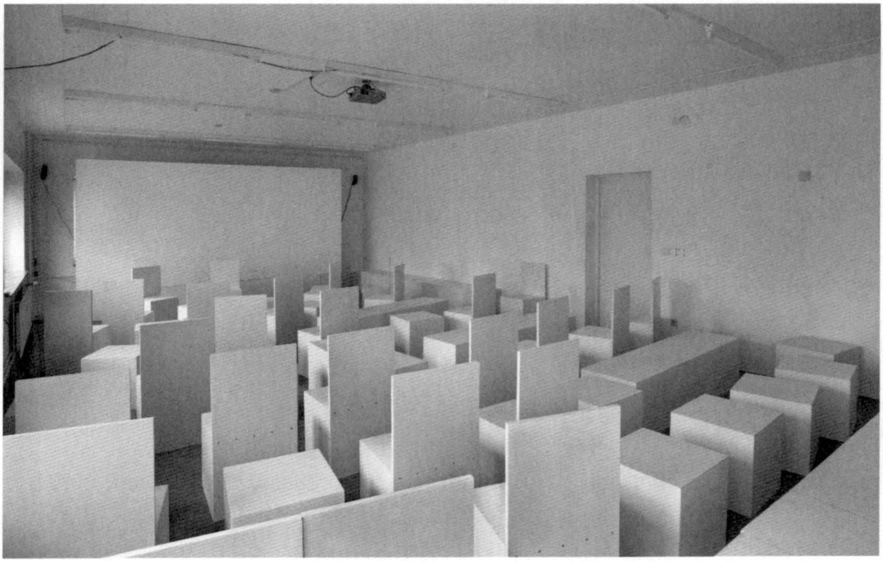

and associations is a definition of collectivity that "manifests itself in some kind of subjectivity that would make the multiplicity of its voice resonate."[30] Sharing the experience of many individual voices coming together and authorizing the experience they have produced together makes for the realization that this process has an effect on—and in this sense acquires a certain authority/credence in relation to—the way people experience themselves and their togetherness with others. The continuous deliberation over one's individual part in a collective event serves to create a loop, an indefinite process of negotiating the individual in relation to the collective and the collective in relation to the individual, to the point where the production of authorship appears as a collective endeavor.

The curated encounter that unitednationsplaza produced can be described as a situation of hospitality in which the host sought to escape the hospitable condition and join in sharing the experience as a guest. However, I would like to argue that this only served to establish a kind of authorship that, even though it has relational qualities, is a form of governance. The collective functioned to disguise the authorial role of the host, but did not replace it.

While unitednationsplaza is an example of a project that attempted to neglect and subvert institutional hierarchies, Vidokle assumes the position of an artist in the pursuit of autonomy. Verwoert calls the demand for autonomy a dream that we inherit from modernity: "the hope and claim that the power of a cultural practice to truly make a difference was inseparable from the freedom to determine its own conditions."[31] It is in this context that Vidokle's understanding of artistic practice as a "demand [...] to engage with society in order to create certain freedoms, to produce the conditions necessary for creative activity to take place at all" is to be read—an understanding that frames unitednationsplaza, as it led Vidokle to exchange the exhibition space for a discursive model of practice.[32] He perceives the function of the exhibition as having been reduced to an economy of negation and an affirmation of conditions—as it falls short of continuing to enquire into the processes of production that could stem from providing space for the building of relations. Liam Gillick values the discursive model of practice for offering the artist "the opportunity to be a relatively unexamined, free agent within a collective project," allowing a critical environment to be devised in which the artist's position is not just expressed, but can be perpetually reformed.[33] Artistic practice produces in this sense a curated encounter in which the relation between host and guest seemingly fades in favor of a collectively produced and shared experience, which in turn, however, is the very result of the artists' positioning in the collective project. The collectively shared experience is no longer just something that can potentially emerge from the curated encounter but is its product, the result of a process in which the artist, in this case Vidokle, proceeded to designate the public realm he created "as art or like art."[34]

In a recently published collection of essays discussing Vidokle's practice, Brian Sholis puts forward two characterizing parameters: (1) the "self-effacing nature of his endeavors," that are "nearly always collaborative"; (2) "his relative freedom from the network of institutions."[35] However, many have described how self-organized processes of institutionalization, despite being founded upon a critique of the institution, fail to establish an alternative to the very idea of the institution as a space for a relationship between art and its socio-political context that is not prefabricated. Andrea Phillips reminds us that these self-organized processes are historically very much linked to the matter of finding new ways of engaging the public and Beatrice von Bismarck describes how the model of the artist-run temporary institution is in fact not a form that transgresses the divisions between public and private, or viewed and viewer, but one that works towards their reinforcement. While the traditional role of an art institution, specifically an educational institution, involves a "gatekeeper" function in that it "creates a link between art production and the formation of its public(s)," the artist-run institution produces the formation of publics alongside art production.[36] In the case of unitednationsplaza, the discursive is conceived as an open structure that Gillick describes as being founded upon the dissemination of information—in opposition to the studio or exhibition space where objects are produced for consideration—producing an element of speculation that opens up spheres of experimentation and risk. As a result of this process, art can deliberate social space by providing room for reflection, and thereby speculation, on the possibilities that arise when a space, people, or things and their relation to other spaces, people, or things, are referenced simultaneously. The host's responsibility lies in the handling of a place as a platform for the production of social spaces, which means making sure that the simultaneity of reflection and production as a form of speculation is possible, and thereby consists of a relational activity. But in this process, as Nina Möntmann explains,[37] new social space is produced that incorporates the participants authorized as social subjects into the discursive artistic process, if not subjecting them to it. This realm of production: concrete, distinguished, and coupled with an analytical interest, is how the curated encounter of unitednationsplaza can be described. Again, the hospitable relationship is the result of an authorial positioning, and the notion of the collective merely functions to adorn it.

The question also remains whether such forms of speculation hold any critical potential, that is, whether the "analytical interest" is to produce a social space for an engagement with reality by means of speculation or within a sphere of speculation. For unitednationsplaza, as the idea has continued to be institutionalized over time, specifically with the later version titled Night School forming part of the educational program of the New Museum, New York, the danger is that the sense of speculation can give in to an instrumentalizing intentionality on the part of the host who confuses art as a medium to generate the conditions for creative activity and social interaction with art that produces a ready-made version of social interaction. Vidokle's interest in using art to deliberate social space is far from unconditional; it presupposes that by bringing people together art can function to transform a curated encounter into a space of real social action, where collaborative discursive practices produce the social. But what is the social other than, in the words of Stuart Hall, "the product of a mobile set of relations of signification whose 'fixings' of the social through the relations between different discursive positionalities that they effect is always provisional, incomplete, and on the way to being unfixed again"?[38] The social is not a positive content that can be instituted or manufactured in the sense of transforming how and by what it is governed. Rather, the question for creating patterns of hospitality in the curated encounter must be how processes of subjectivation and imagination can be instituted in a different way, for example by providing a space in which there is the possibility to track those associations and connections that might end up in a shared definition of a common world. This is what Bruno Latour frequently calls "collective," although he does not thereby speak of the construction of the collective in the discursive as it appears in unitednationsplaza,[39] in which we see a set of practices that produces the collective as a specific form of subjectivity organized in a space devised by the host, who as its author acts rather as a parasite to the collective condition created for his own positioning as an artist in the context of social and political practices.

1 Bruce W. Ferguson, "Exhibition Rhetorics: Material Speech and Utter Sense," in *Thinking About Exhibitions*, ed. Ferguson, Reesa Greenberg, and Sandy Nairne (London: Routledge, 1996), 176.

2 Ibid., 177.

3 For a critical discussion on the exhibition as a space for negotiating not aesthetic but discursive relations see Paul O'Neill, "The Curatorial Turn: From Practice to Discourse," in *The Biennial Reader: An Anthology on Large-Scale Perennial Exhibitions of Contemporary Art*, ed. Elena Filipovic, Marieke Van Hal, and Solveig Øvstebo (Ostfildern: Hatje Cantz, 2010), 240–58. Furthermore, Marion von Osten discusses artistic practices in terms of their modes of production of relations that can be taken into account when debating how exhibitions produce relations: Marion von Osten, "Another Criteria … or, What Is the Attitude of a Work in the Relations of Production of Its Time?," Afterall, no. 25 (Autumn 2010): 56–69.

4 Tony Bennett and Patrick Joyce, eds., *Material Powers: Cultural Studies, History and the Material Turn* (London: Routledge, 2010), 25.

5 Here Bennett refers to the history of the museum as an educational means, particularly in Britain during industrialization in the late eighteenth and early nineteenth centuries. Tony Bennett, "Civic Laboratories: Museums, Cultural Objecthood, and the Governance of the Social," *Cultural Studies* 19(5) (2005): 542.

6 The term governmental is understood within the parameters of Michel Foucault's definition of "governmentality" as an art of government that is not limited to state politics, but applies to various forms of institutions and administrative procedures that have specific strategies and tactics to exercise political economy as a form of knowledge. See Michel Foucault, "Disciplinary Power and Subjection," in *Power/Knowledge: Selected Interviews and Other Writings 1972–1977*, ed. and trans. Colin Gordon (New York: Pantheon Books, 1986), 229–230; Graham Burchell, Colin Gordon, and Peter Miller, eds., *The Foucault Effect: Studies in Governmentality*, with two lectures by and an interview with Michel Foucault (Chicago: Chicago University Press, 1991).

7 Oliver Marchart, "The Curatorial Subject: The Figure of the Curator Between Individuality and Collectivity," in *Texte zur Kunst*, no. 86 (June 2012): 28–42.

8 Ibid., 32.

9 unitednationsplaza was a project by Anton Vidokle in collaboration with Boris Groys, Jalal Toufic, Liam Gillick, Martha Rosler, Natascha Sadr Haghighian, Nikolaus Hirsch, Tirdad Zolghadr, and Walid Raad.

10 The online archive features video and audio documentation of most of unitednationsplaza's events, as well as of the one-month edition of the project in Mexico in March 2008 and Night School, another series of seminars, lectures, and informal discussions Vidokle was commissioned to conceive for New York's New Museum in 2009. http://www.unitednationsplaza.org.

11 The curators outline the way Manifesta 6 was conceived to respond to the conflictive political situation of the divided island of Cyprus in *Notes for an Art School*, ed. Mai Abu ElDahab, Anton Vidokle, and Florian Waldvogel (Amsterdam: Manifesta International Foundation, 2006). The first seminar during unitednationsplaza was titled retrospectively "Histories of Productive Failures: From French Revolution to Manifesta 6," October 27–29, 2006. Guests invited to present included Anselm Franke, Anton Vidokle, Haris Pellapaisiotis, Mete Hatay, Pavlina Paraskevaidou, Rana Zincir Celal, Liam Gillick, Maria Lind, Diedrich Diederichsen, and Tirdad Zolghadr. http://unitednationsplaza.org/event/1/.

12 I am referring here mainly to a set of writings by Anton Vidokle including "From Exhibition to School: Notes From Unitednationsplaza," in *Art School (Propositions for the 21st Century)*, ed. Steven Henry Madoff (Cambridge, MA: MIT Press, 2009); Martha Rosler and Anton Vidokle, "Exhibition as School as Work of Art," *Art Lies* 59 (Fall 2008): 70–77; and Anton Vidokle and Tirdad Zolghadr, "I Can't Work Like This," *Printed Project* 6, Visual Artists Ireland (February 2007). Furthermore, a collection of essays on Vidokle's practice was published shortly after the conclusion of Night School in

2009, with contributions by Liam Gillick, Maria Lind, Monika Szewczyk, and Jan Verwoert. Brian Sholis, ed., *Anton Vidokle: Produce, Distribute, Discuss, Repeat* (New York: Sternberg Press, 2009).

13 — Vidokle, "From Exhibition to School," 192–93.

14 — Anton Vidokle, "Exhibition as School in a Divided City," in *Notes for an Art School*, 8–14.

15 — Ibid., 9.

16 — Rosler and Vidokle, "Exhibition as School as Work of Art."

17 — Vidokle, "From Exhibition to School," 192–93.

18 — On many occasions Vidokle articulates a profound adversity towards any form of sovereignty being attached to the curator, who is perceived as competing with the artist about who has the definitive capacity "to designate something as art or like art." See Anton Vidokle, "Art Without Artists?," *e-flux journal* 16 (May 2010). http://worker01.e-flux.com/pdf/article_136.pdf.

19 — Marchart, "The Curatorial Subject," 28–42.

20 — Katharina Schlieben, "The Crux of Polyphonic Language, or the Thing as Gathering," *Manifesta Journal* 8 (2009/2010): 16–20.

21 — Vidokle, "From Exhibition to School," 198.

22 — Liam Gillick, "Maybe it Would be Better if We Worked in Groups of Three? Part 1 of 2: The Discursive," *e-flux journal* 3 (February 2009). http://www.e-flux.com/journal/maybe-it-would-be-better-if-we-worked-in-groups-of-three-part-1-of-2-the-discursive/.

23 — Jan Verwoert, "Gathering People Like Thoughts," in *Anton Vidokle: Produce, Distribute, Discuss, Repeat*, 12.

24 — Ibid., 16.

25 — Ibid., 16–17.

26 — The seminars ran from March 12 to 23, 2007. Invited guests included Stefanie Wenner, Adrienne Goehler, Florian Schneider, Jackson Pollock Bar, Chris Evans, Jörg Heiser, and Jennifer Allen. http://unitednationsplaza.org/event/5/.

27 — See Hadley+Maxwell, "Find Us At the Kitchen Door," *Art Lies* 59 (Fall 2008): 18–23.

28 — Rebecca Uchill, "Hanging Out, Crowding Out or Talking Things Out: Curating the Limits of Discursive Space," *Journal of Curatorial Studies* 1, no. 1 (2012): 27–43.

29 — Ibid., 36.

30 — Verwoert, "Gathering People Like Thoughts," 16.

31 — Ibid., 17.

32 — Vidokle, "From Exhibition to School," 193.

33 — Gillick, "Maybe it Would be Better if We Worked in Groups of Three?," 2.

34 — Vidokle, "From Exhibition to School," 192.

35 — Sholis, "Anton Vidokle: Produce, Distribute, Discuss, Repeat," 7.

36 — Andrea Phillips, "Public Acting: From Public Art to Art's Publicity" (unpublished manuscript, 2011); Beatrice von Bismarck, "Game Within the Game: Institution, Institutionalization, and Art Education," in *Art and Its Institutions: Current Conflicts, Critique and Collaborations*, ed. Nina Möntmann (London: Black Dog Publishing, 2006), 124–32.

37 — Nina Möntmann, *Kunst als sozialer Raum* (Cologne: Walther König, 2002), 166.

38 — Stuart Hall rephrased by Tony Bennett in *Tony Bennett, Critical Trajectories: Culture, Society, Intellectuals* (Oxford: Blackwell, 2007), 76.

39 — Bruno Latour, *Reassembling the Social: An Introduction To Actor-Network-Theory* (Oxford: Oxford University Press, 2005), 247.

III

Gift and Visibility/ The Gift of Visibility

Beatrice von Bismarck

Showing Showing

Louise Lawler and the Art of Curatorial Hospitality*

At the conclusion of the Berlin exhibition project "The Work shown in this space is a response to the existing conditions and/or work previously shown within the space 3," an invitation to the event for the closing of the show was distributed in May 2000. The idea for and design of the card were the work of Louise Lawler. Listed on the card were all the artists who had participated in the project from January 4 to May 20, 2000—a project that presented the challenge of taking positions in the exhibition space sequentially, each of which reacted to the positions of the previous participants, following the logic of a *cadavre exquis*. In addition to the participants—Christopher Williams, Henrik Olesen, Lawrence Weiner, Simon Starling, Michael Elmgreen & Ingar Dragset, Heimo Zobernig, Manfred Pernice, and Isa Genzken—the card indicated the date and time of the event, the duration of the project, the host institution (neugerriemschneider gallery in Berlin) and its contact details, the title of each artist's contribution, the names of those responsible for the photograph and the type design of the card (Jens Ziehe and Andreas Koch), and the title of the exhibition itself.

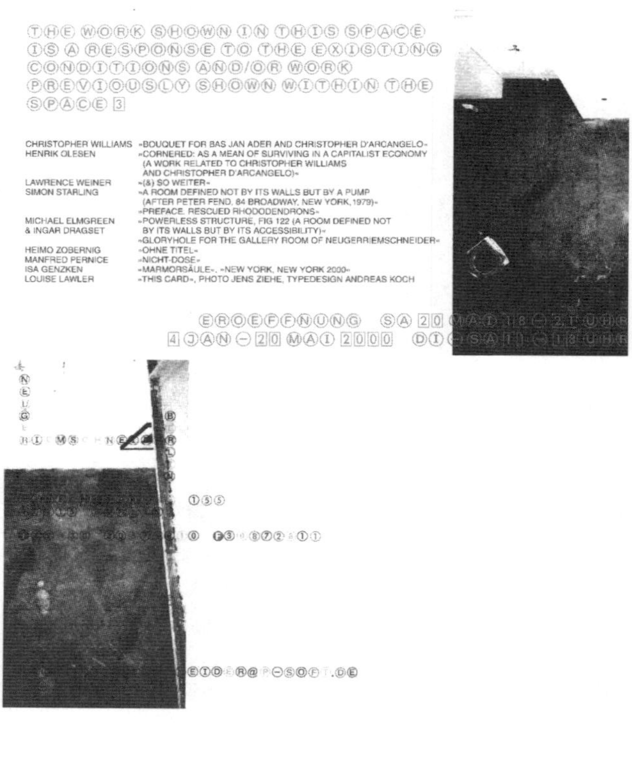

THE WORK SHOWN IN THIS SPACE IS A RESPONSE TO THE EXISTING CONDITIONS AND/OR WORK PREVIOUSLY SHOWN WITHIN THE SPACE 3

CHRISTOPHER WILLIAMS »BOUQUET FOR BAS JAN ADER AND CHRISTOPHER D'ARCANGELO«
HENRIK OLESEN »CORNERED: AS A MEAN OF SURVIVING IN A CAPITALIST ECONOMY (A WORK RELATED TO CHRISTOPHER WILLIAMS AND CHRISTOPHER D'ARCANGELO)«
LAWRENCE WEINER »(&) SO WEITER«
SIMON STARLING »A ROOM DEFINED NOT BY ITS WALLS BUT BY A PUMP (AFTER PETER FEND, 84 BROADWAY, NEW YORK, 1979)«
»PREFACE. RESCUED RHODODENDRONS«
MICHAEL ELMGREEN & INGAR DRAGSET »POWERLESS STRUCTURE, FIG 122 (A ROOM DEFINED NOT BY ITS WALLS BUT BY ITS ACCESSIBILITY)«
»GLORYHOLE FOR THE GALLERY ROOM OF NEUGERRIEMSCHNEIDER«
HEIMO ZOBERNIG »OHNE TITEL«
MANFRED PERNICE »NICHT-DOSE«
ISA GENZKEN »MARMORSÄULE«, »NEW YORK, NEW YORK 2000«
LOUISE LAWLER »THIS CARD«, PHOTO JENS ZIEHE, TYPEDESIGN ANDREAS KOCH

EROEFFNUNG SA 20

4 JAN – 20 MAI 2000

Louise Lawler,
***This Card*, 2000.**
Invitation to the closing of "The Work shown in this space is a response to the existing conditions and/or work previously shown within the space 3," neugerriemschneider, Berlin, 2000

With this invitation card, Lawler was making use of a form of advertising that is certainly common when publicizing events in the art field. At the same time, she was thereby also referring to the conditions under which the exhibition took place: to the institutionally framed space, the participants, the span of time within which the project could be carried out, and to the fact that, with the closing event, it had come to an end and could be considered finished. She provided the information that could be expected from such an invitation in keeping with the conventions of running exhibitions, but not without making visible at the same time the institutional, personal, and media requirements. For Lawler's card is not only the designed medium for invitation to "The Work shown in this space" but is also itself an exhibit, the final contribution to a series of ten attempts to come to terms with an existing situation that took place at irregular intervals over the course of just over five months. For that reason, her name is the last of the artists on the list, and her artistic contribution, *This Card*, the concluding one. Even as the exhibition was still running, she offered a retrospective on it, not unlike the final credits of a film.

In Lawler's contribution to the exhibition, performative gesture, artistic representation of an event, and participation in an event are all inseparably intertwined. The card pronounces the invitation and by doing so already performs the act of invitation; it records the invitation as event, shows all of the invitees who responded to one another in turn, and lists their works and the requirements and conditions that established the framework of the invitation. It is itself also a guest participating in the event it publicizes. Artistic produce and artistic act at once, it is essentially defined processually both by the act of invitation and by its inscription in the exhibition process. The discussion that follows here is focused on the implications of the invitation card's dual status: the extroverted orientation of the gesture of invitation, which entails aspects of both directed address and self-referential advertising, as well as the social information about the hosts, and finally also the material and discursive conditions of a place that can receive guests.

Artistic and curatorial questions intersect here, since the artistically conceived card takes over aspects of the act of invitation that are, according to the conventions of the art field, the responsibility of curators. Moreover, the act of invitation manifests forms of the duties of hosting, a concept that has lately become particularly relevant to both artistic and curatorial practice. According to this notion of the duties of hosting, the offering of food and drink can represent an occasion, but in their function as a locational and metaphorical framing, they can clearly go beyond that. Especially since Rirkrit Tiravanija developed the model of cooking for an art audience, a wide variety of culinary offerings have developed in an aesthetic setting, some of which adopt the ideas of artistic service from the early 1990s while others integrate the ambition of a temporary gathering or even the formation of communities, each placing different demands on discursive formation. Both continuing and distinguishing itself from relational aesthetics,[1] the UNWETTER artists' group, which participated in the 3rd Guangzhou Triennial in 2008, uses the format of a "discursive picnic" for its work. Its stated goal is to combine various contexts and roles in a continuous process of reciprocal exchange. The Berlin-based artist Dorothee Albrecht, a member of UNWETTER but also Research Curator for the 3rd Guangzhou Triennial, took part in both these contexts as contributor to and organizer of the exhibition. In adopting this role she became an example of the significance that the concept of hosting has acquired, especially at the intersection between artistic and curatorial practice.[2]

Hospitality, conviviality, and hosting are becoming qualities demanded in situations occurring in the context of art—be they picnics, invitations to meals, symposia, or exhibitions. Connected with these events are projections of a coming together on equal footing, without any hierarchy or restrictions, for a joint debate and sensory pleasure. Curators and artists feel equally obliged to this practice, integrating their own practice into the economic, political, and social dimensions of a way of working that is giving, generous, and welcoming.[3] This orientation entails expectations of and requirements for the situations to which one is being invited as well as opportunities to forswear self-interest and reciprocity. This interaction speaks both to the deictic quality of art—by which art shows both itself and that which it depicts—and also, in reference to the theories of Derrida in particular, to the social effects of global migration movements supported by an unconditional opening up to the Other.[4] In this context, Lawler's card is a contribution that combines aesthetic and sociopolitical perspectives, that exchanges the lack of specificity of an open, social get-together for a deliberate effort to display and make dynamic the relationships of invitation.

The various discourses concerning the act of presentation as a cultural practice are intersected and compressed in the status of Lawler's invitation card. The focus is on the relationship of artistic works to their presentation. Out of the nature of that relationship, which justifies the work as an aesthetic object but is nevertheless no less conflict-ridden, arise questions of dependencies and the latitude for action that come with presentation. This is fundamentally about the parts of the act of presentation that are internalized or externalized by the practice of art and are brought to bear in the clashes of iconic and deictic difference. The nodal point of this interaction makes it possible to describe the relationship that the presentation of the work has to the presentation *in* the work, *through* the work, or as work.

Concentrating on the acts and processes of presentation means focusing on an aspect that opens up a transitional zone between "art" and "exhibition." In that zone, the modalities, competencies, and responsibilities reveal a form of indeterminacy. Rather than always outsourcing display and delegating it to third parties—the mediator or curator—the personal and material assignments of who or what is involved, and how, are still open to negotiation. In that sense, the idea of a transitional zone differs from that of a "middleman" advocated by Søren Andreasen and Lars Bang Larsen in 2007 with reference to Fernand Braudel.[5] By analogy to the field of economics, they assign the "middleman" the task of introducing the artwork to the field of art. Although this position refers to a transitional zone like the one just mentioned, it is that of a mediating representative, whose subjective mediation separates the process of presenting from art and artists. On the one hand, this designation, as a practice external to art, conceals the fact that, as well as artists, their public, and the various institutions involved, curators constitute part of the art field in the first place; on the other hand, it ignores the fact that presentation and self-presentation are constitutive aspects of artworks by means of which they—as Martin Seel has expressed it—distinguish *themselves* from other things in the field of appearance. Both from a sociological perspective that understands works of art as "social media" produced for an observer,[6] and from the vantage point of a philosophical aesthetics that emphasizes art's mode of presentation, the presentation of art can be understood as a condition that supplements its own constitution as an aesthetic object, if not making it possible in the first place. If we assume along with Seel that it is a specific feature of works of art that they "present themselves in such way that we can find *something* presented by them," this addresses the "iconic difference" described by Gottfried Boehm, according to which a picture always simultaneously reveals itself and that which is in the picture.[7] These descriptions also capture the dual character of Lawler's invitation card as a documentary publication object for the exhibition and as its commenting exhibit. The mode of self-presentation inscribed in and characteristic of the work of art, as Seel emphasizes, also alludes to the fact that the act of presentation used in exhibitions necessarily raises the question of where or what is or can be involved in its presentation in addition to the work of art, and in what form. To put it another way, if works of art are presentations and indeed presentations of a particular kind, which are therefore only realized in the perception of a social other, then what part of the presentation is a component of the work of art and what is an additional, supporting aid?

Lawler's choice of the invitation card as a publication format derives its significance from this question—to the extent that it makes the constitutive property of the artwork that presents itself as artwork indistinguishable from the function of advertising itself as an artwork. It breaks with the apparent separability of the goals of aesthetics and (attention) economy and emphatically locates both in the artwork's mode of presentation. Her contribution to the exhibition puts on display the idea that art not only silently accepts an Other—an audience, however it might be conceived—but also actively and explicitly addresses it. The economic interests stored therein resonate as an accompanying fundamental tone through the interplay Lawler maintains between a physical sales point and an immaterial presentation site, as much as through the medium of an invitation card for a commercial gallery.

Identifying such entanglements is an essential part of Lawler's practice. The media of publicity and advertising are fixed features of her working materials. She has designed a number of invitation cards and posters for various commercial and noncommercial exhibition venues, as well as creating the stationery for documenta 7 in Kassel in 1982, pages in art magazines, and advertising materials for art events and initiatives in the form of series of postcards, paperweights, and boxes of matches. With her paper napkin for "The Museum as Muse: Artists Reflect" exhibition at MoMA in New York in 1999, she designed a practical object that could serve a purpose during lunch and dinner and was indirectly but significantly—as a means of encouraging attention and financial support—involved in presenting art.[8]

By combining in this way exhibition, public relations, and advertising, Lawler takes up a strand of development in the arts that essentially emerged in the 1960s: breaking down the separation between artistic work and publicity. In the circle of conceptual artists surrounding the dealer and curator Seth Siegelaub between 1966 and 1970, as Alexander Alberro has shown, a form of dematerialization of art was coupled with an approach aligned to strategies of mass media publicity.[9] Pursued in different ways in each case by Douglas Huebler, Lawrence Weiner, Joseph Kosuth, and

Robert Barry, the fragmentation of artistic works, their reduction to announcements or descriptions, their serialization, and their discursiveness in keeping with the aesthetic standards of the late 1960s meant that publicity work was required in order for their work to be intelligible to an audience. This was essentially done by Siegelaub, who held exhibitions in his own apartment on Madison Avenue in New York and also in clubs; organized social events including weekend soirées at his home, placed advertisements, and intensively produced easily distributable advertising materials. As a trailblazer for a new type of curator, he took on, independently of any institutional ties, a variety of tasks that created a public for the artists he supported. When Barry, Kosuth, Huebler, and Weiner interviewed themselves in 1969 and declared that to be their contribution to the "Prospect 69" exhibition in Düsseldorf, they were integrating into their own artistic practice a means Siegelaub had employed for them. Siegelaub's distinction between "primary information," which describes the ideas of a work of art, and "secondary information," which refers to the material form of presentation by which a work of art is perceived, breaks down here.[10]

This conceptualized reference to the methods of public relations and advertising emphatically problematized the relationship between aesthetics and media but could not eliminate the economic undertones. On the contrary, rather than avoiding the status of consumer goods the artists around Siegelaub developed and adapted his marketing strategies for their own work.[11] The fact that their works were not entirely assimilated into a pure marketing strategy—as the advertising world had always insinuated in seeking to make strategic borrowings from artistic processes—resulted from this multiple coding. By means of this coding the work was opened up with respect both to its iconic quality and to its deictic quality. In their self-interviews, Barry, Kosuth, Huebler, and Weiner reveal their work as artists as well as the act of showing that they undertake in the process. In addition, by doing so

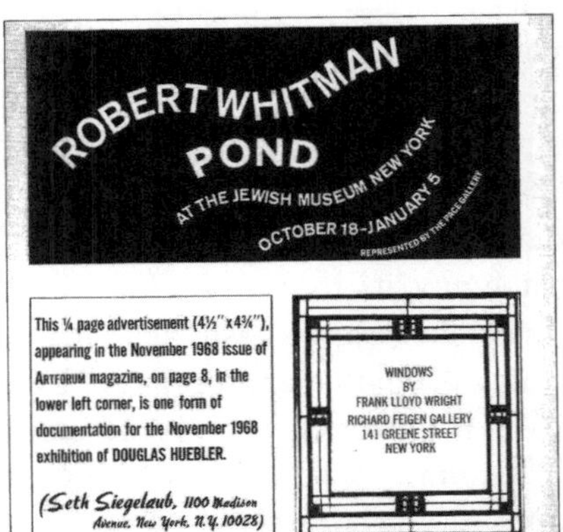

Douglas Huebler, *Douglas Huebler: November 1968*, 1968. Advertisement in *Artforum*

they ultimately neutralized the taboo of modernist art: that economic interests be negated. Their approach passes visibility off as linked to the acquisition of capital. Following Pierre Bourdieu's distinction between types of capital, this was not necessarily economic capital but in any case symbolic or social capital, which could be manifested in reputation and esteem, on the one hand, or contacts and networks, on the other, and these can in turn be transformed into economic capital.[12]

Within Seth Siegelaub's circle, the debates over the relationship of art and its presentation took on a currency in the light of new possibilities of communication through mass media. The explicit invocation of the viewer integrated into the work of art, as in practices of the 1960s and '70s—for example, in Dan Flavin's early work *Mira Mira (to Mrs. Brody)* (1960) or Bruce Nauman's collage *Please/Pay/Attention/Please* (1973)—is found in the self-interviews in a radically dematerialized variant. From a historical perspective, this opens up a field that declares the means of public relations and advertising to be a completely natural part of artistic practice, either for the purpose of self-presentation or with the goal of critiquing institutions or gender assumptions. Lynda Benglis's use of invitation cards and advertisements with her nude body should be mentioned in this context along with the postcards sent by Martha Rosler.[13] Both, in very different ways, drew attention to strategies of communication and public relations. Independent of the use of publicity materials in one sense or another, they shifted the act of and the conditions for presenting art to the work of art itself, in such a way that the showing always explicitly exhibits itself, because of the means that have been chosen, regardless of the other content addressed in the work. They are showing as seduction on one's own behalf.

Lawler's card displays the act of inviting in its generous, giving dimension as well as its interweaving of attention and recognition as it is employed in commercial contexts such as branding and marketing tourism.[14] Lawler takes up the contradictory demands on art, its autonomy, its commodity form, and causes them to confront each other. She thus takes up the basic idea that was the inspiration for the exhibition: eluding economic appropriation by means of the processual and relational. Even if this orientation could no longer be convincingly brought to bear in a commercial gallery in the year 2000—something the card ultimately expresses as well—the work bears within it the goal of the original project to which it can be traced back. Survival in a capitalist economy in which existing structures are transformed or reformed was the motto of the exhibition organized by Peter

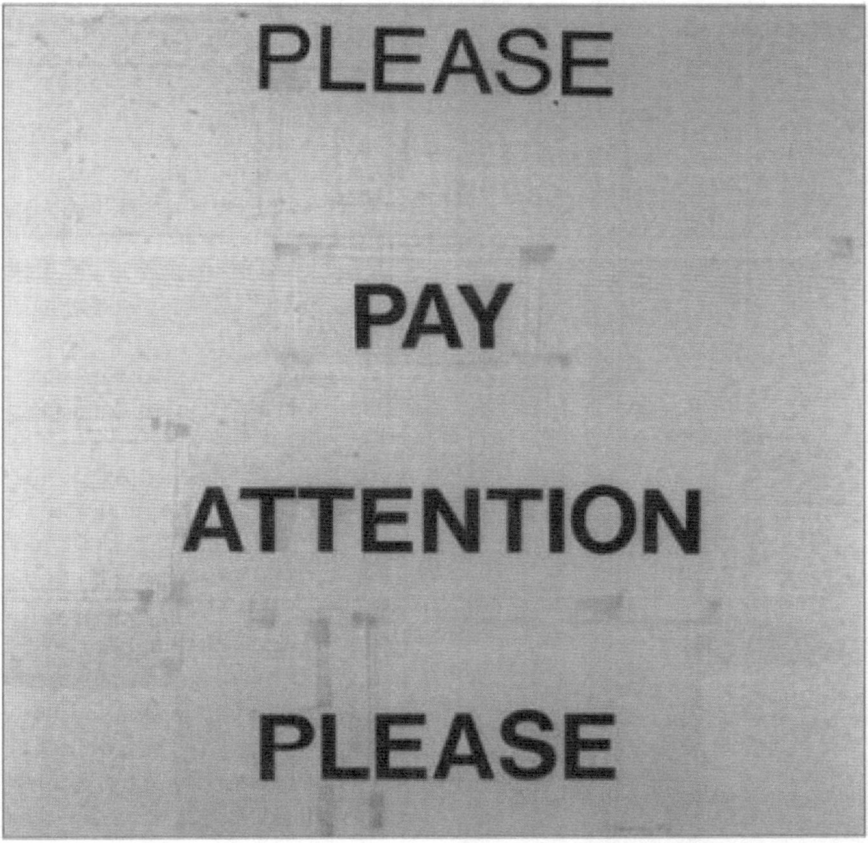

Bruce Nauman, *Please/Pay/Attention/Please*, 1973

Nadin with Christopher d'Arcangelo and Peter Lawson at 84 West Broadway in New York in 1978—a motto Henrik Olesen cited in his contribution in 2000.[15] The flexible, dynamic, and interrelated structure of "The Work shown in this space" is part of the reason this exhibition format has become particularly important in the art field, not least for its tendency to critique capitalism. The original project began on November 9, 1978, with built-ins titled "30 Days Work" by Nadin, d'Arcangelo, and Lawson: craft interventions of the sort that at the time were being done in the lofts of other patrons of the arts and designated as artistic work defined by the time required to construct them.[16] In a loose sequence over the months

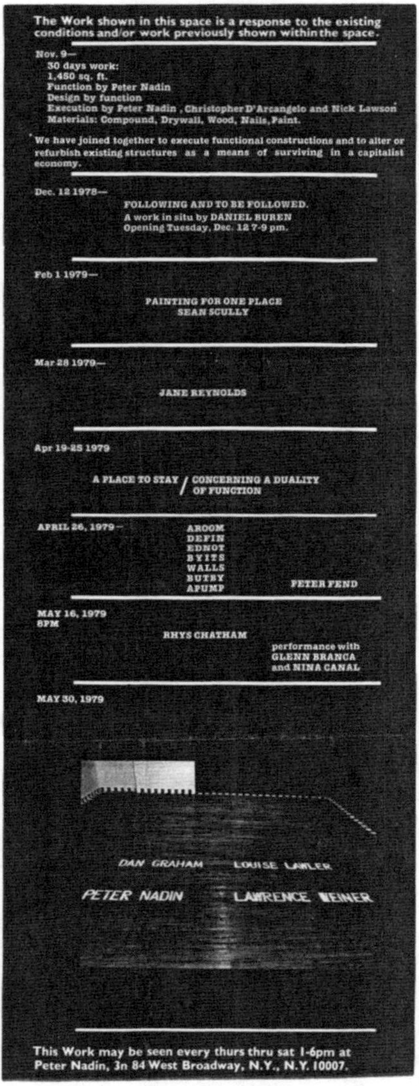
The Work shown in this space is a response to the existing conditions and/or work previously shown within the space.

Nov. 9—
30 days work:
1,450 sq. ft.
Function by Peter Nadin
Design by function
Execution by Peter Nadin, Christopher D'Arcangelo and Nick Lawson*
Materials: Compound, Drywall, Wood, Nails, Paint.

*We have joined together to execute functional constructions and to alter or refurbish existing structures as a means of surviving in a capitalist economy.

Dec. 12 1978—
FOLLOWING AND TO BE FOLLOWED.
A work in situ by DANIEL BUREN
Opening Tuesday, Dec. 12 7-9 pm.

Feb 1 1979—
PAINTING FOR ONE PLACE
SEAN SCULLY

Mar 28 1979—
JANE REYNOLDS

Apr 19-25 1979
A PLACE TO STAY / CONCERNING A DUALITY OF FUNCTION

APRIL 26, 1979—
AROOM
DEFIN
EDNOT
BYITS
WALLS
BUTBY
APUMP
PETER FEND

MAY 16, 1979
8PM
RHYS CHATHAM
performance with
GLENN BRANCA
and NINA CANAL

MAY 30, 1979
DAN GRAHAM LOUISE LAWLER
PETER NADIN LAWRENCE WEINER

This Work may be seen every thurs thru sat 1-6pm at Peter Nadin, 3n 84 West Broadway, N.Y., N.Y. 10007.

Christopher d'Arcangelo, Invitation card to "30 Days Work," 84 West Broadway, New York, 1978–79

that followed, Daniel Buren, Sean Scully, Jane Reynolds, Rhys Chatham, Lawrence Weiner, Peter Fend, Dan Graham, Peter Nadin himself, and Louise Lawler contributed to the exhibition. An invitation card recorded the dates of each contribution, with the final date listed as May 30, 1979. Christopher d'Arcangelo's suicide marked the end of the project.

As a processual and relational concept that also contains an aspect of the playful, the New York exhibition of 1978–79 has had a series of successors that refer to it more or less directly.[17] At neugerriemschneider in 2000, the titles several of the participants gave their works took up this form of ongoing transformation and continuation and emphatically underscored it by alluding in different ways to the original project. Whereas Lawrence Weiner merely speaks of *(&) so weiter* (And so on), Henrik Olesen's quotation, Christopher Williams's dedication to Bas Jan Ader and Christopher d'Arcangelo, and Simon Starling's subtitle *after Peter Fend, 84 West Broadway, New York, 1979*, all make a direct connection. However, it is exactly the show's most prominent features—its processual character and its anticapitalist and sociopolitical connotations—that are clouded by Lawler's contribution, even beyond the inherent advertising logic of inviting. She also removes the idealized pretension that an open, equal coming together can be achieved through hospitality. First, she undermines the assignment of a status to the host, since the card makes it unclear who is the inviter for the exhibition in question: she herself, having conceived the invitation, competed for this role not only with the owners of the gallery, Tim Neuger and Burkhard Riemschneider, who made their space available and made all the logistics possible, but also with Christopher Williams, who made the first contribution. As a guest in the gallery, as one of several guests invited to participate in the show, Lawler is also the host for those she provided space for on her card.[18] Initially, this diffuse distribution of tasks, which dissolves the status of artists, curators, and gallery owners, seemingly underscores the principle of equal responses implied in the format of the exhibition. An argumentative, if you will, exchange among equals in the field of exhibition making. The claim that the UNWETTER collective formulated for its own work, according to which various positions and ways of perceiving and seeing are taken into account for action (including political action), may echo here. But it is precisely the specific quality of Lawler's invitation that it assumes neither an unconditional hospitality, which is not supported by rules or expectations of exchange, nor a nonhierarchical relationship of the participants. She steps in as a representative to mark an emphasized position occupied by means of power within the circle of participants. It is this position that makes it possible for her to annul the exhibition's primary feature—its processual quality. With her card, the artist creates her own exhibition space, one that compresses the passing of time and thus removes the intended meaning of the temporality of the whole project in 1978, that is, to withdraw from commodity status and to evade the mechanisms of the market. Lawler's contribution subjects the project to her own conditions, in that the card is the first, and indeed only, presentation of all the contributions at the same time. Via the card's contents and means the project completes and reveals itself as such. By becoming visible as a whole, the project loses its essential characteristic. By creating a place on the paper that takes form beyond the architecture of the institutional gallery space, while having a functional presence, Lawler causes the existing social and economic conditions to enter into a constant interplay with those that challenge them.[19]

This work does not so much concede authorial power as thematize it. Lawler shows the action of exposing rendered visually to be a sequence in which—in contrast to continual interaction and common discursive and aesthetic movements—the last contributor always has the power to define the overall situation. In its dual nature as the means of providing information in the service of an exhibition and as an autonomous artistic contribution to that exhibition, Lawler's card makes it possible to establish distance from and reflect on the exhibition project, placing it, by means of the announcement, in the shifted, framing conditions of presenting: the card provides information that transforms the loose sequence of artistic presentations, their informal publication, and their transitory appearance into a project with clear, distinctly defined contours, structures, and combinations, replacing the unstable and intangible qualities of the ongoing process with a product that is limited in time and has come to a standstill, as if the slow flow of a sequence of actions had clotted into an image with her contribution. The card thus addresses not least the possibilities and conditions of temporalizing the presentation of art. Lawler produces a standstill, making the ephemeral and processual more available to reception while at the same time—by means of her contribution's oscillating between documentation, advertisement, and autonomous artistic product—raising once again, though now from a different, slightly shifted perspective, the question of the nature of exhibitions as products and potentially commodity-like forms.

* This text was first published in English in *Performing the Curatorial: Within and Beyond Art*, ed. Maria Lind (Berlin: Sternberg Press, 2012), 135–45. Originally published in German as "R.S.V.P. Louise Lawler und die Kunst des Einladens," in *Kunsthandeln*, ed. Karin Gludovatz et al. (Zurich: diaphanes, 2010), 73–86.

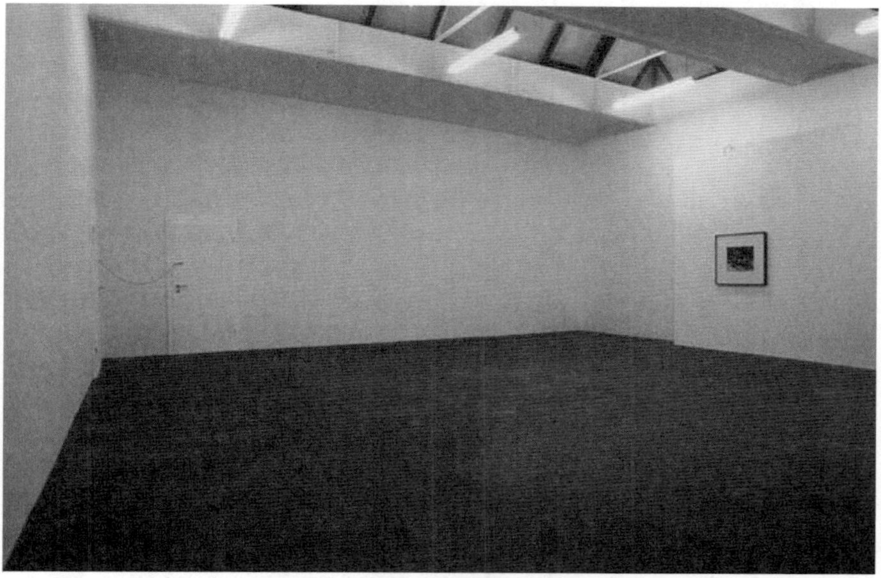

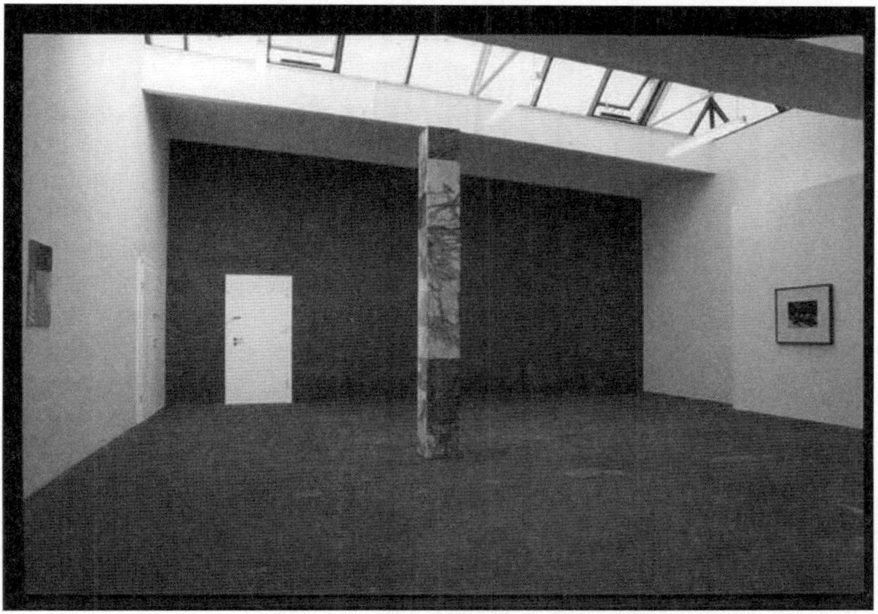

Installation views of "The Work shown in this space is a response to the existing conditions and/or work previously shown within the space 3," neugerriemschneider, Berlin, 2000

1 For a discussion of the social and political implications of relationally constructed art, see Nicolas Bourriaud, *Relational Aesthetics* (Dijon: Les presses du réel, 2002); George Baker, "Relations and Counter-Relations: An Open Letter to Nicolas Bourriaud," in *Contextualize: Zusammenhänge herstellen*, ed. Yilmaz Dziewior, exhibition catalogue, Kunstverein Hamburg (Cologne: DuMont, 2003), 126–33.

2 On UNWETTER's goal, see Astrid Mania, "Walls Fall Down: Berlin's Contemporary Art Institutions," in *Institutional Critique and After*, Southern California Consortium of Art Schools Symposia, vol. 2, ed. John C. Welchman (Zurich: JRP Ringier, 2006), 251–63, esp. 262–63; see also the flyer, "UNWETTER: We/You are invited / Wir/Sie sind eingeladen! TO GATHER: DISCOURSIVE PICNIC on the margins of the 50 years documenta-conference," for their contribution to the conference "documenta zwischen Inszenierung und Kritik / documenta between Staging and Criticism," Evangelische Akademie Hofgeismar, October 27–30, 2005, on the occasion of the exhibition "50 Jahre / Years documenta," Kunsthalle Fridericianum Kassel, 2005.

3 See, for example, "Plato's Table: Hospitality and Participatory Practice," symposium, April 14, 2008, The Drill Hall, Collective Gallery, Edinburgh, with the participation of, among others, Phil Collins, Charles Esche, Gob Squad, Simon Sheikh; the curatorial concept of the artists' collective rum46, "Notes on Hospitality, Community, and Counter-publicity related to Collective Curating as Practice and Method"; the exhibition project "Feast: Radical Hospitality in Contemporary Art," 2011, Smart Museum of Art, University of Chicago: The subjects included artistic positions ranging from Italian Futurism by way of Gordon Matta-Clark and Rirkrit Tiravanija who, as the blog on the exhibition preparations puts it, "are using meals to advance aesthetic goals and foster critical engagement with our current culture."; and *Il dono: Offerta, ospidailtà, insidia / The Gift: Generous Offerings, Threatening Hospitality*, exhibition catalogue for an exhibition of the same name at Palazzo delle Papese, Centro Arte Contemporanea, Siena, September 2001 (Milan: Charta, 2001). The exhibition was concerned with artistic gestures of offering and invitation in relation to the idea of the gift.

4 See Jacques Derrida and Anne Dufourmantelle, *Of Hospitality*, trans. Rachel Bowlby (Stanford, CA: Stanford University Press, 2000); and Derrida, *Given Time: 1. Counterfeit Money*, vol. 1, trans. Peggy Kamuf (Chicago: University of Chicago Press, 1992). For more detail on this, see Kathrin Busch, "Dass gut schenken eine Kunst ist: Für eine Ästhetik der Gabe," *Zeitschrift für Ästhetik und Allgemeine Kunstwissenschaft* 50, no. 1 (2005): 27–55.

5 See Søren Andreasen and Lars Bang Larsen, "The Middleman: Beginning to Think about Mediation," in *Curating Subjects*, ed. Paul O'Neill (London: Open Editions, 2007), 20–30.

6 See Juliane Rebentisch with reference to Niklas Luhmann in Rebentisch, *Ästhetik der Installation* (Frankfurt am Main: Suhrkamp, 2003), 90.

7 Martin Seel, *Die Ästhetik des Erscheinens* (Frankfurt am Main: Suhrkamp, 2003), 176; Gottfried Boehm, "Die Wiederkehr der Bilder," in *Was ist ein Bild?*, ed. Boehm, 3rd ed. (Munich: Fink, 2001), 11–38, esp. 29–36.

8 For a selection of Louise Lawler's ephemera, see Louise Lawler, *Twice Untitled and Other Pictures (Looking Back)*, ed. Helen Molesworth (Cambridge, MA: MIT Press, 2006), 157–94.

9 Alexander Alberro, *Conceptual Art and the Politics of Publicity* (Cambridge, MA: MIT Press, 2003).

10 Ibid., 53.

11 Ibid., 149–69.

12 Pierre Bourdieu, "The Forms of Capital," trans. Richard Nice, in *Handbook of Theory and Research for Sociology of Education*, ed. John G. Richardson (New York: Greenwood Press, 1986), 241–58.

13 For more detail on the interpretation of these works in the spirit of a strategy of publication and advertising, see also Beatrice von Bismarck, "Das Interieur auf der Bühne," in *Auftritt als Künstler* (Cologne: Verlag der Buchhandlung Walther König, 2010), 114–24.

14 On the association of hospitality with marketing tourism and branding, see, for example, Kathleen Lingle Pond, *Welcoming Visitors to Your Community: Training Tour Guides and Other Hospitality Ambassadors* (Washington, DC: National Trust for Historic Preservation, 1998); Greg Richards, ed., *Cultural Tourism: Global and Local Perspectives* (New York: Haworth Press, 2007); and Michael Zinganel and Peter Spillmann, eds., *Backstage*Tours: Reisen in den touristischen Raum* (Graz: Forum Stadtpark, 2004).

15 The card for the 1978 exhibition reads: "We have joined together to execute functional constructions and to alter or refurbish existing structures as a means of surviving in a capitalist economy." Henrik Olesen titled his contribution in 2000: *Cornered: As a Means of Surviving in a Capitalist Economy (a Work Dedicated to Christopher Williams and Christopher D'Arcangelo).*

16 On the exhibition project "The Work shown in this space" in the context of the practice of Nadin and d'Arcangelo at the time, see Ben Kinmont, "Peter Nadin Interview," in *Project Series: Christopher d'Arcangelo* (Paris: Antinomian Press, 2005); and Thomas Crow, *Modern Art in the Common Culture* (New Haven, CT: Yale University Press, 1996), 235–41.

17 See, among others, the exhibitions "Followed and to Be followed," Le Consortium, Dijon, 1999; and "This is the Gallery and the Gallery is Many Things," Eastside Projects, Birmingham, 2008.

18 Jorge Pardo, who designed both the look of the neugerriemschneider gallery for its opening in Berlin in 1994 and for its reopening at a new location in Berlin's Mitte district in 1998, is not mentioned on the invitation card. Although Lawler clearly took the design concept he established into account, for her card she took only the exhibition context and dispensed with a broader contextualization that would have included the gallery itself.

19 The aspect of artistic and curatorial availability addressed by Lawler's contribution to "The Work shown in this space" is underscored by the fact that soon after the distribution of her card announcing the event for the closing of the exhibition she opened another exhibition with her own current works using the title "More Words."

Lorenzo Fusi

It's The End Of Hospitality As We Know It

(And I Feel Fine)

I had the opportunity to muse over the notion of hospitality during the preparation of the 2012 Liverpool Biennial exhibition. My reflections were published in the accompanying book entitled *The Unexpected Guest: Art, Writing and Thinking on Hospitality*.[1] Looking back, I still believe that some ideas originating in that experience are a valid ground for debate.

In the West and the North, the articulation of the idea of hospitality is presently at a standstill. Not much has been added in recent years to the analysis proposed by the *duopole* Derrida-Levinas, whose paradigmatic observations have greatly informed our cultural understanding of the term and its socio-political implications. The lack of alternative readings means that hospitality presently falls under a sort of epistemological hegemony.

Whilst I look forward to new interpretations that are able to decolonize or culturally deterritorialize the Western notion of hospitality, thus challenging our assumptions and position, I wonder whether it is at all possible to dismantle the asymmetrical power structure that the hospitality cycle entails. In the conclusions of my essay, I went as far as hoping for the end of hospitality since, to this day, I doubt it represents a viable cultural and behavioral model for resolving the conflict originating in the recognition/separation of any political "I" in opposition to a political "Other."

One of the crucial knots to be resolved is whether hospitality, outside the set of conditions it entangles and upon which the hospitality pact is constructed, exists in full. And, should this be the case, are we truly willing and prepared to offer a hospitality that might be said to be "unconditional"? Can we even afford or think such a proposition?

Following Slavoj Žižek's reasoning in *The Desert of the Real*, I suspect that in reality we are not in the position to embrace a *total* or *unconditional* hospitality, because the cost of taking seriously the "Derridean–Levinasian topic of hospitality and openness towards the Other" is enormous and so are its consequences. Which brings us to the main point at hand: the coexistence of the terms *unconditional* and *hospitality* in the same discursive realm. Can these two words inhabit the same epistemological space?

Žižek suggests that either the topic of hospitality is extended to all subjects (including problematic guests such as "the immigrants or the Palestinians in Israel") "or it means nothing."[2] I instead suspect that hospitality is defined precisely by its partiality and is only valid within the limitations it poses. I also do not think that hospitality is the right working frame for resolving issues related to immigration, let alone the Israeli-Palestinian conflict, because hospitality is a paradigmatic othering predicate (even when the separation happens within the sphere of the self) not a solution to the otherness of the guest subject. As the notion of hospitality *always* comes with some strings attached, we should simply embrace the idea that hospitality is conditional by definition. Unless we accept that a condition-less hospitality is something else, a *something* other than hospitality per se, we cannot but fail to resolve the conditionality that hospitality poses.

Such an understanding is key, for at the moment we decide to adopt the hospitality mode, we also have to accept the set of conditions that lie at the foundations of the declination of hospitality as a relational strategy.

This is particularly true in relation to duration. I see the relationship between the categories *hospitality* and *unconditional* as one of inverse proportion; they are more than altogether irreconcilable; the measure of their difference increases with time. Linguistically, the process is clearly illustrated in the guest-ghost association and subsequent differentiation. The sudden manifestation of any unexpected, unannounced, inexplicable, not-yet-thought-of phenomenon confronts us with the immediate (pre-conscious) necessity of having to respond instinctually. During this phase, the way we relate to the *unknown* or *pre-known* is not yet intellectualized or regimented by laws or tradition (*mori*). At this time, the guest and the ghost occupy a similar position. It is only then that our hospitality (acceptance/recognition) might be said to be unconditional. Over time, while the ghost might retain its spectral quality, the essence of the guest becomes more clearly determined. And the more we know about our guest, the less we are prone to unconditionally concede. The determination of the guest (which is dependent on the passing of time, duration) also determines the type of hospitality we are willing to offer, and thus establishes our conditional relation to the otherness occasioned by the guest.

Whilst we are becoming more prepared to face our unpreparedness (to paraphrase Derrida, who claimed that in the case of hospitality we should be "prepared to be unprepared"), the territorial, cultural, economic, or socio-political ownership of the space/dimension the host inhabits is reinforced. The sooner the host recovers from the marvel or surprise of the arrival, the stronger his/her position becomes.

In this instance, time determines space (the physical site and the metaphysical dimension of the hospitable) as well as the conditions the host places on the welcome they are willing or capable to extend to their guest.

To stretch the notion of hospitality beyond conditionality equals entering a completely new realm, a relationship that eludes the power structure grounded in the entitlement of the host to act as a host. This can happen only with the condition that the space the host occupies is not clearly marked or identifiable as the host's own. Whereas hospitality insists on and contributes to the crystallization of the powers ingrained in the determination of geopolitical and economic categories such as territoriality and ownership, other interrelational modalities (for example, cohabitation, co-existence) challenge these premises. But such a shift cannot but happen at the expense of those who claim the right to be the host, and in all honesty I doubt that our society is ready for such a radical and revolutionary proposition.

1 – Lorenzo Fusi, "Disappearing Human Beings, Not Problems," in *The Unexpected Guest: Art, Writing and Thinking on Hospitality*, ed. Sally Tallant and Paul Domela (London: ART/BOOKS, 2012), 10–15.

2 – Slavoj Žižek, *Welcome to the Desert of the Real: Five Essays on September 11 and Related Dates* (2002; repr., London: Verso, 2013), 192. The sentence is italicized in Žižek's text.

Nanne Buurman

Hosting Significant Others

Autobiographies as Exhibitions of Co-Authority

Since the so-called "curatorial turn" in the 1990s, curators have been discussed as paradigmatic authors in the art field. In the context of the global biennial culture, they have even gained celebrity status among a wider public. Klaus Biesenbach, to name but one example, is known for his friendships with stars such as Madonna, Lady Gaga, or Tilda Swinton.[1] As masters of networking, contemporary curators epitomize the neoliberal norms of constant cooperation and communication. Their immaterial mode of working as charismatic managers of culture is exemplary of the "project based polis."[2] Consequently, they are discussed as role models of post-Fordist subjectivity, in which well-connectedness and socializing skills are of central significance.[3] Yet, their author status also owes much to modernist conceptions of originality, individuality, and autonomy—characteristics usually attributed to artists.[4]

Indeed, Harald Szeemann is often cited as having authorized curatorial practice by transferring features usually associated with artistry onto his role as curator. According to Søren Grammel, the "Einladeausstellung" (invitational exhibition) "When Attitudes Become Form" (1969) was an important step in Szeemann's acquisition of auctorial status. Basing the show on commissions and inviting artists to work in situ rather than choosing art objects for display allowed him to model his subjectivity on that of the artists by foregrounding individual attitude as the shared principle of curatorial and artistic work instead of assuming the seemingly neutral scholarly stance that defined the traditional profession of the custodian-curator.[5] Apart from thus utilizing curatorial hospitality towards artists as a means to authorize himself, the subsequent gestures of leaving his position in the museum, declaring himself independent as a freelance curator, and treating exhibitions as artworks all added to his reputation as a meta-artist. The same is true for the monograph *Museum of Obsessions* (1981). Subtitled *by/on/about/with Harald Szeemann*, it is perhaps the first "autobiography" by an auctorial curator.[6] Even though he did not edit it himself, the publication, which Szeemann agreed to and cooperated in producing with Merve editors Peter Gente and Heidi Paris, helped canonize his author status as an independent exhibition-maker and thereby also contributed to authorizing the profession of curating. Furthermore, by calling this monograph a museum, he gave it a title that "underscores the possibility for the medium of the 'book' to become an exhibition space in itself."[7] Following this line of thought, my essay looks at the intersection of hospitality and life-writing by considering autobiography as a self-reflexive curatorial format in which authority may be exhibited by hosting significant others.

Thus, my aim is to add another dimension to the discussions about the high level of self-referentiality in the curatorial field, where since the 1990s numerous symposia have served as forums for curatorial self-positioning and promotion. Such events are often dominated by first person narratives on the speaker's own practice, which has led Paul O'Neill to state that curatorial discourse is in "perpetual self-production," with curating becoming the "subject and object of study."[8] Taking the autobiographic character of curatorial events and the publications accompanying them as a point of departure, this essay inverts the perspective and considers the curatorial quality of autobiography.

Instead of once more reiterating the cliché of Szeemann as the founding father of a *curation nation*,[9] I take a historical detour and consider Gertrude Stein as a curator *avant la lettre*. Her open studio at 27 rue de Fleurus in Paris has been considered a proto-museum of modern art.[10] As a salon host, collector, and writer, who fostered the careers of avant-garde artists such as Picasso and Hemingway, her activities in publishing and promoting modern art and literature resemble contemporary curatorial practices. Moreover, her hosting of the legendary Saturday night salons bears similarities with some recently much-discussed contemporary forms of hospitable curating that involve gatherings, conversations, and other relational formats.[11] Nevertheless, my primary concern is not the reconstruction of empirical events but an analysis of how they are retrospectively narrativized in Stein's memoir *The Autobiography of Alice B. Toklas* (1933). Looking at this autobiography as a curatorial format in its own right, I will consider how by hosting significant others it performs a shift of attention from the notion of the author as solitary genius, autonomous artist, or independent curator to the contexts and conditions in which authority is constituted collaboratively—and thereby exposes authorship as necessarily relational.[12] In other words, rather than reiterating the stereotype of curators as independent meta-artists, this essay explores the notion of hosting as a model for reconsidering curatorial authorship as a social process that involves reciprocal hospitalities and mutual interdependencies. Thus, contemplating the figure of the hostess as a precursor of contemporary modes of curatorship also implies an alternative genealogy of the curatorial.[13]

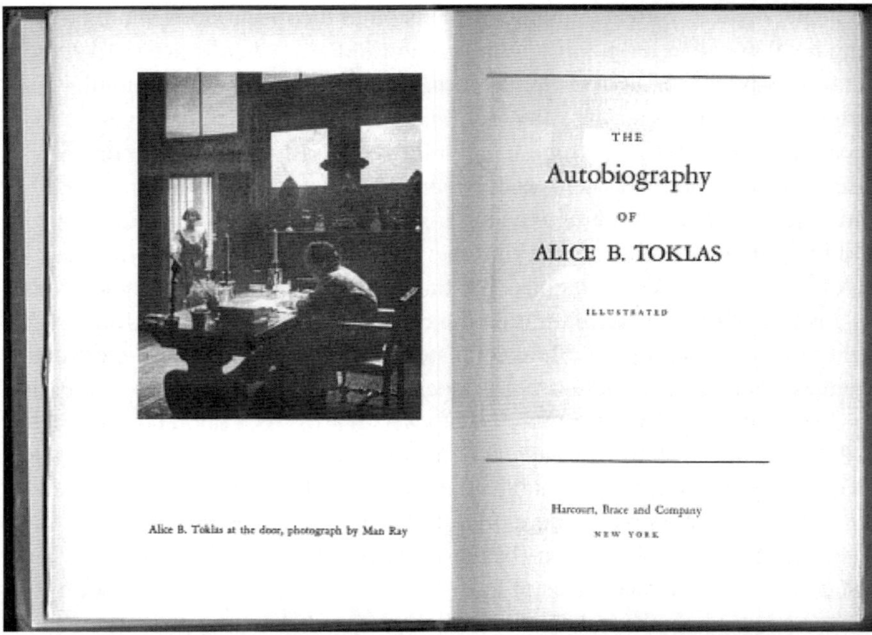

Alice B. Toklas at the door, photograph by Man Ray

THE
Autobiography
OF
ALICE B. TOKLAS

ILLUSTRATED

Harcourt, Brace and Company
NEW YORK

Frontispiece to the first edition of Gertrude Stein's *The Autobiography of Alice B. Toklas* (1933)

The Autobiography as a Self-Reflexive Curatorial Format

The Autobiography of Alice B. Toklas presents Stein's life from the perspective of her partner, Alice Toklas, with a focus on the years 1905–32 as the legendary age of avant-garde Paris. In literary criticism, it is considered a meta-autobiography that problematized the fictional and performative character of life-writing long before this issue had been acknowledged in theory.[14] Due to its non-linear, anecdotal, and repetitive style, *The Autobiography* is noted for its parody of orality, for its unusual treatment of temporality, and for highlighting the flawed workings of memory. What is more, the first edition bears some similarities with a family album: it includes sixteen photographs and facsimiles of people, rooms, and paintings.[15] As these are not present in subsequent editions, I will primarily focus on the text's verbal inducing of images, through which readers are presented with a portrait gallery of Stein's significant others. My concern with the text-as-exhibition is a reversal of the conceptualization of exhibitions-as-texts that has been used by cultural analysts to make exhibitions "readable."[16] These critics stress what has become almost a truism of institutional critique: that exhibitions are not neutral representations but institutional speech acts, which rather than merely presenting objects make use of the power of display.[17] Hence, exhibitions recreate their objects as exhibits with particular significance. The same holds for autobiographies as formats of self-exposure, particularly for Stein's *The Autobiography*, in which she not only turns herself into an exhibit but also creates literary avatars of her friends, relatives, and colleagues, whom she displays alongside herself.

Some years after its publication, Stein commented on the performative effect of the memoir that had brought her fame and made her as important as she had imagined herself in it.[18] The power of portraits to function as self-fulfilling prophecies is foreshadowed in the book itself with regard to Picasso's portrait of *Gertrude Stein* (1906): "Yes, he [Picasso] said, everybody says that she does not look like it but that does not make any difference, she will, he said" (16). Thus, already in the 1930s, Stein problematizes questions of performativity, identity, and referentiality and addresses the impossibility of objective representation.[19] Life-writing theory, in contrast, is said to have started to explicitly question the documentary and mimetic character of autobiographies only around the same time that exhibitions discursively lost their innocence with the deconstruction of the neutrality of the white cube in the 1970s.[20] Notably, *The Autobiography* does not pretend to be a truthful account of historical events. Instead, its obvious inconsistencies and narrative self-reflexivity point to the mediality of the text. By emphasizing its own unusual mode of presentation this semi-fictional self-portrait calls attention to how past activities are framed and negotiated. This is achieved, for example, by the narrator's comments on her own narrating, such as "There are a great many things to tell [...] but now I must describe what I saw when I came" (10). Furthermore, by lending her voice to different characters and by citing how they tell the same story differently, Stein presents readers with a "cubist" description of one incident from different viewpoints.

The technique of "narrating narrating,"[21] with its obsessive use of inquit formulas—for example the "he saids" in the quote referring to Picasso—functions in a way similar to Daniel Buren's *Exposition d'une Exposition* (1972). For this work, which was part of his contribution to documenta 5, Buren applied striped wallpaper in rooms where other artists' works were presented, highlighting the otherwise invisible function of walls as media of curatorial storytelling. As Beatrice von Bismarck points out in "Curating Curators," such institution-critical appropriations of curatorial responsibilities by artists expose curating as an activity "that clearly goes beyond the original meaning of the Latin word *curare* in the sense of looking after and preserving, to increasingly bring the aspect of mediation to the fore."[22] Foregrounding conventionally less prominent narrative framings through the use of "quotation marks," both Stein and Buren shift the focus *from work to frame*.[23] They thereby reveal a polyphony of authorial voices that questions the monolithic individuality of authority, thus putting forward a notion of plural authorship by different interdependent agencies. While many passages in *The Autobiography* literally reconstruct existing exhibition venues—such as Stein's studio (e.g., 12–20) or the Salon des Independents (e.g., 21–24)—as settings for social gatherings, the text as a whole, besides displaying the complicated relationship of author and narrator, may be considered as a curatorial space that houses and exhibits historical figures as fictional characters.

The Making of Co-Authorship

Reading Gertrude Stein's *The Autobiography of Alice B. Toklas* in terms of the curatorial therefore offers an opportunity to rethink curatorship beyond the binaries of hyper-visible versus invisible curatorial figures and individual versus collective approaches.[24] *The Autobiography* exhibits the relationality of authorship by constructing a mental space that hosts significant others as co-authorities. It thereby frames the making of authorship as socially and contextually conditioned.[25] Far from innocent, it reflects the ambivalence of such hospitality, which not only altruistically features other people and their as-yet-unrecognized work but also becomes a self-promotional display of prestigious relationships as social capital. Accordingly, the book-as-exhibition oscillates between centering and decentering authority, staging Stein as a protagonist of high modernism as well as displaying relationships and personal interdependencies as prerequisites not just for subject formation but also for acquiring auteur-status. On the one hand, this narcissistic, autopoietic account somewhat ironically reinforces the idea of exceptional genius, while on the other, it questions authorial sovereignty by showcasing social networks, mutual dependencies, and immaterial mediating activities as constitutive factors for

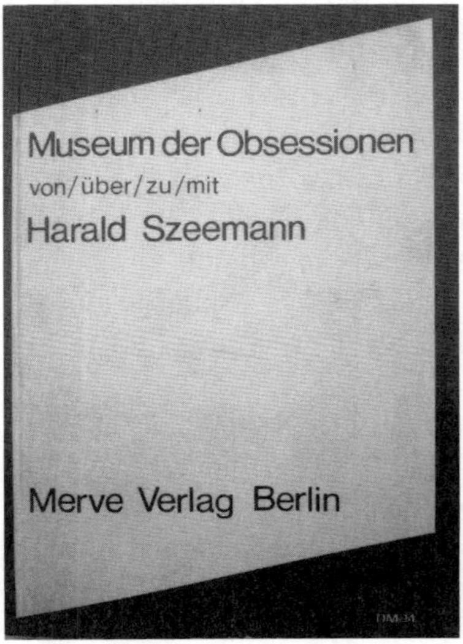

Cover of ***Museum of Obsessions: by/about/ on/with Harald Szeemann*** **(1981)**

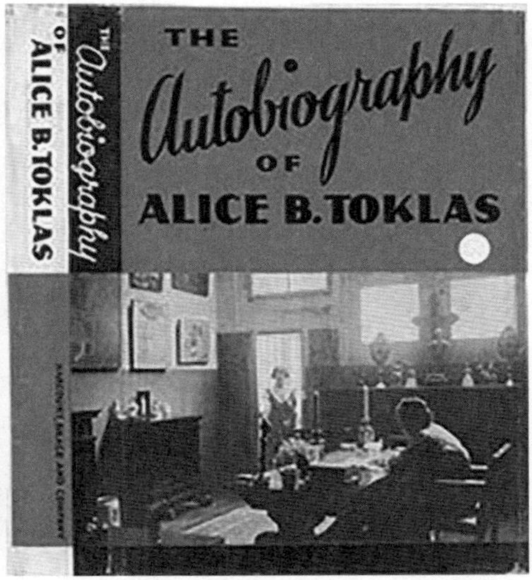

Cover of the first edition of *The Autobiography of Alice B. Toklas* (1933)

establishing authority. Challenging modernist myths of autonomous artistry as well as gendered conventions of self-effacing femininity, Stein —as I will discuss in more detail—simultaneously takes center stage and co-authorizes other actors, thereby queering traditional distributions of roles such as author versus narrator, artist versus curator, host versus guest.

The paradoxical mode of Stein's enterprise already becomes obvious when we look at the cover of the first edition. As opposed to the *Museum of Obsessions*, for instance, which identifies Szeemann as subject and object of this literally egocentric monograph by including his name in the title, Stein's name is missing from the cover of her book. Initially, this effacement seems to echo the long tradition of modesty in women's writing as manifested in anonymity or the use of male pseudonyms.[26] Indeed, at first glance the title *The Autobiography of Alice B. Toklas* masks the book as her partner's memoir. What seems to be a denial of authorship in favor of the narrator, Alice Toklas, however, is subsequently contradicted by the book's content, which presents Stein's brilliance in analogy to the then already recognized genius of Picasso, her artistic mirror image:

> She realizes that in english literature in her time she is the only one. She has always known it and now she says it. She understands very well the basis of creation and therefore her advice and criticism is invaluable to all her friends. How often I have heard Picasso say to her when she has said something about a picture of his and then illustrated by something she was trying to do, racontez-moi cela. In other words tell me about it. These two even today have long solitary conversations. They sit in two little low chairs up in his apartment studio, knee to knee and Picasso says, expliquez moi cela. And they explain to each other. They talk about everything [...]. (85)[27]

Their closeness is stressed repeatedly. Sometimes Picasso and Stein almost appear as twins or *doppelgängers*, who share their creative giftedness (52, 136). By spotlighting their friendship and their common interests as well as by boasting that she discovered Picasso and fostered his career, Stein might have hoped to partake in the aura of his genius. The emphasis on her contribution to the making of his name as well as that of Hemingway, her declared literary foster child, underlines how Stein's authority is mutually entwined with each of theirs and thereby relativizes the idea of the "uncreated creator."[28]

Since she is now regarded as the godmother of not only the Parisian Cubist avant-garde but also the Anglo-American modernist literary movement, it is ironic that "Gertrude Stein was in those days a little bitter, all her unpublished manuscripts, and no hope of publication or serious recognition" (211). It is therefore not unlikely that by emphasizing her influence as a financial and intellectual patron of these famous men, she intended to gain the recognition she felt she deserved. In claiming to have bought everybody's first paintings and depicting herself as an indispensible advisor, she implicitly also admits her own dependency on the artists as testimonies of her significance.[29] The ambivalent reciprocity of hospitality as a means to generously nurture peers while simultaneously profiting from this co-authorization will now be addressed in more detail together with some remarks on the intermediality of the text, which allows for an alternative explanation to the standard view that Stein employed Toklas as a narrator to comply with expectations of humility about oneself.[30]

Reciprocal Hospitality: Text as Image as Space

The Autobiography of Alice B. Toklas is by no means a literary white cube—that is to say, it refrains from suggesting objectivity or auctorial neutrality while simultaneously breaking with gendered scripts of modesty and curatorial codes of humbleness that demand self-abnegation in favor of magnifying significant others, be they men or artists. Many theorists have relativized the selfless generosity often associated with hospitality by calling attention not only to the power inherent in the gatekeeping function of hosts but also to the possible inversion of roles, where the invited host the host.[31] In *The Autobiography*, Stein and Picasso, for instance, are shown as mutually hosting each other in their work. Where Picasso pays tribute to Stein as a hostess by including her visiting card in his paintings (122), Stein in return prominently features his pictures in her writing—but certainly not in a self-effacing manner. In fact, Picasso's famous portrait of *Gertrude Stein* (1906) even functions as a kind of *leitmotif* in the *The Autobiography*. Stein's posing for it is mentioned numerous times. Yet, this should not be mistaken as conforming to traditional gender hierarchies, in which the male artist's gaze objectifies the allegedly passive female model. On the contrary, by making the painting her model, Stein reappropriates her portrait and thus proclaims co-authorship.

Besides explicitly mentioning the picture, the text narratively imitates its visual mode of presentation. As we shall see, it verbally echoes prominent aspects of the portrait, such as masking, posing, and decentering the gaze.[32] Therefore, in addition to playing with literary autobiographical conventions, *The Autobiography* may be said to be modelled on visual (self-)portraits, which explains the much-discussed unconventional decision to use Toklas as the narrator.[33] This mode of display—besides paying homage to her partner—allows Stein to appear as both subject *and* object of representation, something that is the norm in painted self-portraits, but quite unusual for written autobiographies, where readers conventionally identify with the autobiographer's "I" or "eyes" rather than "looking" at him or her.[34] Following this line of thought, the discussion of a photograph taken by Man Ray may also be read as a motto for *The Autobiography* as it demonstrates Stein's literary concern with capturing movement in a single image—another interest she shared with her artist friends.

> [Man Ray] showed us pictures [...] and he asked if he might come and take photographs of the studio and of Gertrude Stein. He did and he also took some of me and we were very pleased with the result. [...] One day she told him that she liked his photographs of her better than any that had ever been taken except one snap-shot I had taken recently. This seemed to bother Man Ray. In a little while he asked her to come and pose and she

did. He said, move all you like, your eyes, your head, it is to be a pose but it is to have in it all the qualities of a snap-shot. (213–12)

Like Man Ray's photograph, Stein's memoir is a carefully composed pose that, due to its informal voice and incoherent treatment of temporality, reads like a series of spontaneous snapshots. Furthermore, the passage relates to his photograph of Toklas and Stein in the latter's studio (1922), which adorns the cover of the first edition of *The Autobiography*.

The photograph's striking similarity to Diego Velázquez's *Las Meninas* (1656) is one of the reasons I take the argument for the text's intermediality even further. Employing both images as a foil, I read *The Autobiography* in the tradition of studio portraits, a genre that conflates studio and cube, atelier and exhibition. It has been repeatedly pointed out that by providing controlled insights into the private realm, such autobiographical pictures have self-promotional functions. *Las Meninas*, for instance, has been interpreted not only as Velázquez's application for knighthood and nobility but also as a manifesto for the ennoblement of painting as a fine art at a time when it was still widely considered a craft. According to Jonathan Brown, it was instrumental for Velázquez's self-authorization as a painter to receive Philip IV as a guest in his studio and to boast of their intimacy by hosting the king in the painting as a significant testimony of his painterly authority.[35] *Las Meninas* also addresses other issues concerning hospitality that are relevant to Stein's auto-portrait: The fact that Velázquez's studio was situated inside the king's palace, in addition to his status as a kind of royal housekeeper and curator of the royal collections, especially raises the question of who hosts whom and to what ends.[36]

When reading the virtual exhibition space of *The Autobiography of Alice B. Toklas* in terms of hosting, it is useful to revisit the etymology of the words host and guest, which stem from the same Proto-Indo-European origin: *ghosti*, simultaneously denoting guest and host.[37] According to J. Hillis Miller, the word parasite today is generally equated with leeching, whereas in the original Greek, *parasitos*, it had positive connotations meaning to share food as fellow guests. In the following close-reading of Stein's autobiography, I employ these two sets of vacillating meanings to explore different dimensions of curatorial relationality: First, looking at the narrative, I talk about *ghosting*, that is, the deliberate confusion of author and narrator that blurs the positions of Stein and Toklas, with both concurrently featuring as host and guest, curator and curated. Thereby, I show how the text authorizes curatorial functions by highlighting its own power of display and the importance of publishing, while it at the same time centers the reader's attention on Stein as an authority. Second, in terms of content, I consider how and to what effect Stein is shown to *parasite*, that is, to literally and metaphorically share food with other characters. Thus, I discuss how the salon, in analogy to painted studio portraits, is presented in *The Autobiography* as a liminal space between public and private where Stein acquires curatorial authority through regulating access as a hostess.

Ghosting

The Autobiography of Alice B. Toklas is probably most famous for flouting the Lejeunian "autobiographical pact," which requires the identity of author, narrator, and protagonist as a guarantee of verisimilitude.[38] The authorial masquerade of Stein presenting her autobiography in the name and voice of her partner was staged most consistently in the first edition of the book. Although any direct reference to Stein as the author is missing on the cover, the Man Ray photograph (1922), a replica of which also faces the title page of the first edition, hints at Stein's authorship, as it shows her in the foreground, sitting at her desk writing, while Toklas stands in the background of the picture as an onlooker framed by the door. The photograph introduces the designation of roles in the spectacle of the book. Even though it seems obvious that Alice Toklas, as an eyewitness, narrates the memoir from her point-of-view, a separation of authorial, narratorial, and writerly responsibilities remains difficult. Early on in *The Autobiography* Toklas claims to be its author (18). On the last page, however, she contradicts herself by declaring that Stein has ghostwritten it:

> I am a pretty good housekeeper and a pretty good gardener and a pretty good needlewoman and a pretty good secretary and a pretty good editor and a pretty good vet for dogs and I have to do them all at once and I find it difficult to add being a pretty good author. About six weeks ago Gertrude Stein said, it does not look to me as if you were ever going to write that autobiography. You know what I am going to do. I am going to write it for you. [...] And she has and this is it. (272)

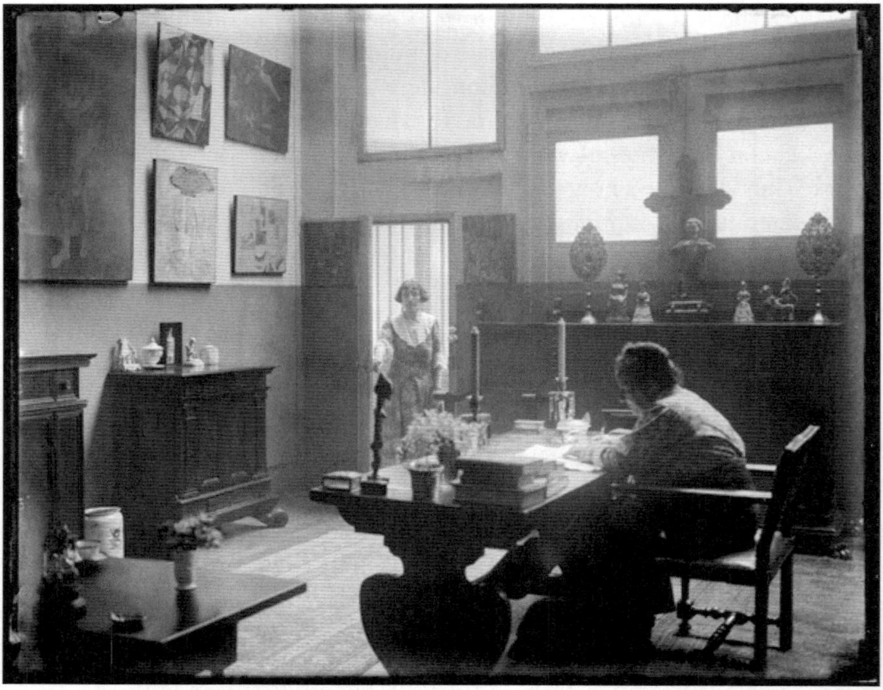

Man Ray, Gertrude Stein and Alice Toklas in the atelier at 27 rue de Fleurus, Paris, 1922

This admission is rendered dubious again by the pains that are taken to prove Stein's true authorship. Despite the inclusion of a facsimile of the handwritten manuscript's first page as evidence that Stein in fact wrote the book, the constellation of guest and host remains crucially irresolvable.[39] "Stein enters the mouth of her lover and takes up lodging in the body of Alice for the purpose of writing *The Autobiography*. Alice in turn enters the mouth of her host writer through whose body she speaks."[40] The deliberate blending of voices and reciprocal inhabitation of each other's bodies is important in so far as it questions the univocality of supposedly sovereign authorship.

This shared voice device, which calls attention to the practical difficulties of telling apart each partner's contribution in a shared effort of cooperating and cohabitating lovers, is not the only way in which Toklas's constitutive participation in authorship is credited. Her contribution as a "midwife"

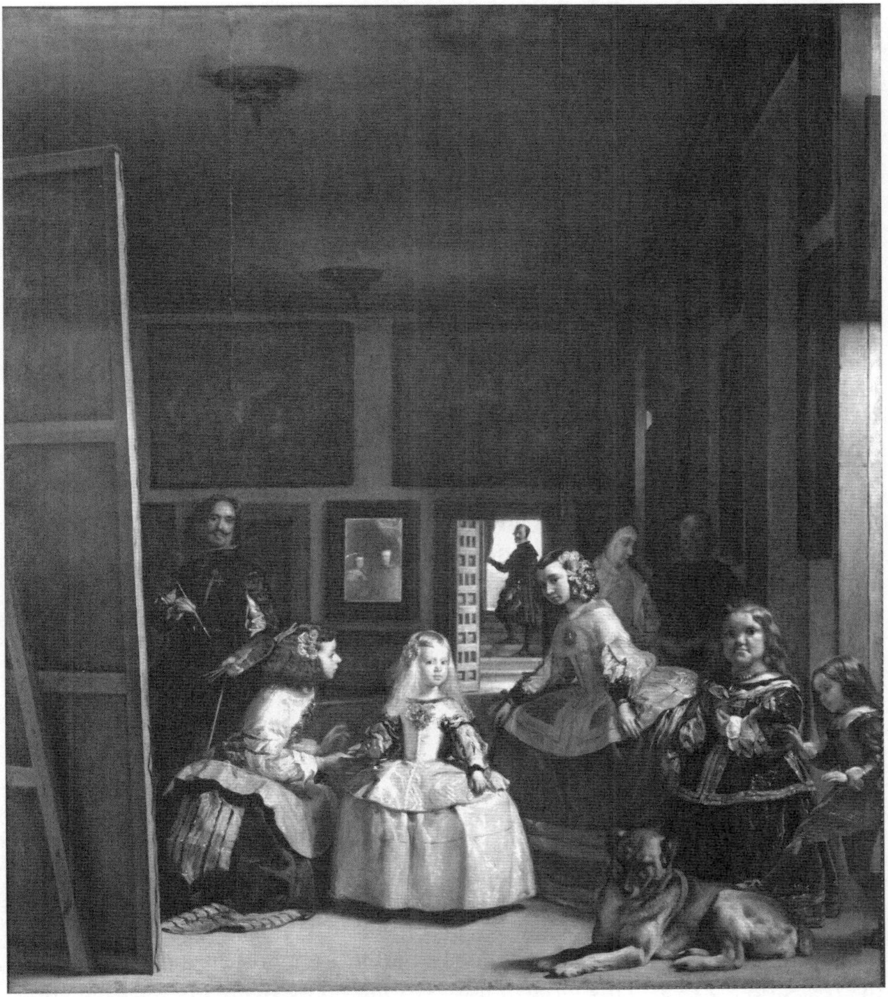

Diego Velázquez, *Las Meninas*, 1656

of Stein's literature is also explicitly mentioned throughout the book. Stereotypically feminized "unglamorous tasks,"[41] such as providing comfort through domestic work, taking care of guests, assisting in proof-reading and copying manuscripts, are prevalent motifs in *The Autobiography* and are treated as seriously as the artistic activities. When Toklas, towards the end of the narrative, describes her founding of the Plain Edition (1930) as an instrument to distribute Stein's literature, she speaks in an almost authoritative voice (261ff.). Thus, Toklas's editorial practice corresponds to Stein's role as an advocate of the avant-gardes. Moreover, in both cases the mediating effort of producing a public for the art of the other is presented as an essential part of the artistic work. Therefore, the highlighting of hitherto widely disregarded but indispensible activities can be regarded as an authorization of "curatorial" functions.

The aforementioned near symbiosis of the two women is suspended by the split between Toklas as an observer and Stein as the observed: The author Stein hosts the narrator Toklas. In turn, Toklas as a narrator hosts Stein as a character of her—or rather their—story. Toklas also in a way hosts the readers by allowing them to look through her eyes. In fact, on the second page of the book, Toklas is explicitly introduced in the role of a "hostess" (8). Following this scheme of making Toklas the exhibitor of her life, Stein manages to position herself center stage. "When we went into the atelier there were already quite a number of people in the room, scattered groups, single and couples all looking and looking. Gertrude Stein sat by the stove talking and looking and getting up to open the door and go up to various people talking and listening" (17). The narrator's repeated description of Stein as a regal presence, who calmly presides over the Saturday night gatherings in a throne-like high-backed chair, in a way prefigures the famous (self-)representation of Harald Szeemann as *primus inter pares*, with both representations relying on iconographic traditions of depicting authorities that are highly gendered.[42] "Miss Stein sat near the stove in a lovely high backed one and she peacefully let her legs hang, which was a matter of habit, and when any one of the many visitors came to ask her a question she lifted herself up out of this chair" (14). The narrative focus on Stein as a protagonist turns her into an icon. "Gertrude Stein sat peacefully in a chair and those who could did the same, the rest stood" (135). This iconization is furthered by the many passages that mention Stein's frequent posing as a model for different artists (51–52, 57, 60, 64, 126, 153). However, neither the topos of Stein's chairing nor that of her modeling is illustrated by the photos included in the first edition. Instead, these topoi are verbally evoked and branded into the mind's eye through continual repetition. Stein is repeatedly portrayed not only as the center of the Paris art scene but also as a literary genius and the most important writer of her time. The constant repetition of her full name as well as the recurrent mentioning of the titles of her other texts foreshadows contemporary marketing strategies such as branding and product placement.

Stein's self-centered, narcissistic claim to fame in a way marginalizes Alice Toklas, assigning her the stereotypical role of the "wife of a genius" (18) who bears witness to her partner's greatness. Nevertheless, in the course of the narrative Toklas gradually moves towards the center of the story, until she regularly refers to Stein and herself in the plural "we" (153). Eventually she enters the scene of action as a character, instead of merely observing it as a narrator from the outside. This coincides with her moving into Stein's house at 27 rue de Fleurus, shortly after she had started to collaborate in Stein's production.[43] Her assistance is explicitly linked with the publication of Stein's work: "When I first came to the rue de Fleurus Gertrude Stein was correcting the proofs of *Three Lives*. I was soon helping her with this and before very long the book was published" (123). In chapter five Toklas recounts her correspondence with T. S. Eliot's secretary about publishing a text of Stein's in the journal *Criterion* (218). Finally, in the last chapter she proudly talks about her own publishing venture: "I now myself began to think about publishing the work of Gertrude Stein. I asked her to invent a name for my edition and she laughed and said, call it Plain Edition. And Plain Edition it is. All that I knew about what I would have to do was to get the book printed and then to get it distributed, that is sold" (261–62). What follows is a comprehensive discussion of her editorial work and the art of bookmaking, including the questions of printing, binding, distribution, advertisement, and "getting reviews." Toklas's "ambitious" (263ff.) efforts reach a climax when she manages "to get the book put in the windows of all the book stores in Paris that sold english [*sic*] books. This event gave Gertrude Stein a childish delight amounting almost to ecstasy. She had never seen a book of hers in a bookstore window before" (262). In sum, Toklas is presented as an indispensible mediator of Stein's work. As a character in *The Autobiography* she transcends the boundary between the space of reception and that of creation, between spectator and spectacle, between production and reproduction. Yet unlike other ghostly figures such as spin doctors, ghostwriters, or the invisible Victorian "Angel in the House," she is given her own voice and is credited in and by *The Autobiography* for many of the marketing activities that made Stein's work public. This tale of the increasingly visible agency of the go-between prefigures the gradual emergence of curators from behind-the-scenes to center stage, which has been taking place since the late 1960s. Thus, the authorization of narrative and editorial functions in the book may be read in analogy to the recognition of the authority of curatorship.

The narrative technique of "ghosting" helps circumvent the conventional confessional character of autobiographical writing, which often pretends to allow readers to participate in the author's most intimate thoughts. Nevertheless, as a consequence of Stein choosing Toklas's perspective, the narrative is hosted in the domestic space of their home as the main setting. Since the text gives controlled insights into the private sphere of Stein's atelier, where life

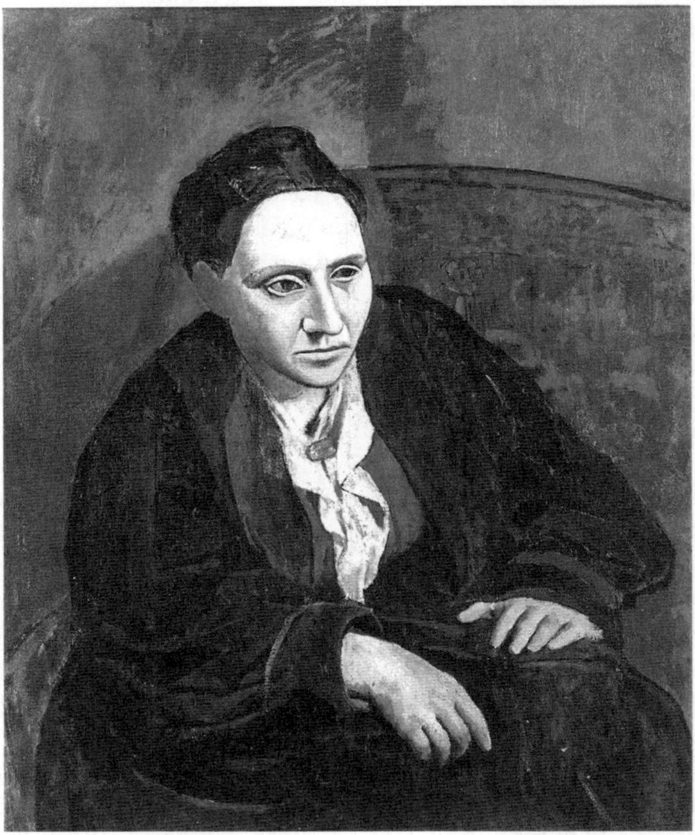

Pablo Picasso, *Gertrude Stein*, 1906

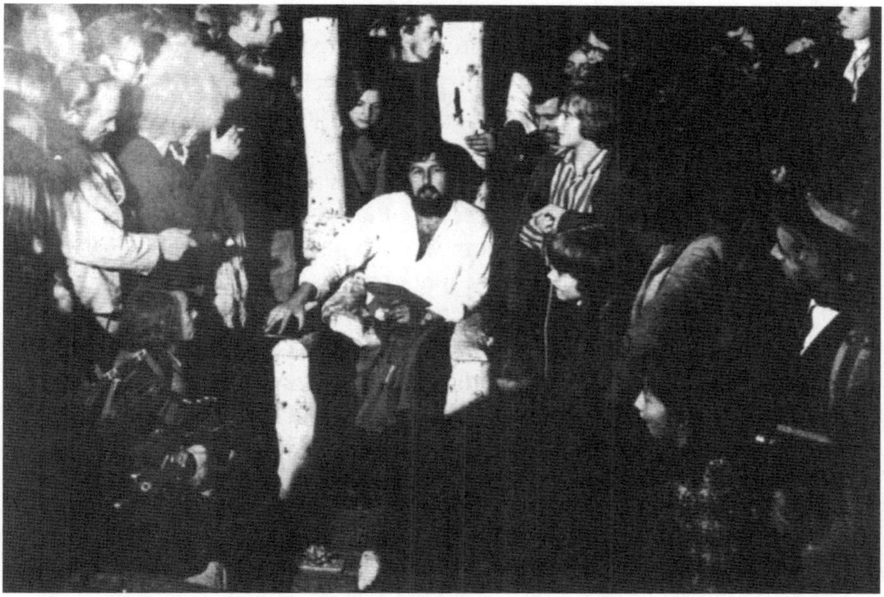

Harald Szeemann on the last day of documenta 5, 1972

and work are hard to distinguish, it can be said to bear traits of painters' studio portraits. Public cube and private studio merge into the semi-public institution of the salon as a space of "co-appearance" where the audience, composed mainly of artists and writers, serves as a forum for Stein to assert her curatorial authority as a host.[44] Not dissimilar from the cast of characters in Gustave Courbet's *The Painter's Studio* (1855), the featured intellectuals in Stein's tale do not really play the roles of protagonists but rather function as a background for Stein to stage herself as an author. Breaking away from the idea of the solitary genius working in isolation, and instead foregrounding the social interactions that accompany cultural production, the text, besides acknowledging domestic support structures as preconditions for artistic work, characterizes Stein as the "mother of Modernism."

On the first page of *The Autobiography* narrator Alice Toklas states: "I like a view, but I like to sit with my back turned to it" (7). It is worthwhile reading this prelude together with Irit Rogoff's elaborations on the participatory potential of *looking away* from the artworks one is supposed to admire.[45] Turning her back on the predefined scripts that hierarchize visual culture, Toklas prefers not to describe the masterworks in Stein's studio. In the second chapter, she constantly promises but postpones her explanation of the pictures. In stark contrast to this disregard, she extensively describes even the most trivial details of the room as well as the actions that she remembers having taken place there.

> Against the walls were several pieces of large italian renaissance furniture and in the middle of the room was a big renaissance table, on it a lovely inkstand, and at one end of it note-books neatly arranged, the kind of note-books french children use, with pictures of earthquakes and explorations on the outside of them. And on all the walls right up to the ceiling were pictures. At one end of the room was a big cast iron stove that Hélène came in and filled with a rattle, and in one corner of the room was a large table on which were horseshoe nails and pebbles and little pipe cigarette holders which one looked at curiously but did not touch, but which turned out later to be accumulations from the pockets of Picasso and Gertrude Stein. But to return to the pictures. The pictures where so strange that one quite instinctively looked at anything rather than at them just first. I have refreshed my memory by looking at some snap shots taken inside the atelier at the time. The chairs in the room were also all italian renaissance, not very comfortable for short-legged people and one got the habit of sitting on one's legs. Miss Stein sat near the stove in a lovely high backed one and she peacefully let her legs hang, which was a matter of habit, and when any one of the many visitors came to ask her a question she lifted herself up out of this chair and usually replied in french, not just now. This usually referred to something they wished to see, drawings which were put away, some german had once spilled ink on one, or some other not to be fulfilled desire. But to return to the pictures. (13)

Focusing on the frame instead of the work, the peripheral instead of the central, absent actions rather than present representations, the narrator shifts the attention away from the original *raison d'etre* of the famous Saturday night gatherings: the modern masterworks. In this chapter, Toklas does not fulfill her promise to tell the reader about the pictures. She only lists the artists' names, reducing the images to mere signatures of their authors (14).[46] In the same chapter, the cook, Hélène, is granted considerably more words of characterization than all the modern masters together. The favorable two-page portrait of Hélène acknowledges her excellent cooking skills and grants her the privilege of voicing her opinions on the painters (11–12). Through her prominent appearance, the usually unacknowledged reproductive labor of providing everyone with meals is credited as a crucial precondition for the artistic conviviality.

Apart from highlighting the material and social context in which the works are implicated, decentering the gaze from the paintings provides room for showcasing Stein's hosting activities. Her studio is recreated as a mental space where the narrator fuses the history of all that has been happening there into one image of "continuous present." This condensation of different temporalities into near synchronicity functions like an imaginary *tableau vivant* of the ongoing history of the Saturday night gatherings. It adheres to the social nature of the event rather than its artistic significance.

> When we went into the atelier there were already quite a number of people in the room, scattered groups, single and couples all looking and looking. Gertrude Stein sat by the stove talking and looking and getting up to open the door and go up to various people talking and listening. She usually opened the door to the knock and the usual formula was, de la part de qui venez-vous, who is your introducer. The idea was that anybody could come but for form's sake and in Paris you have to have a formula, everybody was supposed to be able to mention the name of somebody who had told them about it. It was a mere form, really everybody could come in and as at that time these pictures had no value and there was no social privilege attached to knowing anyone there, only those came who really were interested. So as I say anybody could come in, however, there was the formula. Miss Stein once in opening the door said as she usually did by whose invitation do you come and we heard an aggrieved voice reply, but by yours madam. (17)

Like a stage-set, the setting of the room revives the atmosphere of actions that have taken place there. Hence, the recurrent passages that picture Stein's studio serve as a *pars pro toto* for the entire book. In prominently framing Gertrude Stein as the stable center surrounded by disciples, the book also captures the bohemian conviviality as a group portrait of "everybody" who participated in the artistic carnival. Stein's practice of "portrait-writing" is repeatedly mentioned, and there is an extensive list of everybody she portrayed (124–26, 131).

> This was the beginning of the long series of portraits. She has written portraits of practically everybody she has known, and written them in all manners and in all styles. Ada was followed by portraits of Matisse and Picasso, and Stieglitz who was much interested in them and in Gertrude Stein printed them in a special number of Camera Work. (125)

The book and the salon's guest list read like a *who's who* of the cultural field at the time.[47] Consequently, this "everybody" was not an open public but rather a selected private audience of artists, writers, and other cultural producers. We learn that the Saturday night gatherings, before they were instituted as a response to the increasing interest in the Stein collection, had started as private dinners. Artists such as Matisse and Picasso were welcomed as privileged guests, with whom Stein shares many meals throughout the story (19,52,56,73,113ff.).

> We were talking, [Stein] said, of a lunch party we had in here last year. We had just hung all the pictures and we asked all the painters. You know how painters are, I wanted to make them happy so I placed each one opposite his own picture, and they were happy so happy that we had to send out twice for more bread, [...] because they cannot eat and drink without bread and we had to send out twice for bread so they were happy. Nobody noticed my little arrangement except Matisse [...]. (19)

The importance of food is not only stressed by the elaborate characterization of the cook Hélène; the topos of *parasiting* as a medium of friendship frequently comes up, establishing especially Picasso as a very significant other. "He was sitting next to Gertrude Stein at dinner and she took up a piece of bread. This, said Picasso, snatching it back with violence, this piece of bread is mine. She laughed and he looked sheepish. That was the beginning of their intimacy" (52). Contrary to Stein's generosity towards certain artists—with whom she is literally and metaphorically shown breaking bread—according to the narrator, she only hesitantly gave way to the pressures of the increasing general interest in her collection (47).

It is for this reason that, as the salon grew more public, visitors were supposed to name someone who had told them about it. Toklas stresses that this was just a formula, because supposedly "everybody"—and this is underlined through hyperbolic repetition of the word (11, 17, 47, 135)—could come. Nevertheless, the ritual of admission emphasizes both Stein's role as a gatekeeper and the practice of naming names as an effective door opener, aspects that are fundamental to curating, where the curator's filtering function—to decide who gets into an exhibition and who has to remain outside—often also entails curatorial control over careers. On a meta-level, *The Autobiography* makes use of the strategy of name-dropping in an almost exaggerated manner—literally authorizing the text through accumulating other people's authority. The power involved in this kind of (literary) hospitality is obvious. As host, Gertrude Stein has the curatorial authority to select whom to include. The book therefore shows Stein not only as a collector of art but also of people as co-authorizing others. Since *The Autobiography* is a collection of many people's characterizations, it functions like a portrait gallery or family album of her artistic "relatives." As a veritable Facebook, it allows her to display relationships as a demonstration of her well-connectedness. Following this line of thought, the title of its sequel, *Everybody's Autobiography* (1938), would also have suited *The Autobiography of Alice B. Toklas*. The sequel even more explicitly addresses the importance of networking, of meeting the right people, and of "being photographed together" (*EA*, 4–6)—a phrase that is repeated time and again in typically Steinian manner.

Conclusion

Gertrude Stein's unconventional autobiographical practice sheds new light on quite a few recent curatorial publications. Although *A Brief History of Curating* (2009) is not at first sight an autobiography, Hans Ulrich Obrist uses it to assert his authority in interviews that put him side by side with what he calls the "pioneers of curating."[48] Likewise, *Selected Maria Lind Writings* (2010) is not literally autobiographical, but it portrays Lind from the multiple perspectives of her fellow curators and artists, who were invited to select from her writing and comment on her curatorial practice. *The Logbook* (2012) that accompanied dOCUMENTA (13) includes many pictures of Carolyn Christov-Bakargiev that show her posing with artists and other collaborators as well as her e-mail exchanges with those involved in the making of documenta.[49] Although different in many respects, these publications may be considered as implicit instances of curatorial autobiography that host significant others as exhibitions of co-authority.

Against this backdrop, Stein's *The Autobiography of Alice B. Toklas* proves to be relevant with regard to contemporary curatorial discourse because it reflects hospitality as an ambivalent social constellation that may be instrumental in simultaneously authorizing oneself and others. Oscillating between seemingly paradoxical assertions and subversions as well as centerings and decenterings of authorship, the book—significantly—does not mask the conflicts inherent in acts of authorization. Instead, it exhibits the interplay of benevolence and self-interest as co-existent aspects of authorial positioning in the cultural field. The display of friendship networks as a means of self-authorization goes hand in hand with a foregrounding of hitherto usually unsung care labors as a significant part of artistic work. In *The Autobiography*, the "egoist" employment of relationships as social capital and the more "altruistic" crediting of others' formerly disregarded contributions appear as two sides of the same coin, namely, the relationality of authorship.

Perhaps *The Autobiography* seems so strikingly contemporary because its exhibition of what today would be called immaterial labor was conceived at a time before post-Fordism had dawned and the curator as we know him [*sic*] had appeared on the map. It was written at the height of Fordism, when care work, affective labor, and symbolic production were not yet considered paradigmatic economic forces but seen as either exceptional, privileged, spare-time activities or marginalized feminine responsibilities. Since the biopolitical shift of precedence from the manual production of objects to the immaterial (re)production of subjectivities and relationships, there has been a mainstreaming of tasks, positions, and attitudes formerly considered as primarily feminine, which has coincided with the rise of the curator.[50] Yet, the prototype of the contemporary curator, the "exhibition-maker" Szeemann, was authorized somewhat anachronistically as a reincarnation of the exemplary material producer of industrialism: the creative artist. Such an ennoblement of curatorship as independent meta-artistic craftsmanship mythifies the deeply interdependent practice of curating as the heroic deeds of exceptionally self-sufficient individuals, thus streamlining it with scripts of autonomous authorial mastery that have traditionally been associated with masculinity.

Stein's autobiography provides us with an alternative to this history. Her story reminds us that the curatorial is not so much a sublimation of an "ethics of care" but rather the recognition of being inextricably entangled in the "stuplimity" of a complex network of social relations.[51] Therefore, Stein's autobiography may be read as an early example of curatorial self-reflexivity that complicates the processes involved in the making of authorship. Dramatizing relations between host and guest, display and displayed, curator and curated,

The Autobiography of Alice B. Toklas queers simple notions of curatorial authority as meta-artistry and invites further considerations of the curatorial.

1 See Moritz von Uslar, "Kurator Klaus Biesenbach: Die Kunst der guten Freunde; Mit Lady Gaga und Madonna im Schlepptau; Der erstaunliche Erfolg des Kurators Klaus Biesenbach am MoMA in New York," *Die Zeit*, no. 16, April 14, 2012.

2 Luc Boltanski and Eve Chiapello, *The New Spirit of Capitalism* (London: Verso, 2005).

3 See Oliver Marchart, "The Curatorial Subject: The figure of the curator between individuality and collectivity," special issue, *Texte zur Kunst* 86, *The Curators* (June 2012): 28–40; Beatrice von Bismarck "Curating Curators," ibid., 42–60.

4 See von Bismarck, "Curating Curators," 52.

5 Søren Grammel, *Ausstellungsautorschaft: Die Konstruktion der auktorialen Position des Kurators bei Harald Szeemann; Eine Mikroanalyse* (Frankfurt am Main: Revolver, 2005). See esp. chap. 3.1, "Personifizierung der Ausstellung."

6 The English titles are my translation from the original German *Museum der Obsessionen: von/über/zu/mit Harald Szeemann* (Berlin: Merve, 1981).

7 Anna-Sophie Springer, "Volumes: The Book as Exhibition," *C Magazine*, no. 116 (Winter 2012): 21–29.

8 Paul O'Neill, *The Culture of Curating and the Curating of Culture(s)* (Cambridge, MA: MIT Press, 2012), 38; cf. von Bismarck, "Curating Curators," 44.

9 This term was popularized by Steven Rosenbaum in a publication on online-publishing. See Rosenbaum, *Curation Nation: How to Win in a World Where Consumers are Creators* (New York: Mcgraw-Hill, 2011).

10 Stein's open studio (circa 1905–38) was one of the few permanent institutions where one could encounter art by contemporaries. However, she is by no means the only or first proto-curator. See, for example, Beti Žerovc's interview with Walter Benjamin, "My Dear, This is Not What it Seems to Be," in *What is Modern Art? (Group Show)*, ed. Inke Arns and Walter Benjamin (Frankfurt am Main: Revolver / Archiv für aktuelle Kunst, 2006), 28–34.

11 Parallel to what has come to be called the discursive, social, or educational turn in curating, salons with their relatively intimate convivial atmosphere have gained popularity again alongside phenomena such as dinner parties, reading groups, and seminars, as sites of curatorial relationality. Examples in Berlin include Salon Populaire (by Ellen Blumenstein, Fiona Geuß, Ulrike Bernard, Bryndis Bjornsdottir) and Salon für kritische Kunstvermittlung (initiated by Nanna Lüth, Sandra Ortmann, Maren Ziese); and in London, n.paradoxa Salon (hosted by editor Katy Deepwell) and the ICA Friday Salons, to name just a few. Moreover, many reading groups combine conviviality and domesticity by taking place in the participants' homes or—as in the case of Annette Krauss and Hilde Tuinstra's ongoing Read Ins—in the houses of strangers.

12 The plural "significant others" is used here as a reference to the apparent consensus amongst scholars of women's life-writing that "self-definition in relation to significant others is the most pervasive characteristic of the female autobiography." See Bella Brodzki and Celeste Schenck's introduction to *Life/Lines: Theorizing Women's Autobiography*, ed. Brodzki and Schenck (Ithaca: Cornell University Press, 1988), 1–14, esp. 8. See also Mary G. Mason "The Other Voice: Autobiographies of Women Writers," in *Autobiography: Essays Theoretical and Critical*, ed. James Olney (Princeton: Princeton University Press: 1980), 207–235; Marcus K. Billson and Sidonie A. Smith, "Lillian Hellman and the Strategy of the Other," in *Women's Autobiography: Essays in Criticism*, ed. Estelle C. Jelinek (Bloomington: Indiana University Press, 1980), 163–79. More recently, Adriana Cavarero uses the notion of "the necessary other" with regard to Gertrude Stein's memoir in her argument against an individualist ontology of subjectivity. Cavarero, "The Necessary Other," in *Relating Narratives: Storytelling and Selfhood*, trans. Paul A. Kottman (New York: Routledge, 2000), 81–93, esp. 84.

13 In fact, historiographers describe salonières as organizers, facilitators, and context providers for intellectual and artistic conversation and creation, thus defining the functions, roles, and skills of salon hostesses in terms very similar to those used to characterize curators. Particularly, post-representative curatorial practices that go beyond the making of exhibitions (as mentioned in note 11) may be related to the history of literary salons that goes back to the seventeenth and eighteenth

centuries and beyond. See Dena Goodman, "Enlightenment Salons: The Convergence of Female and Philosophic Ambitions," *Eighteenth-Century Studies* 22, no. 3 (Spring 1989): 329–50. See also Evelyn Gordon Bodek, "Salonières and Bluestockings: Educated Obsolescence and Germinating Feminism," *Feminist Studies* 3, no. 3–4 (Spring 1976): 185–99.

14 See, for example, James E. Breslin, "Gertrude Stein and the Problems of Autobiography," in *Women's Autobiography*, ed. Jelinek, 149–65; Brodzki and Schenck, *Life/Lines*, 1–14.

15 Gertrude Stein, *The Autobiography of Alice B. Toklas* (New York: Harcourt, 1933). Unless indicated otherwise, I cite from *The Autobiography of Alice B. Toklas* (London: Penguin, 2001). For an analysis of the images in the first edition see Paul K. Alkon, "Visual Rhetoric in *The Autobiography of Alice B. Toklas*," *Critical Inquiry* 1, no. 4 (June 1975): 849–81.

16 See, for example, the contributions by Tony Bennett, Bruce W. Ferguson, and Mieke Bal in *Thinking about Exhibitions*, ed. Reesa Greenberg, Bruce Ferguson, and Sandy Nairne (London: Routledge, 2006).

17 Mary Anne Staniszewski, *The Power of Display: A History of Exhibition Installations at the Museum of Modern Art* (Cambridge, MA: MIT Press, 1998).

18 See Gertrude Stein, *Everybody's Autobiography* (1937; Cambridge, MA: Exact Change, 1993).

19 This becomes even more explicit in *Everybody's Autobiography*, where she writes: "The only thing that makes identity possible is no change but nevertheless there is no identity nobody really thinks they are the same as they remember" (72).

20 See Brian O'Doherty, *Inside the White Cube: The Ideology of the Gallery Space* (Santa Monica, CA: Lapis Press, 1986); James Olney, "Autobiography and the Cultural Moment: A Thematic, Historical, and Bibliographical Introduction," in *Autobiography*, ed. Olney, 3–27, esp. 20, 21. Olney explains that before a "refocusing from *bios* to *autos*" in the 1970s "the autos was taken to be perfectly neutral and adding it to 'biography' changed nothing." Biography is perceived as "the recollected life as transmitted through the unclouded, neutral glass of the *autos*."

21 I translated this expression from the German "Erzählen erzählen" coined by Heide Volkening to refer to the shift from a focus on narrated events to the narrating of events. See Volkening, *Am Rand der Autobiographie: Ghostwriting–Signatur–Geschlecht* (Bielefeld: Transcript, 2006), 129.

22 von Bismarck, "Curating Curators," 48. See also von Bismarck, "Den Kurator kuratieren: Daniel Buren," in *Auftritt als Künstler: Funktionen eines Mythos* (Cologne: Verlag der Buchhandlung Walther König, 2010), 167–76.

23 Craig Owens, "From Work to Frame, or, Is There Life After 'The Death of the Author'?" in *Beyond Recognition: Representation, Power, and Culture* (Berkeley, CA: University of California Press, 1997), 122–139.

24 The first of these oppositions structures O'Neill's argument in *The Culture of Curating*. The second serves as a foil for several articles in *Texte zur Kunst* 86. See, for example, Marchart, "The Curatorial Subject," 28–40.

25 For the relationality of subject formation and authorship with regard to autobiographical writings see Cavarero, *Relating Narratives*; see also Michel Foucault, "Über sich selbst schreiben," in *Ästhetik der Existenz: Schriften zur Lebenskunst*, ed. Daniel Defert, trans. Michael Bischoff et al. (Frankfurt am Main: Suhrkamp, 2007), 137–54; Judith Butler, *Giving an Account of Oneself* (New York: Fordham University Press, 2005).

26 For modesty as a feature of women's autobiographies see, for example, Patricia Meyer Spacks, "Selves in Hiding," in *Women's Autobiography*, ed. Jelinek, 112–32. See also Mason, "The Other Voice," 207–35.

27 Early on in the text, Toklas announces: "The three geniuses of whom I wish to speak are Gertrude Stein, Pablo Picasso and Alfred Whitehead" (9).

28 See Pierre Bourdieu, "But who Created the Creators?," in *Sociology in Question* (London: Sage, 1993), 139–48. Bourdieu's sociological macro-analysis is interested in the objective relations between positions, whereas this text is more narrowly concerned with Stein's portrayal of interpersonal relationships that

contribute to the making of authorship. Nevertheless, one could indeed read Stein and Picasso's relationship in terms of a "structural homology between the space of production (the artistic field) and the field of consumers (i.e., the field of the dominant class)" (ibid., 143–44). Leo Stein's contribution to Gertrude Stein's career, however, diminishes throughout the book. He is not mentioned by name and only rarely referred to as "her brother." In *Everybody's Autobiography*, 70–80, Stein talks about him as the significant other of her youth.

29 — As Toklas recalls, "They were however all very grateful to her in later years because practically everybody who later became famous had sold their first little picture to her" (60). Furthermore, the narrator describes how Stein acts as a literary authority and career counselor for Hemingway: "He and Gertrude Stein went over all the writing he had done up to that time. [...] Begin over again and concentrate, she said. [...] He and Gertrude Stein used to walk together and talk together a great deal. [...] If you keep on doing your newspaper work you will never see things, you will only see words and that will not do, that is of course if you intend to be a writer" (230). In return, Stein is described as being very grateful to Hemingway for allegedly having caused the first publication of *The Making of Americans* in the *Transatlantic Review* by talking the review's editor Ford Madox Ford into it (232–33).

30 — See, for example, Philippe Lejeune, "Autobiography in the Third Person," *New Literary History* 9, no. 1 (Autumn 1977): 27–50.

31 — Jacques Derrida, *Von der Gastfreundschaft* (Vienna: Passagen, 2001), 90. See also Michel Serres, *Der Parasit*, trans. Michael Bischoff (Frankfurt am Main: Suhrkamp, 1987), 31–32.

32 — Torsten Jost also addressed these aspects in his presentation, "Von Maskenspielen in Literatur und Malerei zum Theatralen: Gertrude Stein, Pablo Picasso und die Aufmerksamkeit," at the research colloquium of the international research training group InterArt Studies, Freie Universität Berlin, November 21, 2012.

33 — On this, Brodski and Schenck write: "Gertrude Stein […] also poses as a biographer in order to write her own autobiography […] *The Autobiography of Alice B. Toklas* is a mediated text as well, but in this case, Stein's verbal self-portrait is framed in the autobiographical narrative of her devoted secretary-lover, in a transgressive generic practice foregrounded by the title page." *Life/Lines*, 9.

34 — Elizabeth W. Bruss problematizes the translatability of conventional introspective autobiography into film, since there seems to be "no 'eye' for an 'I'." See Bruss, "Eye for I: Making and Unmaking Autobiography in Film," in *Autobiography*, ed. Olney, 296–320, esp. 298.

35 — See Jonathan Brown, "Über die Bedeutung von Las Meninas," in *Las Meninas im Spiegel der Deutungen: Eine Einführung in die Methoden der Kunstgeschichte*, ed. Thierry Greub (Berlin: Reimer, 2001), 150–69.

36 — For "Velázquez [...] as curator" see Svetlana Alpers, *The Vexations of Art: Velázquez and Others* (New Haven, CT: Yale University Press, 2005), 4.

37 — For a discussion of these etymologies see J. Hillis Miller, "The Critic as Host," *Critical Inquiry* 3, no. 3 (Spring 1977): 439–47.

38 — See Philippe Lejeune, "The Autobiographical Pact," *On Autobiography*, ed. Paul John Eakin, trans. Katherine Leary (Minneapolis: University of Minnesota Press, 1989), 3–30.

39 — Heide Volkening insists that the book does not provide a definite answer to the question of who wrote the book but rather keeps it open deliberately. See Volkening, *Am Rand der Autobiographie*, 103–72.

40 — Sidonie Smith, "'Stein' is an 'Alice' is a 'Gertrude Stein,'" in *Subjectivity, Identity, and the Body: Women's Autobiographical Practices in the Twentieth Century*, ed. Sidonie Smith (Bloomington: Indiana University Press, 1993), 64–82, esp. 80.

41 — Nora Sternfeld, "Unglamorous Tasks: What Can Education Learn from its Political Traditions," trans. Steven Lindberg, *e-flux journal*, no. 14 (March 2010).

42 — For an analysis of Szeemann's posture see Dorothee Richter, "Artists and Curators as Authors: Competitors, Collaborators, or Teamworkers?" in *Cultures of the Curatorial*, ed. Beatrice von Bismarck, Jörn Schafaff, Thomas Weski (Berlin: Sternberg Press, 2012), 229–48, esp. 230–31.

43 — The date Toklas joined the Stein household (1909/10) is not given in *The Autobiography*. As it is not addressed explicitly, the event of her moving in can only be inferred from the narrative.

44 — The "space of appearance," according to Hannah Arendt, "predates and precedes all formal constitution of the public realm." See Arendt, *The Human Condition* (Chicago: University of Chicago Press, 1958), 199. For the proto-public character of salons see Jürgen Habermas, *Strukturwandel der Öffentlichkeit: Untersuchungen zu einer Kategorie der bürgerlichen Gesellschaft* (Frankfurt am Main: Suhrkamp, 1990), 86–96. See also Lauren Berlant and Jay Prosser, "Life Writing and Intimate Publics: A Conversation with Lauren Berlant," *Biography* 34, no. 1 (Winter 2011): 180–87.

45 — See Irit Rogoff, "Wegschauen: Partizipation in der Visuellen Kultur," *Texte zur Kunst* 36 (December 1999): 86–112, esp. 101.

46 — This is reinforced in the following chapters where Toklas tells the stories of buying the paintings, elaborating the circumstances of the acquisitions in great detail while only giving very short abstract descriptions of the pictures themselves—if at all. Connections, scandals, and gossip make up most of the text. With regard to the purchase of Matisse's famous *La Femme au Chapeau* (1905), for instance, readers learn much more about the model, Madame Matisse, than about the painting. Her housekeeping qualities, her taste in clothes, and her marriage, as well as the Matisses' family life and their changing economic situation cover almost ten pages (39–48). The pictures seem to function as excuses for Toklas to characterize those involved in their production, distribution, and reception. Through these digressions, Stein's practice of portrait-writing is superimposed on the featured masterpieces, providing an ekphrasis set off-focus.

47 — In *The Autobiography* the following cast of characters (and several more) are reported to have visited rue de Fleurus. Many of the visitors are mentioned repeatedly and characterized both in and outside the salon context while others remain flat characters: Pablo Picasso, Henri Matisse, Henri Rousseau, Juan Gris, Georges Braque, André Derain, Marie Laurencin, Guillaume Apollinaire, Robert Delaunay, Jacques Lipschitz, Francis Picabia, Man Ray, Francis Rose, Bernard Faÿ, Djuna Barnes, Alfred North Whitehead, Edith Sitwell, Clive Bell, Erik Satie Sylvia Beech, Tristan Tzara, Virgil Thomson, Sherwood Anderson, Paul Robeson, Jo Davidson, Pavel Tchelichev, Ford Madox Ford, Richard Wright, Alfred Stieglitz, Carl Van Vechten, Henry McBride, Mildred Aldrich, Mabel Dodge, Ernest Hemingway, T. S. Eliot, Ezra Pound, William Carlos Williams, F. Scott Fitzgerald, Mina Loy, Thornton Wilder, Mary Borden-Turner, Elliot Paul, Ernest Walsh, Robert McAlmon.

48 — Obrist's more literally autobiographical *Ways of Curating* (2014) was published after this text was finalized.

49 — See also Nanne Buurman, "CCB With…: Displaying Curatorial Relationality in dOCUMENTA (13)'s *The Logbook*," *Journal of Curatorial Studies*, 5.1, special issue, *Affect and Relationality*, ed. Jennifer Fisher and Helena Reckitt (June 2016).

50 — For a discussion of the relations between immaterial labor, biopolitical production, and the feminization of work see, for example, Michael Hardt and Antonio Negri, "Metamorphoses of the Composition of Capital," in *Commonwealth* (Cambridge, MA: Harvard University Press, 2009), 131–50.

51 — For a virtual glorification of care, see, for example, Anthony Huberman, "Take Care," in *Circular Facts*, ed. Mai Abu ElDahab, Binna Choi, Emily Pethick (Berlin: Sternberg Press, 2011), 9–17. For the notion of "stuplimity" see Sianne Ngai, *Ugly Feelings* (Harvard University Press: 2005), 248–96. Drawing on Stein's writing, Ngai elaborates on stuplimity as a kind of "aesthetic overpowerment" that diverges from the Kantian sublime, describing it as "less dramatic" and not confirming "the self's sense of superiority over the overwhelming or intimidating object" (270).

Jörn Schafaff

Hospitality Exhibited

Rirkrit Tiravanija's *untitled 1994 (meet tim & burkhard)*

On September 30, 1994, the neugerriemschneider gallery in Berlin has an opening for an exhibition by the Thai artist Rirkrit Tiravanija.[1] It is his first exhibition at this still young gallery, which just opened its space on Goethestraße a few months ago. The guests who have made their way to Charlottenburg for the opening are encountering the following situation: the exhibition space is fitted with several colorful pieces of furniture; music is playing from a portable stereo; a television monitor showing a video is sitting in a corner. The guests who are already present are helping themselves from a refrigerator, drinking beer from the bottle or choosing between a screwdriver and a vodka tonic. At some point the room is quite full; several of the visitors are sitting on the sofa, the chairs, or the barstools placed in front of the display window, but most are standing in the middle of the room. Thus far everything is pointing to a typical scene at an opening: the usual mix of networking and party that this just emerging Berlin gallery scene experiences every couple of days. Only one thing seems strange: there are no works of art. It could hardly be the furniture, since it is being used. Perhaps it is the video? It is titled *meet tim & burkhard*. It shows the owners of the gallery, Tim Neuger and Burkhard Riemschneider, in several scenes obviously shot in their premises on Goethestraße, telling the story of how they met and decided to open the gallery. The video looks more like art, but what then would be the status of the other elements in the space? This is no video installation; the arrangement doesn't give the impression that everything is focused on the video,

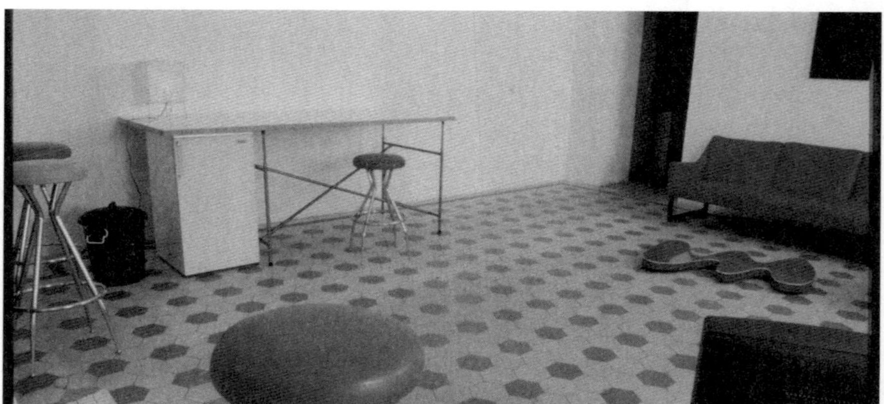

Rirkrit Tiravanija, *untitled 1994 (meet tim & burkhard)*, 1994. Installation view at neugerriemschneider, Berlin, 1994

even though the title of the exhibition does seem to point to its central importance: "untitled 1994 (meet tim & burkhard)." The gallery's owners are, however, themselves present, so *untitled 1994 (meet tim & burkhard)* could also be a call to interact with them directly. Tiravanija's first solo exhibition in Germany is an invitation to the art world to get to know the gallery's owners a little better, through the video, in personal conversation, and on the basis of the furniture, which, word spreads quickly, is from their private living quarters. The framework furnished and installed by Tiravanija defines the meeting of the gallery's owners and the attendees of the exhibition as an act of hospitality. Because this happens in the mode of an exhibition, however, the exchange between the hosts and the guests does not just happen but also becomes the object of aesthetic reflection. Those who otherwise display the art of others in their rooms are on display themselves this time, just like the other participants and the very act of meeting.

Rirkrit Tiravanija is considered the hospitality artist par excellence. His works seem to be the perfect instrument for institutions to attract the public with the promise of an unusual but easily accessible and enjoyable experience of art. Since the early 1990s the cliché of the friendly Thai artist has hardened, who with his cooking events initiates easily digestible get-togethers by which, in a generous gesture, he transforms the exhibition budget into free food for everyone. "Would you consider to include in Campo one of your food/feed piece[es]? So that at the opening we would could [*sic*!] have a moment of real conviviality?" asked Francesco Bonami in 1996 in advance of the "Campo 6" exhibition he curated.[2] A video that MoMA released on YouTube in 2012 also leaves the impression that the Tiravanija work it presents is primarily about the surprising experience of being fed in a museum and talking with others on that occasion—as art.[3] The faces of visitors to the exhibition who speak in the video radiate a good mood as well as joy that they were welcomed in a museum in such an unusual way and invited to stay. What they don't mention is the reflexive structure typical of Tiravanija's art, as I have outlined using the example of *untitled 1994* (*meet tim & burkhard*). But it is precisely this structure that can potentially enable the oscillating movement by which the experience of hospitality can become understandable as a curated encounter. The framing devices that Tiravanija precisely places—including not least the cultural format of the exhibition itself—serve as construction parts for an experiential space that opens up between the situational experience and situation-related reflection; a space in which the relationships between the host and the guest can be measured. This is relevant to the field of the curatorial because Tiravanija himself works curatorially and often employs the format of the exhibition for his art. Above all, however, the situations he initiates do not simply mirror the attributions, behaviors, and relationships of host and guest that predominate in the exhibition world but rather open their typical roles and responsibilities for negotiation. In order to discuss how that happens and what conclusions can be drawn from that, let us begin by returning to the exhibition in Berlin.

Hosting the Exhibition

By placing the gallery's owners as the focus of his exhibition, Tiravanija marked their central position within the structure of the gallery. "They have the site, and hence cultural power, at their disposal. Guests have only delimited room for play," a reviewer remarked aptly at the time.[4] In *untitled 1994 (meet tim & burkhard)*, Tiravanija explored the scope of this room; more than that, he transformed the entire exhibition situation into the set of a role play to be played according to his rules. By taking this step, he demonstrated that the guest's position is by no means powerless, just as the power of the gallery's owners is by no means unlimited and unconditional. The furniture suggested that the site of the event was their home, which meant that whoever was to enter their premises should follow the rules that applied there. However, the fact that the game proposed by Tiravanija included providing beverages for the visitors to the exhibition reminded the hosts that their position too is associated with obligations. In addition, even before the play of hospitality unfolded in the exhibition, the very act of attribution—the fact that the gallery's owners had to go along with the game proposed in order to be able to exhibit Tiravanija's art—had introduced an awareness of the mutual dependency that marks the relationship between host and guest: I decide who I invite to my house, but the invitee has the opportunity to turn down the invitation. And that person can formulate conditions I must meet if I want to have him or her in my home—explicitly so in a functional relationship such as that between an artist and a gallery owner. I will arrange things so that he or she feels welcome.

The conditions formulated by Tiravanija in a first step went so far as to invert the positions of the inviter and the invited. The artist took over the role of the inviting curator who puts together the elements of the exhibition, asks lenders for works to exhibit, and arranges the exhibits into a set of relationships in space and time. In addition, he underscored the claim to power associated with the curator's position by conceiving for himself yet another powerful role: that of the director, not only of the video but also of the activities that would take place within the stage-like setting of the exhibition space. Equipped with a triple authority—as artist, curator, and director—he directed the filming with the gallery's owners, who switched into the role of actors, but ultimately oscillated between the theatrical or cinematic role they took on and their social role as owners of the gallery. Although they were performing as themselves, the framing of the gallery situation added a symbolic level to their activities, just like any artifact gains symbolic meaning when exhibited, or any actor's move is structurally defined not only as the move itself, but also as meaningful within the framework of the stage performance.[5] In a similar but even more obvious manner, the very act of filming and the fact that their scenes had been scripted by Tiravanija introduced a difference into their actions, a point of oscillation from which they could—or even had to—consciously observe their social role behavior. It was precisely this oscillation point that marked Neuger and Riemschneider as exhibits in the exhibition—or, more precisely, as exhibited exhibits, since the reflexive structure of the double encoding of the artistic work as exhibition made the exhibition itself the subject of the exhibition.

In a second step, the reflexive structure also transformed the exhibition audience into actors in the theatrical sense. Tiravanija receded into the background and passed the authority that he had initially demanded on to the actors. As guests in his play, it was now up to them to take responsibility and explore their room to play. He had already left it to Neuger and Riemschneider to "attribute" their roles themselves; at the beginning he had asked each of them to write a report about how they met. The passages that coincided then provided the basis for the selection of scenes. He had also left it up to the gallery owners to decide which furniture they wanted to set up in their gallery. During the exhibition itself he no longer influenced the unfolding events at all, and thereby called into question the position of the artist within the existing constellation. Although he had, on the one hand, argued for the switch from guest to host, on the other, he claimed the role of the artist to be nothing more than that of the initiator of the starting situation. How it would develop was the responsibility of the other participants. Here, too, the relationship between the artist-host and the viewer-guest, who has been transformed into a fellow actor, manifested the recognition of a mutual dependence—in relation to both carrying out the work of art and producing its meaning.

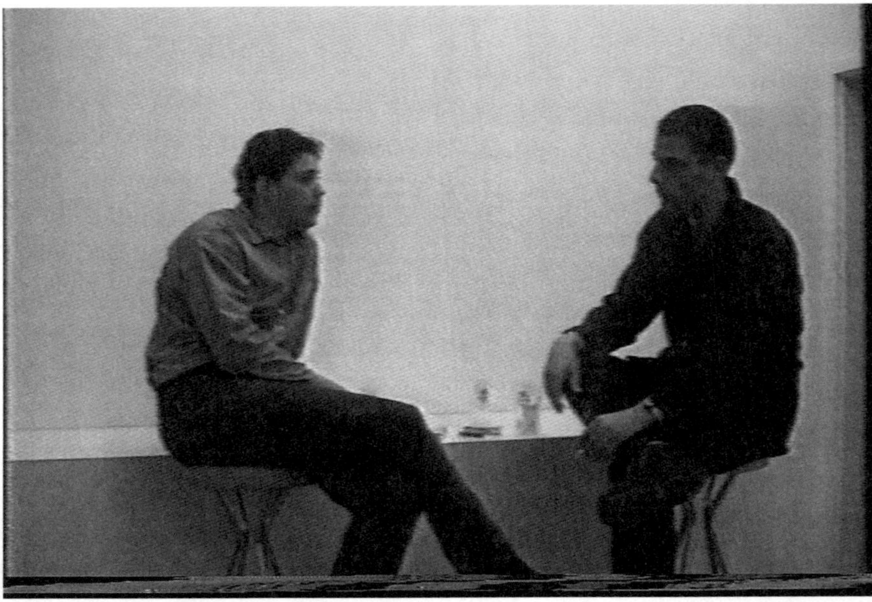

Rirkrit Tiravanija, still from the video *meet tim & burkhard*, 1994

The Work and the Guest as Host

Any exhibition can be analyzed in terms of the relations between hosts and guests. In the case of *untitled 1994 (meet tim & burkhard)*, I have so far identified the position of the host as being that of the gallery owners, the curator, and the artist. As I have argued, all three also took on the position of the guest, just like the exhibits, and the visitors. What I would like to suggest now is that the latter two can also play the role of hosts. A crucial factor for the identification of the work of art or the visitors as hosts derives from the relationship between responsibility and possibility. Responsibility results where possibilities exist. If a work of art permits different possibilities for how to approach it, the viewers have the responsibility for their behavior within the framework of possibility. Conversely, the artist is responsible for the possibilities for behavior that he allows the viewers within the framework of his art.[6] "Each particular artwork is a proposal to live in a shared world, and the work of every artist is a bundle of relations with the world, giving rise to other relations, and so on and so forth, ad infinitum."[7]

If we, like Nicolas Bourriaud, understand the work of art to be a statement that seeks to be perceived and accepted by one or more viewers, this points to the fundamentally social dimension of the work of art, an ethics of encounter. Referring to the work of the Cuban-American artist Félix González-Torres, Bourriaud proposes what he calls the "criterion of co-existence": "Does it [the artwork] give me a chance to exist in front of it, or on the contrary, does it deny me as a subject, refusing to consider the Other in its structure?"[8] One feature of *untitled 1994 (meet tim & burkhard)* is that the structure of the work did not entail a position "in front of" anything. As soon as you entered the gallery, you were in the middle of it. The work of art thus took on the role of a host who unconditionally integrates those who arrive. The pressure toward inclusion was balanced to a degree by the relative openness and incompleteness of the situation one entered on arriving. Tiravanija's framing left it up to those attending the exhibition how much they wished to engage with what they found there. In principle this could be applied to any work of art, to the extent that a work of art can only ever be an offer to engage with its materiality, its form, its meaning, or the context to which it refers. Nevertheless, it is part of the traditional understanding of art that a work of art is linked to a particular aesthetic experience, a particular point of view, and a particular message. In the case of *untitled 1994 (meet tim & burkhard)* the artistic setting merely marked an initial situation, necessarily and explicitly, so a judgment about what would be an appropriate or sufficient engagement with the work was tied to those who entered that situation and reacted to it—as part of the work of art. Whichever of the possibilities inherent in the work one availed oneself of—whether someone enjoyed the drinks, relaxed a little, sought conversation with the others present, looked at the furniture and the video, thought about the gallery as an institution or the exhibition as a cultural format—depended on the decision of the individual visitor.[9] But exactly by doing this the visitors to the exhibition were also acting as hosts to the possibilities provided by the structure of the work, in that they accepted, rejected, ignored, or simply overlooked the possible actions, relations, and meanings that Tiravanija brought into play by setting up the framing devices. More than that, only by accepting as hosts the possibilities inherent in the work of art did they lend the possibilities a current reality, which brought into focus all the more emphatically the responsibility of the viewer in the reception process. Reception is understood here as a reply tied to the obligation to take responsibility for that reply, or, in the words of Bourriaud: "Producing a form is to invent possible encounters; receiving a form is to create the conditions for an exchange, the way you return a service in a game of tennis. [...] someone shows something to someone who returns it as he sees fit."[10]

What Kind of Hospitality?

Recognizing the other is a central motif of hospitality. As the discussion here shows, it is possible to discuss the relationship to the other in terms of the relationships between the work of art and the viewer. In connection with a work of art that explicitly addresses the relationships between the guest and the host, it makes sense to address the relationship to the other from the perspective of hospitality. If this work of art is structured in the format of an exhibition, it not only permits inferences about aspects of hospitality in the framework of exhibitions but also, conversely, makes it possible to employ the relationships found in exhibitions as models for broader reflections on hospitality. The extent to which that makes sense depends on which concept of hospitality we base it in each case.

In the third defining article of his philosophical essay "Zum ewigen Frieden" (1795; translated as "Toward Perpetual Peace"), Immanuel Kant defines hospitality as "the right of a foreigner not to be treated with hostility because he has arrived on the land of another." He adds, as qualification, "The other can turn him away, if this can be done without destroying him, but as long as he behaves peaceably where he is, he cannot be treated with hostility."[11] By using the word *Hospitalität*, which is hardly common in German today, he distinguishes his concern from a broader hospitality (*Gastfreundschaft*)—that is, the rule that guests should be treated in a friendly manner. For, as he emphasizes right at the beginning of the article, it is "not a question of philanthropy but of *right*." This right, according to Kant, is "the *right to visit*; this right, to present oneself to society, belongs to all human beings by virtue of the right of possession in common of the earth's surface on which, as a sphere, they cannot disperse infinitely but must finally put up with being near one another; but originally no one had more right than another to be on a place on earth." Human rights take precedence over the rights of the state; hospitality is one foundation of the rights of the citizen of the world. Because territorial borders and attributions of belonging and property are reality, however, the meeting of those who seek to stay in a territory and those who claim to own that territory must be regulated. It is striking that Kant formulates these relationships from the perspective of the visitors, as a right. It is also striking that for him this is not connected with an unconditional claim to stay, to remain for an extended period, or even to participate, since hospitality is, according to Kant, "not the *right to be a guest*."[12] Only the risk of an existential threat to the visitor if turned away could justify the visitor remaining without the agreement of the residents.

Can the legal discourse on access to and staying in states be applied to the relationships between the actors in a cultural field and its institutions? There is one objection to such an expectation that would prematurely end the discussion. States and cultural institutions are, from a legal and practical perspective, different matters, and the borders of a cultural field are not defined in a way comparable to those of a country. Any direct application of Kant's concept of hospitality to the curatorial field would thus necessarily lead to distortions and constrain the discussion concerning the context of an exhibition. Surely one could ask, following Kant, what rights can be associated with the territorial behavior of curators, artists, and visitors—and questioning whether works of art fundamentally have the right "to *seek* commerce with the old inhabitants" would presumably elicit interesting answers.[13] However, as this discussion of *untitled 1994 (meet tim & burkhard)* suggests, many aspects of a discourse on hospitality focused on "curated encounters"[14] —the understanding of the roles of artists, gallerists, and visitors, for example—rather belong to the sphere of cultural conventions. Such issues are however not a matter of right in the legal sense (even if they can have an influence on it) but rather involve debates over ethical norms and power relationships in society.

Another objection to the call to apply Kant's idea is that in his text he was trying to formulate the claim to a right of those who arrive without being invited. Art institutions are, however, by definition corporate bodies that extend invitations, at least insofar as they are dedicated to presenting art. Museums invite visitors to an exhibition, and curators invite exhibits and artists. So who could be an unexpected stranger? Perhaps an uninvited artist who, like André Cadere, puts his works in others' exhibitions.[15] What purpose would it serve to reflect on the right to visit in relation to such a stranger?

Like Kant, Jacques Derrida focused his concept of hospitality on dealing with the other who is not invited. In an interview published in 1999 he explains: "I try to dissociate the concept of this pure hospitality from the concept of 'invitation.' If you are the guest and I invite you, if I am expecting you and am prepared to meet you, then this implies that there is no surprise, everything is in order. For pure hospitality or a pure gift to occur, however, there must be absolute surprise. The other, like the Messiah, must arrive whenever he or she wants. [...] I must be unprepared, or prepared to be unprepared, for the unexpected arrival of any other."[16] This pure or "unconditional hospitality," too, can only be applied to a limited degree to the sphere of exhibitions.[17] As I have already stated in the discussion of Kant, the arrival of the other in the exhibition is the declared goal of making art public and is therefore not unexpected. Moreover, the other cannot arrive whenever he or she wishes but only during the established opening hours. Only the fact that "any other" could come seems to apply to the situation of an exhibition. There are, however, mechanisms at work that limit the unexpected, for example, in the form of cultural and social codes that discipline even those who are not familiar with them.[18] What we are dealing with in exhibitions is rather what Derrida—with reference to Kant—calls "conditional hospitality": welcoming a visitor in the expectation that he or she will also offer something, even if it is only recognizing the rules of the head of the household, and submitting her- or himself to those rules.[19] Such a definition is also closer to a common understanding of hospitality, namely, that rule by which guests—no matter whether they are foreign or familiar, unknown or known—should be received in a friendly fashion, catered to, and offered protection, which is inseparable from the expectation that the guest does her or his part to ensure the encounter is successful.

"Not so much friendly as perhaps familiar"

Throughout its duration, the exhibition "untitled 1994 (meet tim & burkhard)" offered an opportunity to playfully work through this intersubjective structure of hospitality. In contrast to the conventional distribution of roles, the work was constructed, as already described, in such a way that all of the participants played or at least could play the role of the host as well as that of the guest.[20] With the exception of the artifacts, those involved could give in to an oscillating movement, experiencing the switch from one role to another and back again. The gallerists remained hosts insofar as they saw to their tasks as owners of the gallery and catered to the guests, even if the nature of the welcome—providing drinks, offering a place to stay in their living room—could be understood as a commentary on the usual activ-

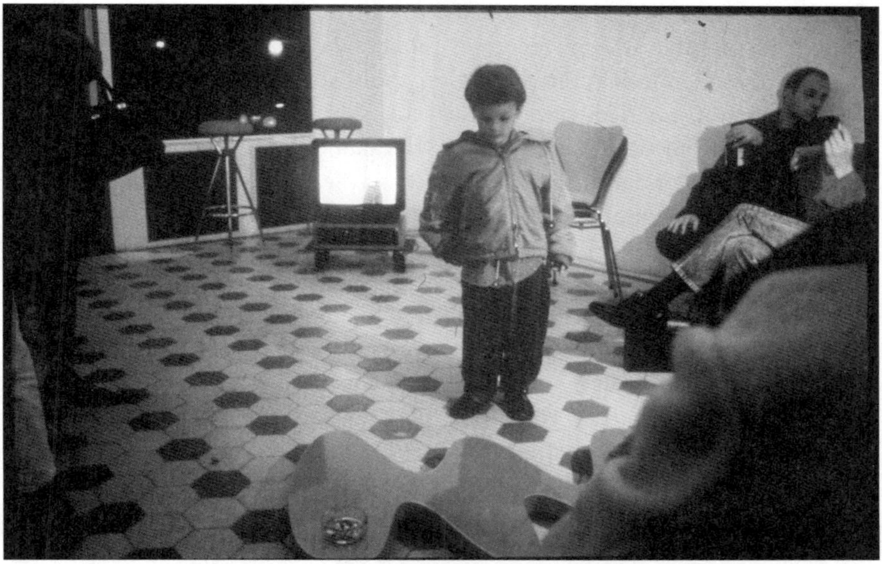

Rirkrit Tiravanija, *untitled 1994 (meet tim & burkhard)*, 1994. Installation view at neugerriemschneider, Berlin, 1994

ity of gallery owners. They were also guests in the constellation arranged by Tiravanija, which, moreover, presented them as new arrivals in Berlin who were presenting themselves, in accordance with certain conventions, to the residents of the city or to its art world, at least.[21] The artist remained a guest insofar as he too was presenting himself with his work to an art metropolis that was just emerging. Likewise, with his art he offered himself as a guest to the gallery's owners and to the exhibition visitors. What he was offering, however, was his switching into the role of the curator, and he thus functioned as the host of the situation for which he was responsible. The guests in this situation, who were part of the work of art, were not only the gallery's owners, the video, and the items of furniture but also the visitors to the exhibition. Thus they too remained in their traditional role, though, thanks to the structure of the exhibition, there was the potential for them to experience it in a different way, namely, as viewer *and* exhibit. By doing so, they took responsibility as hosts not only for the possibilities offered by the situation Tiravanija had constructed but also for themselves, as exhibited actors of a work of art whose basic features had been determined in advance but was ultimately taking shape in real time. Finally—insofar as the work of art is, in relationship to the viewer, what is already present in the exhibition, and is therefore that which welcomes, in one way or another, the arriving visitors—the attendees at the exhibition could also see themselves as hosts, namely, when it was their turn to integrate others entering the scene in the gallery. Each element, including the nonhuman exhibition objects and the curated, exhibited relationships to hospitality, was thus a guest in the gallery, a guest of the curator, a guest in *untitled 1994 (meet tim & burkhard)*.

The same year in which *untitled 1994 (meet tim & burkhard)* was exhibited, Tiravanija corrected an interviewer's assumption that one important aspect of his works was to produce a friendly context conducive to conviviality. He stated that the environments he creates are "not so much friendly as perhaps familiar."[22] In the context of this discussion, this distinction reads like an effort on the part of Tiravanija to distance himself from the cliché of himself as the generous host who is friendly in the conventional sense. Nevertheless, working with the familiar can in this case be understood as an aesthetic strategy that responds to hospitality: to the offer of being prepared for the arrival of some other. This work in Berlin is an example of an inclusive approach that keeps the threshold of access as low as possible and still includes the offer to advance in some way further into the space of possibility that the work of art holds out as a potential.

At the same time, Tiravanija was aware that the familiar could become its opposite in certain situations. The invitation to come to the gallery for a drink was likely to appear disquieting to some uninformed visitors to the exhibition, just as there would have been uncertainty about whether the ordinary objects should be regarded as readymades or as objects to be used. After all, anyone who saw her- or himself as an actor inscribed in the situation experienced it as a moment of self-alienation, though admittedly an alienation that opened up a perspective of reflective distance. From that point it was possible to reflect, without the artist having made a prejudgment, about the existing positions, roles, and relationships. As Tiravanija explained in general in the aforementioned interview, he was not primarily concerned with changing behaviors in the art world. Rather, he was working with cultural behaviors familiar from everyday life that were emphasized in the framework of the exhibition, put on display, and thus delivered to a certain conscious experience. As stylized as these emphasized, constructed situations may have seemed as a result, Tiravanija maintained the idea that they would solidify into an aesthetic experience that would affect the cultural habits of the participants:

The situation is dictated in many cases by the presence of the viewers.
They are, in most cases, confined to the art context.
A sense of relief (perhaps after disorientation).
Introducing a different kind of attitude
(perhaps this could translate in the behaviors)
(perhaps cultural habits).
I am not interested in the artworld and its codes.
I am interested in opening possibilities rather than closing them.[23]

1 "untitled 1994 (meet tim & burkhard)," October 1–November 5, 1994, neugerriemschneider, Berlin.

2 Francesco Bonami to Rirkrit Tiravanija, fax, March 19, 1996, Rirkrit Tiravanija Archive, Berlin. "Campo 6" was a group exhibition curated by Bonami for which Tiravanija produced the exhibition architecture. "Campo 6: The Spiral Village," September 27–November 3, 1996, Galleria Civica d'Arte Moderna, Turin.

3 The video was released on the occasion of MoMA's presentation of *untitled 1992–1995 (free/still), 1992/1995/2007/2011*, a reminiscence of Tiravanija's now legendary work *untitled 1992 (free)*. YouTube, http://www.youtube.com/watch?v=0xRx2s3FpSg.

4 Peter Herbstreuth, "Rirkrit Tiravanija," *Kunstforum International* 129 (January–April 1995): 342–43, esp. 343. The quote is translated from the German: "Sie verfügen über den Ort und also über kulturelle Macht. Gäste haben nur Spielraum." The term "Spielraum," translated here rather literally as "room for play," is usually used in a figurative sense, describing the scope, range, or area in which something or someone can argue, negotiate, move, or act.

5 For the parallel between the symbolic structure of theater and that of visual art see Juliane Rebentisch, *Aesthetics of Installation Art*, trans. Daniel Hendrickson and Gerrit Jackson (Berlin: Sternberg Press, 2012). In relation to this, see also my discussion of the theatrical quality of Tiravanija's work in "Sets and Scenarios: Rirkrit Tiravanija's *untitled 1992 (free)*," in *Assign & Arrange: Methodologies of Presentation in Art and Dance*, ed. Maren Butte et al. (Berlin: Sternberg Press, 2014), 153–70.

6 This is particularly true of art that is conceived with the active, even physical participation of the audience, but it is a problem that has arisen generally, at least since the turn to an aesthetics of reception in which the viewer is the authority that assigns meaning.

7 Nicolas Bourriaud, "Relational Form," in *Relational Aesthetics*, trans. Simon Pleasance and Fronza Woods with Mathieu Copeland (1998; Dijon: Les presses du réel, 2002), 11–24, esp. 22.

8 Nicolas Bourriaud, "Joint Presence and Availability: The Theoretical Legacy of Felix Gonzalez-Torres," in *Relational Aesthetics*, 49–64, esp. 57. Bourriaud mentions other perspectives, but the one mentioned suffices in our context.

9 This in turn offered an opportunity to reflect on the conditions of the possibility of making this or that decision.

10 Bourriaud, "Relational Form," 23.

11 Immanuel Kant, "Toward Perpetual Peace: A Philosophical Project," in *Practical Philosophy*, ed. and trans. Mary J. Gregor (Cambridge, UK: Cambridge University Press, 1996), 311–51, esp. 328–29.

12 Ibid., 328, 329.

13 Ibid., 329. According to Kant, the right to hospitality extends only as far as "the conditions which make it possible to *seek* commerce with the old inhabitants." In the original German text the term translated into English as "commerce" ("Verkehr") has a more open connotation regarding the kind of exchange the guest has the right to seek. This right to try to establish a mutual exchange could be related to Bourriaud's criterion of co-existence, for example.

14 Quoted from the brochure for the "Hospitality—Hosting Relations in Exhibitions" conference, Hochschule für Grafik und Buchkunst (HGB) / Academy of Fine Arts Leipzig, December 13–14, 2012.

15 Cadere used exhibition openings to present his *barres de bois rond* (round bars of wood)—wooden sticks painted with patterns—temporarily next to other works of art. See, for example, Simone Neuenschwander, "André Cadere, L'Incompatibilité," in *André Cadere*, ed. Magda Radu, exhibition catalogue (Bucharest: National Museum of Modern Art, 2011), 251–59.

16 Jacques Derrida, quoted in Richard Kearney and Mark Dooley, eds., *Questioning Ethics* (London: Routledge, 1999), 65–83, esp. 70. In contrast to Kant, Derrida was primarily interested in the ethical behavior of members of state structures toward those who wished to be accepted. For Derrida's perspective, see Stuart Hall and David

Scott, "Hospitality's Others: A Conversation," in *The Unexpected Guest: Art, Writing, and Thinking Hospitality*, ed. Sally Tallant and Paul Domela, exhibition catalogue, Liverpool Biennial (London: Art Books, 2012), 291–304.

17 — Derrida, in Kearney and Dooley, *Questioning Ethics*, 70.

18 — See Tony Bennett, "The Exhibitionary Complex," in *Thinking About Exhibitions*, ed. Reesa Greenberg et al. (London: Routledge, 1996), 81–112.

19 — Derrida, in Kearney and Dooley, *Questioning Ethics*, 69–70.

20 — The fact that the word "hospitality" derives from a Latin word, which depending on the context can mean guest or host, already seems to suggest an interchangeability. In any case, it has often been employed as a starting point in the evolution of philosophical concepts, not least because this double meaning is also retained in the French word *hôte*. On the meaning of *hôte* in the work of Jacques Derrida and Emmanuel Lévinas, see François Raffoul, "The Subject of the Welcome: On Jacques Derrida's *Adieu à Emmanuel Lévinas*," University of Alberta website, accessed October 22, 2014, http://www.artsrn.ualberta.ca/symposium/files/original/72670ea211748e23c49a337e21d99b78.PDF.

21 — In the early 1990s, Tim Neuger was an assistant at Galerie Max Hetzler in Cologne; Burkhard Riemschneider was also working in Cologne for Gisela Capitain. In one scene in the video, Neuger remarks to Riemschneider that he was thinking about opening a gallery in Berlin because a lot was happening there. In retrospect, the video thus documents the beginning of the shift of the center of the German art world from Cologne to the German capital.

22 — Rirkrit Tiravanija, quoted in Éric Troncy and Nicolas Bourriaud, "Rirkrit Tiravanija," *Documents*, no. 5 (February 1994): 33–37, esp. 37.

23 — Ibid.

IV

Asymmetrical Gatherings / Encounters and Asymmetries

Erik Hagoort

Pertaining Asymmetry

It happens that we have come to think of social art practice in terms of reciprocity. Ever since the rise of this art practice, reciprocity has been widely identified as the main condition for it to function as *social*. Yet, social art practice also produces experiences, which are not necessarily reciprocal by nature: responsibility, generosity, hospitality, friendship, confidence, trust, faith. Practitioners and theoreticians have acknowledged this, but the question of how these experiences relate to the condition of reciprocity, in which they function, still needs to be addressed.

1. Promise of Reciprocity

Over the last three decades social art practices have come into existence, with artists genuinely inviting others to cast off their role as observer, not just in order to participate in a scenario predetermined by the artist but to forge together "a relationship that may *itself* become the artwork."[1] Encounter and art merge. The encounter is the art practice.

To refer to these art practices, different terms circulate, among them new genre public art, community art, connective aesthetics, conversational art, participatory art, collaborative art, or socially engaged art. Next to these general terms, theoretical concepts have been developed to understand what these artistic encounters are about, such as relational aesthetics, coined by French curator Nicolas Bourriaud in 1998 in his now well-known essay collection *Esthétique relationnelle*,[2] or dialogical aesthetics, first proposed by American art historian Grant Kester in 2004 in his elaborate study *Conversation Pieces: Community and Communication in Modern Art*.[3] Sometimes a concept refers only to specific art projects, such as the concept of confidentiality used by Russian curator Viktor Misiano, in his essay *The Institutionalization of Friendship*,[4] to identify the core of projects in which friendship was deployed as an artistic strategy.

It seems hardly possible to compare all these different terms and concepts. Yet I would say they all share at least one major presumption: that encounter is reciprocal. And it is presumed that because of the reciprocal dynamics of encounter, social art practices can overcome a fundamental division in the arts, that of the artist giving and the audience receiving. It is believed that because of their reciprocal dynamics social art practices can break down this division, and in doing so can dismantle the hierarchies and inequalities that go together with that division.

In the words of curator Michael Brenson, social art practices may create situations in which "all participants will be, at once, giver and receiver, producer and consumer, artist and audience."[5] Then it would no longer be possible to make a distinction between the creator and the receiver because both would participate in the artwork as equals and their roles would be reversible. Art would stop being a one-way affair; it would turn into the social process itself. At least, that was, and is still, the promise. It is the promise of reciprocity.

If social art practices live up to this promise of reciprocity, isn't that relevant? It is relevant that a discourse has evolved through which reciprocity is not only a promise, but is identified as the leading principle of social art practice, a discourse to which artists and theoreticians contribute, or which they comply with. I use this discourse here to refer to an order of thinking, a normative order that frames the way we experience, reflect on, and make sense of social art practice. This discourse lays down criteria for what an artistic encounter should be and how it should work, and promotes reciprocity as the "*conditio sine qua non*" of social art practice.

Such discourse clearly shows in the writings of curators who have played an important role in our current understanding of art practices of encounter. I will discuss here Mary Jane Jacob from Chicago and Viktor Misiano from Moscow. From the beginning of the 1990s both have initiated and curated artistic encounters and participated in them. Their curatorial practices are geographically miles apart. They developed their theories independently from each other. Yet, their theories share in the discourse of reciprocity.

But there is something intriguing in their writings. While reading their texts, one can discern a theoretical unrest, which makes them interrupt their own discourse of reciprocity. It is a fruitful unrest, which comes from a twofold sensibility. Partly the authors show a sensibility for the complexities of reciprocity, which subsequently makes them question their own expectations concerning reciprocity. And partly they show a sensibility for experiences of encounter that don't match with the discourse of reciprocity. Something in encounter happens outside of reciprocity. This something I call asymmetry in encounter, a term I loan from the French-Jewish philosopher Emmanuel Levinas (1906–1995). I use his philosophical category of asymmetry to articulate the awareness of these curators to what interrupts their own discourse. My question is: What space is given to this asymmetry in encounter, and to what effect?[6]

First I will elaborate on reciprocity by following a remarkable study by the Dutch philosopher of law Dorien Pessers. It is remarkable because she adds to existing theories of reciprocity her idea that reciprocity is not so much about reaching equal social balance as it is about *alternating* inequalities. Second I will address asymmetry in encounter. What does Emmanuel Levinas mean with this philosophical category? Third I will address how Jacob and Misiano deal with the complexities of reciprocity as well as with asymmetry in encounter.

2. Reciprocity

Together with other authors on social art practices (amongst them Grant Kester, Suzanne Lacy, Maria Lind, Lars Bang Larsen, and Nicolas Bourriaud), Mary Jane Jacob and Viktor Misiano hook onto an existing discourse of reciprocity, of which sociologist Marcel Mauss (1872–1950) and anthropologist Claude Lévi-Strauss (1908–2009) are among the most famous spokesmen.[7] Their ideas clearly resonate in the way human encounter is perceived by authors writing on art and social life, such as Lewis Hyde, in his still influential *The Gift: How the Creative Spirit Transforms the World* (1985). And more recently in a collection of essays on social art practice *What We Want is Free: Generosity and Exchange in Recent Art* (2005), edited by Ted Purves.

Rather unknown is the exploration of the Dutch philosopher of law Dorien Pessers. She defines reciprocity not in terms of equality, as Mauss and Lévi-Strauss do, but in terms of inequality, that is to say: reciprocity as *alternating* inequality.

Pessers shares the conviction of both Mauss and Lévi-Strauss, that reciprocity pervades our social life, that reciprocity is a total social fact: “Reciprocity is our necessary way of existence,”[8] she writes. But unlike Mauss and Lévi-Strauss she emphasizes the precarity of reciprocity: the fact that reciprocity is fundamental does not mean that it is stable.

Her basic definition of reciprocity stays close to the etymological meaning. The Latin verb *reciprocare* means to bring back or to return along the same path, to stream back and forth. And that is exactly how Pessers defines reciprocity: “the returning of one’s own via the other.”[9]

This recognition of the self via the other is in no way self-evident. Pessers emphasizes that we are always caught between our longing for recognition on the one hand and our assertiveness, our desire to demand and to take what we want, on the other. In order to receive recognition, we have to give recognition. That means to give in, to be able to restrict one’s assertiveness.

This ability, however, is not produced as some kind of blueprint of our mental structure, Pessers contends, our human psyche is not as well-structured as Lévi-Strauss presumes. Here she criticizes Lévi-Strauss, for whom our mental structure in itself is reciprocal, as it is capable of recognizing and integrating distinctions at one and the same time. The famous example he gives of the custom of reciprocating wine between strangers in French restaurants, illustrates according to Lévi-Strauss an immediate, transformative effect of reciprocity: making strangers communicate and integrate, producing social cohesion.

Against Lévi-Strauss's rather optimistic stance, Pessers argues that we are persons with flaws and desires, which can undermine the precarious balance of giving and receiving. Alongside that we form part of political, economic, cultural, and religious contexts, which push and pull on our ability to "perform" reciprocity. Reciprocity doesn't necessarily produce social cohesion, empathy, or solidarity. For Pessers, "Reciprocity as a moral principle is just as fundamental as it is precarious."[10]

This precarity also shows, as Pessers explains, in the paradoxical nature of reciprocity. She illustrates this with an example that might be familiar to everybody. When you are invited to a birthday party, you give a present. The one who receives it usually reacts by saying, Oh, what a surprise, I never expected to get anything, it's too much, you shouldn't have done that, I don't deserve it. The giver usually responds by saying, Oh, it's nothing, it's just a gesture, it doesn't mean anything. Both of course lie. The receiver does expect a present. The giver wouldn't dare to show up with empty hands. Why then do we play this strange game of hiding intentions?

According to Pessers this awkward game shows reciprocity's paradox of obligatory voluntariness. Giver and receiver both want to express the voluntariness of their relation. Therefore they must deny that they are obliged to one another. Otherwise their bond would show as a contract, instead of as the free, voluntary commitment of love or friendship. This paradox becomes even stronger when the bond is tighter. The more one trusts the other, the less immediate the return has to be. If the bond is very close, you don't even need to be sure whether your gift, your gesture, your commitment, or generosity will ever be returned, or how, or in which quantity, or in what kind of quality: "the expectation of reciprocity is indefinite."[11] Pessers makes us attentive to this indefiniteness and openness of what she calls "positive reciprocity" or "affective reciprocity."

Pessers also points to what is often overlooked: inequality as the motor of reciprocity. The horizon of reciprocity certainly is to balance inequalities. But it is inequality that makes the wheel turn round in the first place. Reciprocity is set in motion by inequality. Here she connects to Paul Ricoeur's idea that reciprocity stems from the initial experience of existence as a gift: I experience the world and my own existence as "being given" by nature, by ancestors, by gods. And also by all those persons who care for me and by society, all of which make my existence possible. The urge to return stems, according to Ricoeur, not from *do ut des* (I give in order that you give) but from *do quia mihi datum est* (I give because I was given to). To give is second, not first. That is the initial drive of reciprocity. Reciprocity stems from an experience of verticality, unevenness, imbalance, inequality.

With this in mind we can understand Pessers's extended definition of reciprocity, in which the alternation of inequality is crucial: "Reciprocity is a sustainable relation—based on intersubjective or institutionalized trust—of *alternating inequality*, through which indefinite achievements in time will be evened."[12] For reciprocity the alternation is crucial, or at least, both parties must have at least the expectation that positions will alternate. This does not mean that equality is established. Reciprocity means that inequality is alternating.

Concluding, Pessers describes reciprocity as being inherently precarious, paradoxical, unequal. Therefore, in her view reciprocity doesn't automatically establish social cohesion, as is presumed by Mauss and Lévi-Strauss. To do so reciprocity must be directed. But how? Positive or affective reciprocity is most likely to prevail among family, friends, and likeminded groups. The openness and indefiniteness, which for Pessers stand for the ethical dimension of positive reciprocity, especially thrive amongst those who are already familiar with each other: family, friends, communities.[13] The bond of positive reciprocity tends to deny others access. Trust is choosy. We are reluctant to include the stranger but willing to include the one in whom we can already recognize ourselves. So, if we stick to Pessers's basic definition of reciprocity, in which the self can return to itself via the other, how other can the "other" actually be? Is the other allowed to be other?

Pessers addresses this problem as a philosopher of law. Her answer is that a symbolic order is needed, with its institutions and regulations, in order to connect the exclusivity of affective reciprocity with the responsibility of social reciprocity. Law in her opinion can change affective reciprocity into rational reciprocity, so that the stranger still can be recognized as belonging to the community that abides by the law. "In this way a rational reciprocity or rational solidarity becomes possible among people who are strangers to one another."[14]

My point is that the rational reciprocity of law may offer a solution but does not take away the difficulty that reciprocal trust and generosity (not expecting something in return for what you do) happens between people who know and trust one another already. So the stranger is excluded. Which means that the positive, ethical dimension of reciprocity seems to produce a negative flipside.

I believe this problem comes about because Pessers—along with Mauss and Lévi-Strauss—still adheres to a normative discourse that regards reciprocity as a *total* social fact, one that is *completely* pervading our social life. There would be no social life outside of reciprocity. Pessers does acknowledge the fact that people can do "something for nothing," referring to A. W. Gouldner's article *The Importance of Something for Nothing* (1973),[15] in which it is made clear that one should also fulfill the needs of people who can never pay back any service. Gouldner calls this beneficence, which for him goes beyond reciprocity's circular and closed movement of the self returning via the other back to the self. Pessers, however, regards beneficence as an extreme ethical, indefinite form of positive reciprocity. In doing so she firmly embeds beneficence within a reciprocal economy of relations, in which, as she has shown, it is hardly possible to do something for nothing.

3. Asymmetry

"It is the great merit of Emmanuel Levinas," says Adriaan Peperzak, one of the leading experts on Levinas, "to have fought the belief that all pesons, things, and events are entirely caught up in the structures and rules of a universal 'economy.'"[16] Levinas's philosophy indeed can be regarded as a critique of the discourse of reciprocity. Levinas points out that something in encounter happens that cannot be placed as an element of our economy of relations. This he calls the face, *le visage*. With the face he does not mean what we look like, the face does not refer to the contours of our complexion. The face is not a phenomenon; it has no substance. In Levinas's philosophy the face is a philosophical category that points to a specific dynamics that occurs in encounter. For Levinas encounter is an event of asymmetry.

Let's follow Adriaan Peperzak's explanation of this event. In an encounter "I am faced by you." Your face invites me to welcome you, to be hospitable, to feed, help, console, to stand in for you, "just because of your being you: this concrete and unique other whom I happen to encounter."[17] Your presence comes to me as a moral command, to put it strongly, or as a moral invitation, to put it in a friendlier way, that has an effect on me, "that regards me or speaks to me in the naked, vulnerable, powerless, but infinitely obligating face of the other."[18]

The face of the other commands/invites me to be responsible. The face of the other sets me free to be responsible, it makes me able to respond or not, to be responsible. I don't have this freedom already; freedom doesn't come from me as an autonomous individual. Freedom comes about through the address to me by someone in need. This address gives me the freedom to respond or not. Levinas calls this an election to freedom and to responsibility. I am invested with freedom.

This happens through encounter. And the dynamics of this are marked, according to Levinas, by asymmetry, not by reciprocity. If I am addressed, then it is my freedom and my responsibility to do something with this command/invitation, or not to. This responsibility is only mine. It is not your responsibility; it is nobody else's. My obligation to be "for you" does not at all depend upon your fulfilling the obligation my face imposes on you. So, in each encounter the potential is there for something extraordinary to happen: within the ordinary, reciprocal economy of relations an asymmetry occurs. I can stand in for you or I can turn my back on you, but this movement towards you or away from you does not have to correspond with your movement towards or away from me.

Peperzak points to the main objection that can be made against this. If the face of the other makes me responsible for the other, then this would also count vice-versa, then all human beings would be equally and reciprocally obliged to each other, everybody would be mutually responsible. So then in fact there is reciprocity again. The answer Levinas would have given, is that this objection can only be made when we abstract from concrete encounter, when we, as it were, step out of encounter and look at it from a distance, from a reflective position outside or above the relation of the other and the self.

Levinas, however, always tries to talk of encounter from within, as the event happens, because there is "a radical impossibility of seeing oneself from the outside and of speaking in the same sense of oneself and of the other."[19] I just cannot step out, I just cannot swap positions with anybody else. Neither can I transfer my responsibility. "A non-transferable responsibility, as if my neighbor called me urgently and called none other than myself," Levinas writes. "It is ethically impossible to transfer my responsibility for my neighbor to a third party."[20]

Sure, we live and function in this reciprocal economy of relations, but we shouldn't take that economy of relations as primary—according to Levinas, it is secondary. Reciprocity is the result of a reflective comparison afterwards; it is not simultaneous with the event, but is secondary, it comes after the revelation of a more original, ethical asymmetry. Primary is this ethical asymmetry of being invested by the other with the freedom to respond and in that way to be responsible for the other. That is the point of view of Levinas.

Levinas's ideas on encounter have only marginally been discussed in art theories about social art practice. There are only a few references, as far as I know. In a compelling part of his collection of essays titled *Relational Aesthetics*, Nicolas Bourriaud comes quite close to Levinasian terminology in his discussion of film critic Serge Daney's idea that each form can be regarded as a face looking at me: "it summons me to dialogue with it."[21] Levinas's philosophy, however, doesn't bring about dialogue, according to Bourriaud, it comes down to "interservility."[22]

Contrary to Bourriaud I think that encounter in Levinas's philosophy is not about an exchange of servility; it is not about reciprocally being of service to one another. In Levinas's thinking the "service" is asymmetrical.

American art historian Grant Kester discusses Levinas in his book *Conversation Pieces* (2004). He appreciates Levinas's critique of the ways in which our interest in and curiosity for the other can happen for the sake of self. But Kester contends that the way Levinas puts it the other way round, by giving absolute priority to the address by the other, is so radical and uncompromising that it cannot be applied to dialogical aesthetics. Levinas contests reciprocity, according to Kester, who writes: "In fact, 'reciprocity' itself is anathema [to Levinas], as it could open the door to an interested or calculating relationship in which we could expect something from the other in return for our submission before it."[23] But reciprocity, Kester argues, is fundamental to any dialogue and therefore also to dialogical aesthetics.

It seems to me that the writings of Mary Jane Jacob and Viktor Misiano show sensibility for the complexities of reciprocity that are addressed by Dorien Pessers, and for experiences of asymmetry, which are addressed by Levinas. The reason for this twofold sensibility might be that they not only curated art practices of encounter but also participated in these practices, in person, and have done so over longer periods of time.

In a recent article for a collection of essays *What We Want is Free: Generosity and Exchange in Recent Art*, curator Mary Jane Jacob looks back at her curatorial practice since her curatorship of "Culture in Action" in 1993. She concludes that for her a central question of her curatorship has been "Can generosity be a reciprocal practice?"[24] This question comes from art experience, through the work of artists by which Jacob is inspired, such as the candy and the poster sheets of Félix González-Torres and the food-events of Rirkrit Tiravanija. She also points to the pioneering function of Gordon Matta-Clark, especially his collaborative *Food project* (1971). In these art practices, the division between audience and artist indeed seems to fade. In the work of González-Torres this happens in very subtle ways, within an institutionalized art context. In a more raw form, out in the social context, this happens in Gordon Matta-Clark's event.

Jacob calls these examples "art-as-offering." She sympathizes especially with projects in which "the thing given away gains importance by being of use to someone in need."[25] This is indeed about offering, about generosity. Nothing is expected from the other, generosity means that the other does not feel that he or she owes something to the giver. But at the same time this "art-as-offering," this generosity, seems to reinstall the situation in which the artist is the giver, and the audience is the receiver who lacks creativity. Again, the audience is pinned down as "being in need, lacking, or deficient."[26]

Jacob would instead like artists to allow others entry, to allow the audience to become a participant. For her, this means that social art practice needs to combine both generosity and reciprocity. How can this be?

Together with her companion curator Jacqueline Baas, Jacob organized a two-year-long project titled "Awake: Art, Buddhism, and the Dimensions of Consciousness" (2001–03). The project comprised a manifold process of research, meetings, meditations, workshops, lectures, and presentations on the relationships between Buddhism and the arts in the United States. Over the course of the project a range of "art workers" from the United States—

including artists, curators, museum directors, art administrators, art educators—were invited to gather regularly for three-day retreats: to take time for, to think of, and to meditate; to achieve "buddha mind" or the "mind of don't know." The book titled *Buddha Mind in Contemporary Art* (2004), edited by Jacob and Baas, gives an impression of the experiences brought about by this process.

The "Awake" project I regard here as a performative way for Jacob to address the central question of her curatorship: the *contradictio in terminis* of reciprocal generosity. She introduces the concept of interconnectedness as a solution. This concept enables her to experience generosity and reciprocity as no longer contradictory to each other. Interconnectedness is a fundamental Buddhist concept which "provides space for situations that allow contradictory states to co-exist," as Jacob writes in her essay on reciprocal generosity.[27] Situations in which generosity and reciprocity seem to exclude one another are embraced instead of opposed, she explains. And "When we understand in a deep and pervasive way our interconnectedness, compassion flows."[28]

Let's try to think along with Jacob here. She is inspired by the Buddhist teacher and artist Chogyam Trungpa, who was an influential artist in Chicago in the 1970s. He seems to take a step further than Jacob. His sayings come down to the conviction that the split between generosity and reciprocity is an illusion. In meditative art, as he calls it, there are no such separations: "In meditative art, the artist embodies the viewer as well as the creator of the works."[29]

Trungpa's thoughts are not easily understood. His sayings are there to be meditated on and practiced over a long period of time—that is if you want to practice your life as a Buddhist. What I think is important in Jacob's focus on "the presence of buddha mind,"[30] is that she dismisses neither reciprocity nor generosity as illusions, which might be the consequence of becoming a Buddhist. In a recent interview with art critic and poet Caroline Picard on the Chicago art-blog "Bad-at-Sports," Jacob says that Buddhism as a wisdom tradition inspires her.[31] Buddhism helps her in trying to appreciate and account for both generosity and reciprocity, to see them not as contradictory but as interconnected.

While Jacob bends the prevailing discourse of reciprocity, Viktor Misiano interrupts this discourse in a compelling, personal way. In 1996 he was invited to participate in an artists' project titled "Transnacionala," set up by the Slovenian artists' collective IRWIN. The collective invited some of its Slovenian and Russian friends, among them artists Vadim Fishkin, Alexander Brener, Yuri Leiderman, and Viktor Misiano himself, to partake in a project that consisted of group travel in two campers through the United States. Circumstances meant that Misiano couldn't take part in this. He stayed in Russia. At home he was the first to receive all the transcriptions of the conversations that took place during the road trip. On the basis of what he read, he wrote the essay "The Institutionalization of Friendship" (1998), which has become widely known. In this essay Misiano addresses the question of whether friendship can be artistic, whether friendship can be used as an artistic strategy. The way he describes the precarity of friendship resembles the precarious balance in reciprocity between our longing for recognition and our will to demand, which Pessers describes. "Transnacionala" proved to be a laboratory of reciprocity's precarity.

For the initiators of "Transnacionala" friendship was the one and only criterion, Misiano concludes. In choosing the participants, neither the work nor the artists' way of working played an essential role. It was not the intention to *make* work together. *Being* together as friends: that was the work. Therefore the initiators selected their companions on the basis of friendship, not on the basis of any match with their professional or artistic interests. Because friendship, writes Misiano, doesn't need to justify itself by any motive at all. Therefore among these friends there was "freedom from any preliminary judgments. There was nothing preliminary except the friendship itself."[32] This all resulted in an absolute equality in friendship, or so it seemed.

It seemed indeed that in "Transnacionala" Michael Brenson's promise of reciprocity, that "all participants will be, at once, giver and receiver, producer and consumer, artist and audience," had come true. The participant-friends operated on an equal level in equal positions, as Misiano suggests. Following Pessers, this would mean that they reached the horizon of reciprocity, some kind of paradise in which no inequality needs to be alternated anymore.

Misiano makes us move, as it were, towards this absolute horizon of reciprocity dissolving in equality, until he interrupts his own discourse of reciprocity. He reveals an asymmetry that he cannot explain. Somehow the equality pushed the singularity of each of the participants to the front. The more they treated one another as equals the more the singularity of each of their characters showed. In his account Misiano gives ample space for this experience of singularity among the friends. In the end he exclaims in a desperate mood: "What made this friendship possible? What made all these people get together? [...] They can agree on almost nothing!"[33]

Misiano describes how the road-trip more and more became a hardship, a test case of friends living through and coping with one another's singularities. Partly this hardship can be understood in terms of reciprocity's precarious balance between self-assertiveness and recognition of the other, referring to Dorien Pessers. And partly it can be understood by referring to Levinas's event of asymmetry. Even among friends asymmetry occurs. Even among friends who know one another through and through, there is still the "radical impossibility of seeing oneself from the outside and of speaking in the same sense of oneself and of the other." The other doesn't mirror me, the other commands and invites me.

To understand more about this asymmetry in friendship and how it relates to reciprocity, we need to look at Levinas's colleague in philosophy Jacques Derrida (1930–2004). Derrida was strongly influenced by Levinas's ideas on asymmetry. In his collection of essays *The Politics of Friendship* (1994), Derrida discusses disproportion in friendship. In his essays on Aristotle, Montaigne, and Nietzsche, Derrida brings to the fore "a certain rupture in reciprocity or equality."[34]

Referring to Michel de Montaigne's essay *On Friendship*, Derrida writes about the distinction that Montaigne makes between common friendship and great friendship. In common or customary friendship both friends keep the reins in their hands. Their bond, Derrida explains, is just "the knot of an attachment between two, between two equals, subjects, or two symmetrical wills."[35] In great friendship there is something else happening, there is an acknowledgement of asymmetry. This asymmetry places me "under the law of the other," the bond of friendship "disjoins and disproportions me, inspiring a confidence, a faith, a 'fidence,' greater in the other than in myself, [...]."[36]

Derrida makes us attentive to this strange, yet so naturally heteronomic character of friendship, quoting the famous phrase of Montaigne: "Our souls were yoked together in such unity, and contemplated each other with so ardent an affection, [...] that I would have entrusted myself to him with greater assurance than to myself."[37] This trust or confidence of great friendship is a sign of a positively valued asymmetry and imbalance, and this is in contrast with the symmetrical working in which both friends keep the reins in their hands.

This acknowledgement of disproportion in great friendship brings Derrida to the question of whether this friendship would not "endanger the principle of equality, mutuality and autarky,"[38] which lives in the political realm. Derrida searches in his essays for an equality, "a certain equality" that recognizes and respects "disymmetrical and heteronomic singularities."[39]

Conclusion

I think curators such as Jacob and Misiano are on the same track as Pessers, Levinas, and Derrida. These curators also acknowledge experiences of disproportion within our reciprocal economy of relations. Neither Jacob nor Misiano denounce reciprocity. For both, reciprocity has the positive effects that they search for: the breakdown of the division between artist and audience; the possibility of a genuine relationship becoming an art practice, and in their case a curatorial practice. But, to their merit, they also try to account for experiences that interrupt and break open the circuit of reciprocity.

To say that asymmetry pertains does not just mean that some hiccups are allowed to occur within the reciprocal economy of relations. It means that encounters, which are crucial for these practices to happen in the first place, continuously and fundamentally produce experiences of disproportion in relation to others. This asymmetry in encounter has an effect on social art practice, which we have to think about and deal with.

1 Suzanne Lacy, ed., *Mapping the Terrain: New Genre Public Art* (Seattle, WA: Bay Press, 1994), 20.

2 Nicolas Bourriaud, *Esthétique relationnelle* (Dijon: Les presses du réel, 1998), translated by Simon Pleasance and Fronza Woods (with the participation of Mathieu Copeland) as *Relational Aesthetics* (Dijon: Les presses du réel, 2002).

3 Grant H. Kester, *Conversation Pieces: Community and Communication in Modern Art* (Berkeley, CA: University of California Press, 2004).

4 Viktor Misiano, "The Institutionalization of Friendship" [1998], in *Transnacionala: Highway Collisions between East and West at the Crossroads of Art*, ed. Eda Cufer (Ljubljana: Koda, 1999), 182–92.

5 Michael Brenson, "Introduction to 'Conversations on Culture,'" in *Conversations at the Castle: Changing Audiences and Contemporary Art*, ed. Mary Jane Jacob and Michael Brenson (Cambridge, MA: MIT Press, 1998), 31–37, esp. 37.

6 I don't address here the fundamental question of how Levinas's philosophical category of asymmetry can be applied to an analysis of social art practices. It is a question I address in my current PhD research, "Resuming Encounters: Reciprocity and Asymmetry in Social Art Practice," at the Royal Academy of Fine Arts Antwerp and the University of Antwerp.

7 I don't discuss Mauss's and Lévi-Strauss's theories here because their writings circulate widely. Their main publications on reciprocity are: Marcel Mauss, "Essai sur le don: Forme et raison de l'échange dans les sociétés archaïques," *Année Sociologique*, n.s., 1 (1925); Mauss, *The Gift: The Form and Reason for Exchange in Archaic Societies*, trans. W. D. Halls (London: Routledge, 1990); Claude Lévi-Strauss, *Les structures élémentaires de la Parenté* (Paris: Presses Universitaires de France, 1949), translated by James H. Bell and John R. von Sturmer as *The Elementary Structures of Kinship*, ed. Rodney Needham (London: Eyre & Spottiswoode, 1969). Mauss's ideas in relation to social art practices I've discussed elsewhere, see Erik Hagoort, "Being Able to Receive," in *The New Conversations 1: La chaîne est belle*, ed. Nico Dockx (Antwerp: Academie voor Schone Kunsten, 2011), 10–17.

8 Dorien Pessers, *Liefde, solidariteit en recht: Een interdisciplinair onderzoek naar het wederkerigheidsbeginsel* [Love, Solidarity, and Law: An Interdisciplinary Research into the Principle of Reciprocity] (Amsterdam: Universiteit Amsterdam, 1999), 51.

9 Ibid., 80.

10 Ibid., 51.

11 Ibid., 79.

12 Ibid., 139, (italics Hagoort).

13 Ibid., 78.

14 Ibid., 139.

15 A. W. Gouldner, "The Importance of Something for Nothing," in *For Sociology; Renewal and Critique in Sociology Today* (London: Allen Lane, 1973), 260–99.

16 Adriaan T. Peperzak, *Thinking: From Solitude to Dialogue and Contemplation* (New York: Fordham University Press, 2006), 48.

17 Ibid., 49.

18 Ibid., 47.

19 Emmanuel Levinas, *Totalité et infini: essai sur l'extériorité* (The Hague: Martinus Nijhoff, 1961), translated by Alphonso Lingis as *Totality and Infinity: An Essay on Exteriority* (Pittsburgh: Duquesne University Press, 1969), 53.

20 Emmanuel Levinas, *Hors sujet* (Saint Clément: Fata Morgana, 1987), translated by Michael B. Smith as *Outside the Subject* (London: Continuum, 2008), 33.

21 Bourriaud, *Esthétique relationnelle*, 24.

22 Ibid., 23.

23 Kester, *Conversation Pieces*, 120.

24 Mary Jane Jacob, "Reciprocal Generosity," in *What We Want is Free: Generosity and Exchange in Recent Art*, ed. Ted Purves (Albany: State University of New York Press, 2005), 3–10, esp. 6.

25 Ibid., 4.

26 Ibid., 5.

27 Jacqueline Baas and Mary Jane Jacob, eds., *Buddha Mind in Contemporary Art* (Berkeley, CA: University of California Press, 2004), 168.

28 Ibid.

29 Jacob, "Reciprocal Generosity," 6.

30 Baas and Jacob, *Buddha Mind*, 11.

31 Caroline Picard, "The Energetic Persistence of Water Part 2: An Interview with Mary Jane Jacob," *Bad-at-Sports: Contemporary Art Talk* (blog), February 28, 2012, http://badatsports.com/2012/the-energetic-persistence-of-water-part-2-an-interview-with-mary-jane-jacob/.

32 Misiano, "The Institutionalization of Friendship," 186.

33 Ibid., 191.

34 Jacques Derrida, *Politiques de l'amitié* (Paris: Editions Galilée, 1994), translated by George Collins as *The Politics of Friendship* (London: Verso, 2005), 62.

35 Ibid., 194.

36 Ibid.

37 Ibid., 195.

38 Ibid., 196.

39 Ibid., 197.

Stefan Römer

Invitation to my ~~Studio~~ *in* the Libertarian Inter-esse

1. Invitation

I am inviting you into a specific space. It is an artist's ~~studio~~ that is defined by the fact that it refers genealogically to very specific developments in art since the discussions of Post-Minimalism and Conceptualism in the 1960s. This space is characterized neither by a specific architecture nor by the production of standardized objects.[1]

It is, rather, about a space that results from specific sociocultural practices in relation to specific forms of artistic thinking. My invitation is to everyone who shows an interest in art in some fashion. I am therefore making myself into a host for all who find this interesting.

My invitation is based on readings of the artist's studio: in Daniel Buren's "The Function of the Studio" (1979), Brian O'Doherty's "Inside the White Cube" (1976), Robert Smithson's reflections on "site" and "non-site," Mary Kelly's *Post-Partum Document* (1976), and Ian Wallace's *In the Studio* (1993/2005). I thereby relate these readings to my own art projects. My idea is to understand the historical formation of the studio in a de-conceptual way and thus paint another picture. When I identify the "interest" of artistic practice I imply the production of the studio.[2]

Buren's statement that "It is therefore only in the studio that the work may be said to belong"[3] is contradicted by Smithson's view that the proper place of art should be regarded as a "site" in the landscape and not a "non-site" in a gallery. Buren's statement brings with it one hard consequence, namely: if the work remains in the studio, the artist runs the risk of starving to death.[4] Another consequence of this formulation, that the work is completely alien to the site of its presentation, can be summed up as follows. Daniel Buren got by without a studio by moving his artistic work directly to the space of presentation (the gallery, the museum, etc.). This designing, conceiving, organizing, and managing activity, assembling in situ installations from materials prepared elsewhere, can be regarded as the prototype for today's exhibition art. "Exhibition art" means works of art created specifically for an exhibition; they do not exist beforehand in the artist's studio. There is, however, a fundamental difference in that Buren articulated his interest in institutional critique in the texts that accompanied each of his exhibitions, and earlier even called for the elimination of the "code of art" in the sense of an avant-garde Utopia. By contrast, contemporary artists producing exhibition art usually work with a studio (for architecture or graphic design) or a staff of employees in the sense of the manufacture of high-quality products. A curatorial invitation to contribute to a show of contemporary exhibition art thus represents above all a task to produce art. In that sense, on the part of the curator, the production of such an exhibition also entails the intellectual activity of presenting a proposal and managing the project. For that reason, it seems to me that the traditional activity of the curator—the optimal conception of space for works of art—has, in general, become secondary.

From the in-situ practice of Buren and others, various "non-" and "post-studio" practices were developed that are relevant to so-called exhibition art. In the early 1990s I myself sought out a production space for art in collective and public spaces (see the formation of the group FrischmacherInnen). This production space made the relationship between the presentation space of the white cube and the space of representation, so-called public space or the public sphere, into an increasingly important political question for the production of art itself. With this critical interest in this genealogy, it is possible to designate a "post-post-studio art" with a graphic mark in the manner of Jacques Derrida's deconstruction: I strike through the term "~~studio~~" to make clear that there is a polyphonic discourse when I write or use the word. Similarly, since the mid-1990s I have been striking through the word "~~public~~" in order to distinguish its new corporate, economic dimensions from its previous meanings. I have myself presented projects for which I worked with activism, photography, and performance/installation in urban space or in and with the public, and my thinking in these projects revolved around Buren's two main points: the negation of the traditional artist's studio and the strategic relationship between the space of production and the space of presentation as ~~publication~~.

The space of artistic production should itself become the space of presentation. To that end, I looked at self-portraits and portraits of artists in their studios. I was made uncomfortable, for example, by the isolation of the "ivory tower" as seen in Georg Friedrich Kersting's portrait of Caspar David Friedrich (1819), in which there is no view of the outside world, no books, no music, and no other people around him. Friedrich is painting from the introspection of a white cell. By contrast, I found Gustave Courbet's self-portrait in *The Artist's Studio* (1855) interesting because he situates his artistic practice within a group of more or less good friends, benefactors, muses, and so on, and thus emphasizes the social connections of his work. All of the photographs or films of artists working should be added to these forms of artistic self-portrayal.

2. “The ~~Studio~~ *in* the Libertarian Inter-esse”

In the context of the term “hospitality,” I developed an artist’s text and an exhibition. The two forms had different subject matter and themes but shared the basic assumption of a collectively produced situation and were based on inviting various people and the content associated with them to enter a specific social life in an artist’s studio. In my text “Das ~~Studio~~ im libertären Inter-esse” (The ~~Studio~~ *in* the Libertarian Inter-esse, 2004), I formulate a specific studio:

> I imagine people in a bright room. Pictures in various media and formats are spread all over the table, the walls and the floor, with all different kinds of color and material rests, and also notes and sketches. Despite the disorder, one can speak of a gallery, a library, an observatory, or a music room; others would think of it as being a boudoir or even a cabinet of curiosities. Perhaps this space of artistic production is a scenery of a strong, specific interest, something which would explain its association with archives. Artists work here, apparently without a reason, on a multidimensional tableau, which is to be understood more as a visual regime than as a painting. It is a regime with many plateaus dealing with art and hospitality, and with the art of hospitality—a Mallarméan casting of the dice of interest on the tableau.
>
> I also imagine that everything is possible here. With a long vibrant feather, a bearded transvestite caresses the breasts of a woman sucking on a straw, while at a festively set table there is a weltering discussion on the culture of the “gift,” and photographs of this scenery are edited on a laptop; some watch while smoking marijuana and drinking wine. The bubbling sound of an analogue synthesizer is digitally transformed into new samples, and a flirt on a sofa is the sign of devotion to this tableau. Some just hang around, others seem to rest, or follow lectures, concerts, or performances, which occasionally even turn into orgiastic revelry. This discursive activity surely exceeds the possibilities of an image. All (interest) belongs to everyone/everything here. That is precisely the risk of fame.
>
> The artistic life-design in the studio defines where the invitation ends and delimitation begins. Thus, in the ideal studio with affected authenticity

> even a (conceivably) unconditional invitation is made. Yet it would be naive or even ideologically mistaken to claim that the interest design of the studio only applied to the decor or the embellishments, or only to the politics of invitation. Rather what is at issue here is thought. A special dietetics, all the way to the shaping of genders, yes, even sex, is enjoyed here—so it is ultimately about the expanded existential design of (self-) invitation: Fall in love with yourself anew. You may. The studio as self-representation in the circle of the ones you love, as the ultimate name-dropping of crossing a threshold to total openness: every day a casual auto-tune-masterpiece.
>
> Can a studio in libertarian interest be staged as a tableau of bureaucratic art DNA? Or would this be a contradiction, like a programmatically un-ironed designer shirt? And: How can such a politics of invitation betray one's own country in a grandiose way? Call me expressively narcissistic, but I paint (not) one painting of you but many. We love it expensive! And please keep in mind, talk here is not (only) about my networked computer, that audiovisual omnivore.[5]

This text describes an ideal ~~studio~~ situation that emerged from an invitation to a transmedia party or symposium. The basic idea was that many people would spend time in a room where—in the spirit of libertinage—everything is supposed to be possible: speaking, eating, drinking, reading books and showing pictures, sex, listening to and playing music, making paintings, and so on. Where does one want to put a limitation, or how can one conceive of ungoverned behavior in this space at all? Moreover, how can this line between personal freedom and the freedom of others be drawn at all? With this imagined space, the text raises the question of whether the ~~studio~~ can house the absolute autonomy or artistic practice—the *dérive*, the idiosyncrasy, the excess, and so on, all of which lend difference to the concept of originality.

If we depart from the idea of the ivory tower in this spirit, the imaginary space determines the crucial question of the threshold. Invitation is joined by the traditional binary function of inclusion or exclusion: Who is invited and who isn't? Only then does the question arise: What is permitted in the studio and what isn't?

Formulated as an act of imagination, as a positive project, the rhetorical questions in this text refer to artistic and theoretical precursors: The cliché of the artist's studio, Stéphane Mallarmé, Charles Baudelaire, advertising slogans, Jack Smith's film *Flaming Creatures* (1963), Larry Clark's photographs, Pierre Klossowski's *Les Lois de l'hospitalité*, and Jacques Derrida's *Of Hospitality*, among others.

The concept of an unconditional invitation as I transmuted the phrase from Derrida represents the definitional threshold of this "hospitality":

> Assheuer: In your recent texts, one can find a subject that was also central to the thinking of Hannah Arendt […]: the absolute valuation of unconditional hospitality. In what way might such a hospitality lead to responses to the problems of the refugees of global society?
>
> Derrida: Unconditional hospitality is inseparable from a thinking of justice itself, but as such it remains impracticable. It cannot be written into the rules or in a piece of legislation. If one wanted to translate it immediately into a policy, it would always carry the risk of having perverse effects. But even as we watch out for these risks, we cannot and must not abandon the reference to hospitality without reservations. It is an absolute pole, outside which desire, the concept, and experience, the very thought of hospitality, would be meaningless.[6]

Derrida speaks of a maximally "unconditional hospitality" as the "impossible." By that he does not, however, mean the fictional content of a Utopia of the term but, quite the contrary, the "concrete urgency, here and now."[7] He relates this to all forms of communitarianism that are responsible for "cultural identity," and thereby attributes a political dimension to the laws of hospitality: "Everything possible must indeed be done to get the laws of hospitality written into actual law. When that is not possible, everyone must judge in their own soul and conscience, often 'privately,' what must be done (when, where, how, up to what point) without the laws or against them."[8]

The political significance Derrida associates with "hospitality" directly concerns the exhibition context as a constellation of interests accommodated by the curator, the artist, the sponsor, and the viewer. Focusing on the terms in the invitation to the conference one may ask: What can a model of interest provide for hospitality?

In the exhibition "Conceptual Paradise: The ~~Studio~~ of Interest,"[9] I presented my documentary film project and a research project on the evolution of the

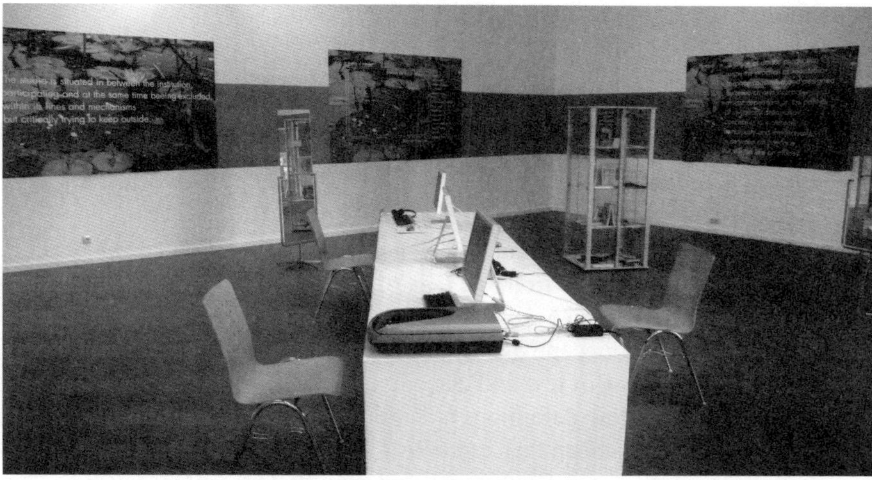

Stefan Römer, *Mise en Scène*, 2009. Installation view of "Conceptual Paradise: The ~~Studio~~ of Interest," Kunstraum der Leuphana Universität, Lüneburg

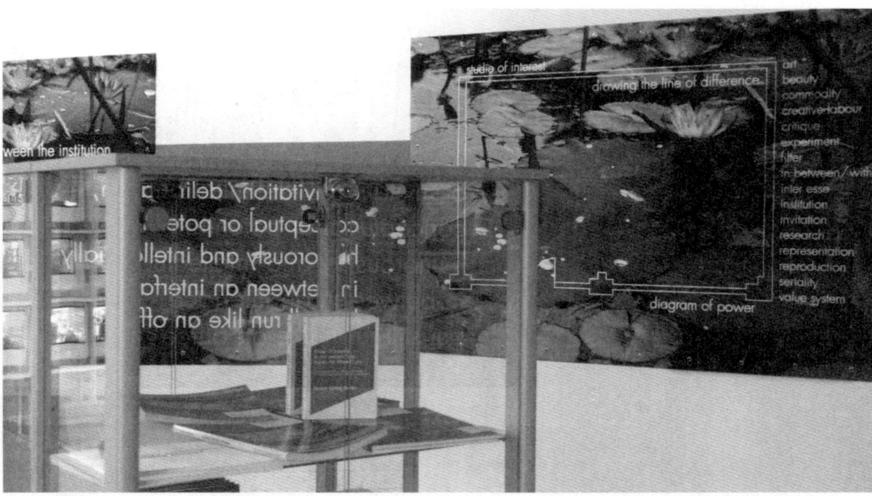

Stefan Römer, installation view of "Conceptual Paradise: The ~~Studio~~ of Interest," Kunstraum der Leuphana Universität, Lüneburg

international discussion of Conceptualism. Four banners on the walls, a video installation with all of the artists and theorists interviewed appearing on monitors in alternation, two labeled mirrors, and several computer screens that provided access to the video database were used to present the exhibition and WikiProject. This project on Conceptualism, which is one of the central research focuses of the Kunstraum at Leuphana Universität, was worked out in cooperation with Eva Birkenstock (art history), Kathrin Busch (philosophy), Martin Warnke (digital media), and Ulf Wuggenig (sociology, cultural theory), as well as a group of students from the departments of Art and Visual Studies, Cultural Theory, and Digital Media at the Leuphana Universität Lüneburg.

Today, practices of Conceptualism cover a broad field, which should not be reduced to the production of text and discourse, but rather is characterized by a large number of competing definitions and artistic approaches. Updating the discussions on Conceptualism thus represents a terrain of the most diverse historical, Post-Conceptual, neo-Conceptual, and even de-Conceptual artistic practices.

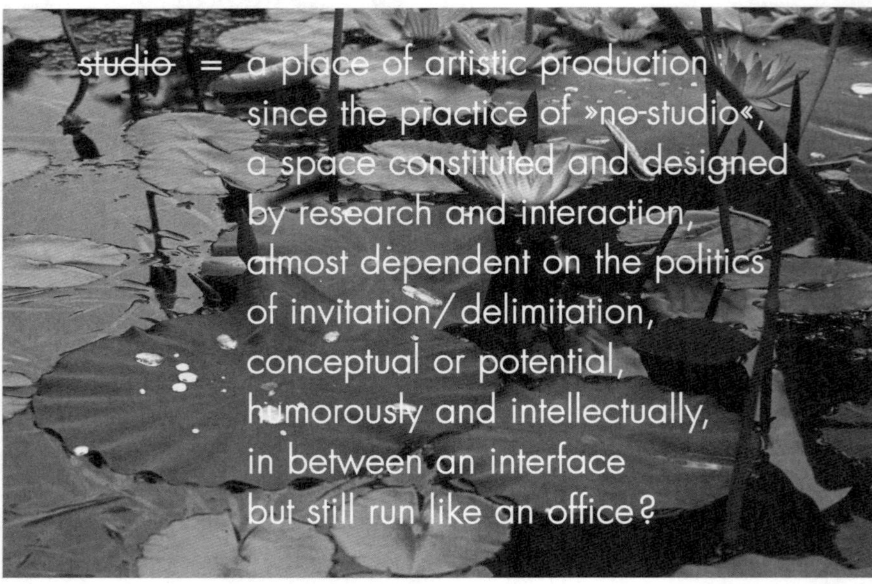

Stefan Römer, *Banner 4*, 2009. Installation view of "Conceptual Paradise: The ~~Studio~~ of Interest," Kunstraum der Leuphana Universität, Lüneburg

The point of departure for the project was my film *Conceptual Paradise* (2006): an effort to come to terms intellectually with the subject through conversations with three generations of conceptual artists (www.conceptual-paradise.com). Using a specific means of cinematic reflection, the film opens with insights into the discourses that are fundamental to contemporary practices, such as artistic research, immaterial work, institutional criticism, and Internet-based projections. Beyond the sequences used in the film, extensive material from conversations with some fifty artists and theorists was made available in full at the website. Hence not only rare film material but also the interview transcripts were made available to a wide audience for research and discussion.

The website is a platform for the practice of art, art criticism, and future online exhibitions that is intended to inspire new art projects and theoretical texts. It thus functions not only as an archive and cultural memory but also as a space for discussions of artistic and scholarly projects. The "Conceptual Paradise" exhibition was a prelude that will be followed by the formation of a continually growing international platform for information, discussion, and production on Conceptualisms, replacing art historical writing's traditional concentration on the northwestern part of the world. Having emerged in an era marked by neoliberalism, the website aims for critical reflection on working conditions in the artistic field in which the initiators themselves are active.

Immediately following on from a series of project seminars I had been giving since 2007 at the Kunstraum at Leuphana Universität, the exhibition presented the current state of the *Conceptual Paradise* website, which was developed in close collaboration with the students involved in the project. For this first public presentation, I conceived a specific installation that revolved around the subject of the artist's ~~studio~~. Ever since the "non" or "post-studio" idea of Conceptualism, the artist's studio has been a subject in various discussions. Whereas artistic research and Internet-connected computers have been playing an increasingly important role in the production of art, the exhibition space has been becoming a display that generates meaning.

The installation included four large-format banners (225 × 150 cm) asking questions about how the ~~studio~~ functions today, with texts and diagrams printed over the water-lily motif from the film *Conceptual Paradise*. Basically, what interests me is a deconstructive reading of what is today regarded as the classic definition of Conceptual art, which in essence states that visual formulation is of secondary importance. In that context, differentiating between the terms "conceptional" and "conceptual" plays a fundamental role, as I have explained elsewhere.[10] Last but not least, "Conceptual Paradise" pursued the goal of using the website and its presentation to encourage further reflection on the epistemological foundations of artistic production. It is my attempt to designate the realm of artistic production in space and time that specifically overlaps with the aims of the Kunstraum at Leuphana Universität. Each banner was given a motivic title. The intention was that the first banner would get the viewers to focus their interest on the exhibition. This was not so much a didactic measure as a narrative of exhibition design intended to encourage identification with the work—whether visual or literary—from which we expect an intense experience of art.

Banner 1 (Who are you?)
Entering the libertarian-interest ~~studio~~
you may ask yourself if you are appropriator,
projector, reflector, sampler, or mode selector.

The second banner asks about the localization of artist's ~~studios~~:

Banner 2 (Where is the ~~studio~~ situated?)
The ~~studio~~ is situated in between the institution,
participating and at the same time being excluded,
within its lines and mechanisms
but critically trying to keep outside.

On the third banner, the terms are positioned around a frame over the motif of water lilies; the individual terms are printed on the right, directly next to the frame. The frame echoes the floor plan of the art space:

Banner 3 (The ~~studio~~ of interest)
~~studio~~ of interest – drawing the line of difference
art, beauty, commodity, creative labour, critique, experiment, filter, in between/within, inter-esse, institution, invitation, research, representation, reproduction, seriality, value system
diagram of power

The fourth banner is about the "politics of inviting or disinviting," and it sketches the concepts of the epistemology of the ~~studio~~:

Banner 4 (How can the ~~studio~~ of interest be defined?)
~~studio~~ = a place of artistic production
since the practice of "no-studio,"
a space constituted and designed
by research and interaction,
almost dependent on the politics
of invitation/delimitation,
conceptual or potential,
humorously and intellectually,
in between an interface
but still run like an office?

The motif of water lilies behind the four constellations took the place of decor in this installation. Central attention was attributed to the role of decorative forms, above all to vines and flowers, which have traditionally played a marginal role in the history of art. In addition to referring to the "Warhol flowers," their iconographic significance is a reference to the mind that has reached the highest stage in the philosophical system of Buddhism. This ambiguity echoes the "Conceptual Paradise" project's gesture of invitation: on the one hand, to the conceptual artists who publish their replies as part of the project; on the other hand, to the viewers who move within this exhibition and beyond and get involved in the website project.

The four banners were placed on a mural painted in the yellowish-gray color RAL 7034, which was one meter wide and ran continuously along the four walls of the exhibition space, with a meter of free wall beneath. Two pivoting mirrors (167 × 50 cm) were set up, labeled on the reverse: "ambient and mirror" and "original and mirror." These two thematic constellations have for many years been the fields of my activity as an artist. The theme of the white cube that becomes an ambient and the theme of the original that becomes a strategic fake outline my interests in the substance of the artistic, which is traditionally defined as the originality of an artistic achievement and the exhibition space that the multimedia "ambient" makes possible.

3. The ~~Studio~~ *in* the Libertarian Inter-esse: Summary

The projects presented here bring together two objects of my artistic research: the concept of "inter-esse" and that of the "~~studio~~." Whereas I conceive the "inter-esse" as an epistemological figure of coexistence based on respective interests ("esse"), I understand the artist's ~~studio~~ between ("inter") the artistic space of imagination and autonomy, the public sphere, the real world, production space, and exhibition space, as critically programmatic antipodes both to the ivory tower and to the romanticization of Warhol's Factory. I define the "~~studio~~ *in* the libertarian inter-esse" as a social and collective practice in-between the archive (of books, audio, or video) and the party or informed and theatrical feast (symposium). This thinking is directly connected to the discourse of Plato's or Xenophon's *Symposium*, the happenings of the Vienna Actionists, and rock concerts by way of the techno parties of the 1990s (with their idealization of immediacy and ecstasy), all the way to artists' conferences, each of which have rituals that can be defined as discursive, ethical, dietetic, and artistic orientations. It is the invitations to parties, events, or happenings of very different structure and form that make such occasions interesting. My concern is to study the fundamental performative aspects of human coexistence that cannot be separated globally from the culture industry.

The concepts "hospitality," "interesting," and "interest" belong to this field of synthetic conception, which can also only be hinted at here. Without the interest of the native (das Heimische) in the guest or the foreigner/other, the relationship of hospitality would be just as weak as it would without the interest of the guest or of the foreigner in the native, as the channel to find/live/practice what he or she previously lacked. I regard this complex and complicated relationship as dependent on the genealogy of interest and interestingness. Elsewhere I have described a deferring reading of this relationship as the epistemological praxis of the inter-esse.[11] This graphic marking of "inter-esse" with a hyphen stands for my deconstructive research coupled with my artistic practice.

It is known of Marcel Duchamp that he considered himself someone who liked to be alone in the studio and elsewhere as well. As he noted, that did not make it easier for him in art. That fits with the following quotation of Thomas Bernhard concerning the ambiguity between solitarily concentrated, perhaps even solipsistic, work and companionable production that perhaps even follows a collective flush:

> Everyone wants to participate and at the same time be left alone. And because that is not really possible, to have both, one is always in conflict. One closes the door in order to be alone again, at the moment when one closes the door one is at the same time aware that it is wrong, that it

> is a wrong action, because essentially one doesn't want it: First, because one knows that being alone is much less pleasant, but on the other hand you can't do anything about it. Together with a woman, you can't write books or even just, ultimately, … it doesn't work. When together with a man, he gets on your nerves as well, because it is no different, so being together, it's all very critical and difficult.[12]

Perhaps with his famous equation Duchamp was summing up precisely this split and the ambiguity of hospitality: "a guest + a host = a ghost"? But, as expressed in the invitation to the conference for which this lecture was written, "It can thus also be treated as a paradigmatic situation within the cultural field exemplifying the generous, but often also ambivalent and problematic, interdependencies between hosts and guests under the conditions of globalization."

But this ambiguity, for which I have tried to provide a framework in my projects, also has a documentary aspect that marks, frames, and exhibits the given institutional situations in situ, often resulting in a new but complicated invitation being extended. Nevertheless, this documentary moment is based on a certain normative attempt to define what concerns the relationship of interests and interestingness. Again unframing the image.

1 I have repeatedly dealt with questions related to the artist's studio: as Artist in Residence, Studio of Resistance, "100 Tage keine Ausstellung," Kunstverein Salzburg, 2000; in the lecture "The Libertarian-Interest ~~Studio~~: Zu einer Theorie des künstlerischen Interesses – Politiken des Künstlerstudios," given at the conference "Wo entsteht die Kunst? Das Atelier seit Caspar David Friedrich," Alfried Krupp Wissenschaftskolleg, Greifswald, April 1–4, 2009; for the exhibition "The Libertarian-Interest ~~Studio~~," ECA Gallery, Kolkata, India, February 17–25, 2009; in the lecture performance "Artistic Spatial Models in Three Songs by Stan Back," for "Post-Studio Tales," Berlin, April 18, 2012; and the lecture "The ~~Studio~~ of Libertarian Inter-esse," given at "Hospitality—Hosting Relations in Exhibitions," International Conference: Cultures of the Curatorial, Hochschule für Grafik und Buchkunst (HGB)/ Academy of Fine Arts Leipzig, December 13–14, 2012.

2 I draw artistic meaning from the space in-between the artwork, the passe-partout, and the frame (inter-esse), since I refer to my de-conceptual mis-reading of Jacques Derrida's "Parergon" with Cézanne's phrase, that he owes the truth "in" painting. See Stefan Römer, *Inter-esse* (Berlin: Merve, 2014), 128–31.

3 Daniel Buren, "The Function of the Studio," trans. Thomas Repensek, *October* 10 (Fall 1979): 51–58, esp. 53.

4 Ibid.

5 Translated from the German by Karl Hoffmann. There is an acoustic version of the original text as a sound file (2:22 mins), recorded with radio disturbance, which was part of "ZEIGEN: Eine Audiotour durch Berlin," an exhibition curated by Karin Sander, Temporäre Kunsthalle, Berlin 2009–10.

6 Jacques Derrida, "Not Utopia, the Im-possible," in *Paper Machine*, trans. Rachel Bowlby (Stanford, CA: Stanford University Press, 2005), 121–35, esp. 131.

7 Ibid., 131.

8 Ibid., 132.

9 "Conceptual Paradise: The ~~studio~~ of Interest," Kunstraum der Leuphana Universität, Lüneburg, December 10, 2009–January 28, 2010.

10 See Römer, *Inter-esse*, 66.

11 Ibid., 167.

12 Kurt Hofmann, *Aus Gesprächen mit Thomas Bernhard*, 2nd ed. (Munich: dtv, 1991), 11–12.

Maja Ćirić

The (Un)spoken Abuse

Curatorial Hospitality through the Lens of Criticality

Starting with the premise that the interdisciplinary practices of curating are often characterized by a complex language that consists of borrowed terms, notions, and inspirations from allied fields, I will place special focus on their relation to hospitality. The aim of this paper is to underline the impact of the spontaneous use of hospitality in curating and to promote an internalized hospitality in the curatorial—one that would be capable of producing a meaningful difference in the art system. The term "internalized hospitality" stands for the complex notion of an inclusion of the history of hospitality in curating by curators who will curate projects related to hospitality in the future.

In order to avoid a spontaneous flow of inspiration on the topic of hospitality, let us look at some of the ambivalent patterns and different positions from which hospitality can be addressed, and at the same time label some of the correlated curatorial outcomes.

From the perspective of cultural studies, there are context-specific rituals related to hospitality. In Southeast Europe, for example, the ritual of taking one's shoes off before entering a host's territory serves to prevent guests from spoiling the established territory with traces of their shoes; the gesture also keeps guests from running away quickly.

In an art context, hospitality could be manifested in practice by hosting curators, artists, audiences; but also conceptually, by hosting all possible concepts of hospitality. To further highlight the complexities of hospitality, let us recall two philosophical interpretations of the concept: Immanuel Kant's universal hospitality and Jacques Derrida's radical hospitality.[1]

One example of applied hospitality is curator Massimiliano Gioni's exhibition "A Guest + A Host = A Ghost" at the Deste Foundation, Athens, in 2009. The overall work appeared to be a compilation of solo displays by specific artists, each of which was represented in the collection by many works. According to Gioni, "the creations by other artists have been placed within these "sub-groups," hence creating parasitic relations between the exhibits."[2] Another mainstream example of curatorial hospitality is the 9th Istanbul Biennial's "Hospitality Zone," housed in a former warehouse that Charles Esche and Vasif Kortun had given over to local artists' initiatives, a gesture that, according to some, felt strategic rather than heartfelt because the zone was positioned as an antidote to the newly opened Istanbul Modern museum next door.[3] A more substantial particular manifestation of hospitality would be one embedded in an institutional vision, or even hospitality used as a tool for institutional critique. For example, Charles Esche, as director of the Van Abbemuseum, explains in a panel discussion on hospitality that he was inspired by the director Želimir Žilnik's radical hospitality in *Black Film* (1971), in which Žilnik picks up ten homeless men from the streets of Novi Sad and brings them home one night, to help "solve the homeless problem." The Van Abbemuseum have claimed radical hospitality as their core value: When Charles Esche talks about institutional hospitality, he is inspired by Derrida, and he encourages the institution "to hand the keys over, to just say yes to what comes along, to say yes before knowing what is going to happen, before determination, anticipation, identification."[4] Esche points to the challenging aspects of Derrida's hospitality, aspects that Europe fails miserably to pick up on when facing the reality of contemporary European politics in a xenophobic climate.[5] He also addresses the hospitality within an art institution that would like to have people knocking at its door but doesn't—because people have questions that the art institution cannot answer. Esche highlights the failure of universal hospitality by pointing out the impossibility of expanding the social circle of people that an art institution might host, as this space is dedicated to those who are familiar with the codex of art institutions and who use the institution to confirm their taste.

Another aspect of the discourse on hospitality lies in the theory-institution axis, which returns to theory. For example, Alex Farquharson's argument in his lecture "Institutional Mores" is grounded on the thesis "that curatorial practices that integrate social values such as generosity, curiosity, and hospitality through the curatorial concepts [...] within the institutions, are opening up the institutions by abandoning and exchanging the space of requests for the space of desire."[6] Later on, he argues that the unstructured space of desires is a way of reproducing the existing institutional order. If the unstructured space of desire is manifested through the spontaneous flow of ideas, then it leads towards the potential abuse of hospitality in curating.

What I propose here is to promote an internalized hospitality that will recognize the contradictions of hospitality as it has been promoted in the curatorial so far.

In the history of curating, the anthropological turn has been manifested through the practice of "curators-as-ethnographers" who have tried to frame a transcultural worldview with their exhibitions, although in most instances they have reinforced the otherness perceived through a Western aesthetic gaze.[7] The real question—one that Esche asks indirectly when he reflects on what capacities institutions can offer and whether an institution can encourage the guest (the (Other) to ask questions that match the institutions resources—is whose requests and whose desires are being considered?

Since the "Primitivism" exhibition at MoMA (1989), "Magiciens de la terre" at the Centre George Pompidou (1989), and the 1993 Whitney Biennial numerous attempts have been made to use hospitality to expand the hegemonic discourse of contemporary art. However, although these and similar exhibitions expanded the geopolitics of the curatorial, they preserved its hegemonic character and were unable to produce new horizons or to integrate the non-Western art worlds in a manner that does not present them as a projection of the exoticized Other. In another text one could analyze the positive outcome of hospitality in exhibitions such as the first Gwangju Biennale "Beyond the Borders" (1995) that "conveyed messages of global citizenship that transcends divisions between ideologies, territories, religion, race, culture, humanity, and the arts."[8]

One form of invisible abuse comes after the curatorial project has expired and the hospitable situation is over: when the guests are sent away from the hegemonic center without resources to exploit their newly acquired symbolic capital. This is exactly how hospitality was employed in those exhibitions—to confirm the existing territory by keeping the potential enemy under control. In a different interpretation, it could also be said that the guests, who enter a predetermined field structured by someone else's resources, could abuse the host.

In practice, I have faced the difficulties of reaching new horizons while dealing with hospitality in the context of an art institution. In their New York main offices, the International Studio & Curatorial Program (ISCP), one of the most renowned residency programs in the world, has a map of the world full of pins marking the places of origin of every former resident. The exhibition "Power to Host," which I curated, was conceived at the ISCP in June 2011 as a critique of the fact that most pins were located on the European and North American continents, while Africa, the Middle East, and Central and South America had few pins or none at all. Besides the display of the artworks, an integral part of the exhibition was a Hospitality Shelf, with the portfolios of artists and curators from underrepresented areas. Although this exhibition was envisioned as a form of institutional critique, paradoxically, its effect was not to change the power structure, but to reinforce the institution's stake in that structure. Hosting the portfolios did not contribute to an expansion of countries at the ISCP immediately. However, four years later it has been unofficially announced that some of the ISCP studios will host artists from the Middle East in the near future.

The abuse of hospitality becomes transparent when it reaches an extreme, even more so than when it is the subject of critical examination. Take, for example, Manifesta 8 in Murcia, Spain, whose geographical location was ostensibly chosen to expand the Western art world into the Arab world and the African continent. Le Colonel, an artist performing institutional critique, hopped on the bus during the Manifesta 8 preview days, and asked the people on the bus how many of them were from the Arab world or the African continent. It turned out that only one person on the bus was of Arab origin, and even she was based in the West.

Another extreme situation came about during the dOCUMENTA (13) seminar in Cairo. According to Angela Harutyunyan, one female student asked to have all cameras and microphones switched off before she would

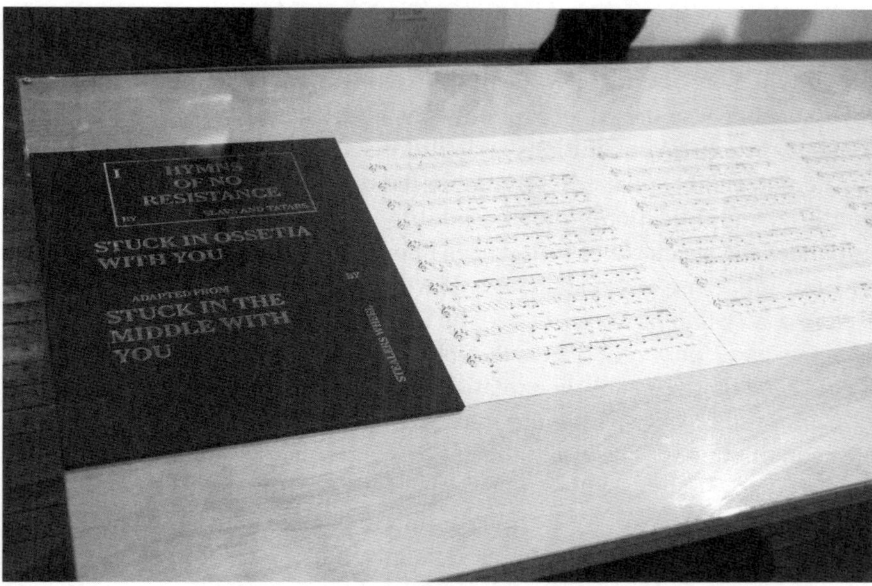

Slavs and Tatars, *Hymns of No Resistance*, 2009. Installation view of "The Power to Host," ISCP, Brooklyn, New York, 2011

utter a word.[9] For the student, it was not the content of the speech, the linguistic barrier, or the elitist jargon that created a wall between the various segments of the "audience," the keynote speakers, or the students, but, rather, it was the means through which the event was staged, including the technical equipment that turns such an event into a seemingly harmless convention. By asking for the technical apparatus to be turned off, she seemed to demand to change both the very conditions upon which the speeches were produced and the manner in which the event was staged.[10]

If the curatorial has borrowed the term hospitality, has it borrowed the best of it? As Kant noted in his essay "Perpetual Peace," the state of peace among men living in close proximity is not the natural state (*status naturalis*).[11] The natural state is one of war, which does not just consist of open hostilities, but also in the constant and enduring threat of them.[12] Analogous to this, if the state of the art world is one of permanent war, then hospitality is used as an illusion to perpetuate existing conditions, while we, the art workers, flatter ourselves with the idea that we are making continuous progress within curatorial discourse towards artificial perpetual peace by practicing hospitality.

The abuse of hospitality as a form of institutional critique is manifested in a way that keeps the Other at a distance. If this abuse is to be looked at through the lens of criticality, then the existing models of examination can not apply, because the way hospitality has been abused in the art world perpetuates the existing conditions and reinforces "the axis of the unloved."[13]

If curatorial hospitality operating in the realm of desire is an effect of curatorial simplification,[14] then hospitality is being abused in a way that stimulates the spectacle of differences in order to prevent the institution of art from achieving any real change. If we agree that hospitality has been used in a way that has perpetuated the already historicized socio-political, what this paper promotes then is the application of a form of hospitality that is not based on the established relations, but is instead contemporary.

Curatorial hospitality should thus be examined through the (ethical) issues and dilemmas. The internalized hospitality that I am arguing for is a curatorial hospitality that would be capable of creating new realities, connections, and positions, by learning from previous exhibitions. This hospitality would not reproduce existing relations, nor use exhibitions as mere tools of cultural diplomacy, but would be capable of stimulating new relations.

The search for an approach to hospitality could be grounded in criticality (pace Irit Rogoff) as a method that would allow for interpreting hospitality in such a way as to create new grounds.[15] Criticality would imply systems of selection and labeling that are different from the institutionalized systems of classification and hierarchization. In practice, this would involve perceiving how much we can learn from past patterns of curatorial hospitality in order to create a new paradigm. We assume that hospitality has up until now been employed to redistribute existing structures in which power is exerted in such a way that it does not change the art world, but serves as an illusion that maintains the art world's coherence and thereby prevents us from perceiving and redistributing the real conditions of the hegemonic art world(s).

The aim of this paper is to point out what has been instituted. Most important is not calculating the abuse produced by hosts or guests but understanding the abuse of the very term hospitality in the curatorial—the abuse of its active, productive aspect, which stems from the lack of a meta-position, which has not been reached despite the numerous attempts to produce discursivity on hospitality and curating. Instead of establishing the history of exhibitions in relation to hospitality, it is important to be aware of the history of using hospitality in curating. Achieving such meta-positioning implies scanning the history of the implementation of hospitality in curating. So far, looking at things historically, in terms of the geopolitics of the curatorial, meta-positioning has been envisioned from the hosts' point of view. However, instead of seeking to represent the history of curatorial hospitality, we have to try to figure out what has been neglected. Presuming that the social and political have already been historicized, it is perception through the lens of criticality that would break with the already instituted social and political in order to derive something new.

Ideally, hospitality in the context of the anthropological turn in curating should be humanism on the move, which, according to Immanuel Kant, is a basis for cosmopolitanism.[16] However, this hospitality is not to be implemented as a Western concept that ignores differences and is based on a Eurocentric worldview. Humanism on the move should articulate the entire dynamics of the post-Other. It should not be articulated through the Western perspective, because even when geographical distance is overcome, psychological difference remains. Curators as agents of circulation should be thinking in terms of the post-Other or, even more properly, in terms of the "unsame." Not abusing hospitality would mean acknowledging the anthropological turn in curating, in the sense that one may find a way to avoid dealing with the Other, but should start, at least, to deal with the unsame.

The multiplicity of positions and interpretations of hospitality in curating calls for the recognition of internalized hospitality. It calls for a language transformation that would lead to the transformation of curatorial practices. In order to keep this text from becoming just another rhetorical gesture of institutional critique, herein we promote internalized hospitality, understood as the result of a meta-positioning of the curatorial, which should be a

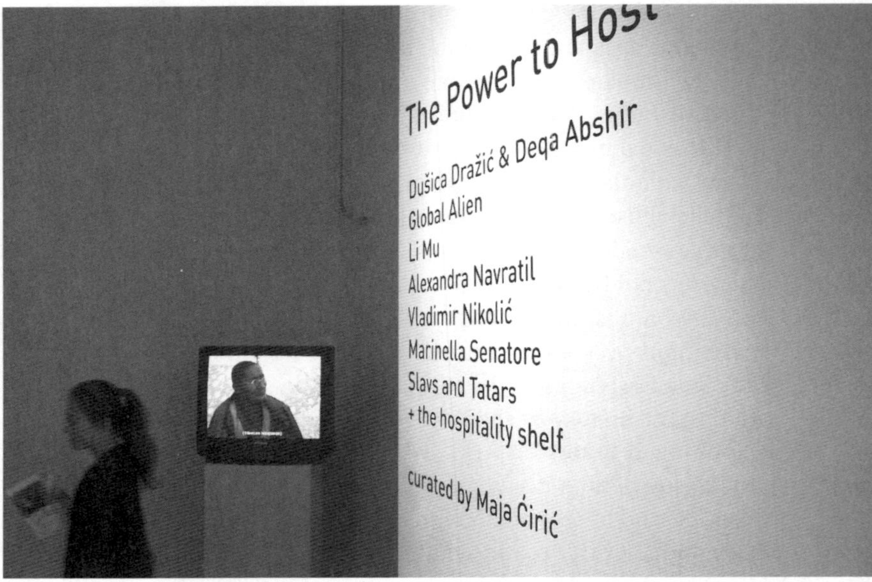

Installation view of "The Power to Host," ISCP, Brooklyn, New York, 2011

question, not only of ethics, but also of the self-interest of those who have the resources to host future exhibitions.

The abuse of hospitality in curating in terms of curatorial geopolitics

1. reinforces existing relations
2. conceals the natural state of "war"
3. neglects the need to reflect on what has been left out
4. neglects the dynamics of struggle
5. conceals the need to think in terms of post-Other (Homi Bhaba) or the "unsame"
6. does not transform or update the language used because the social and political have already been historicized
7. allows the more powerful to play the card of desire
8. represents existing norms and regulations, which are reproduced without being questioned
9. leads to self-abuse when former guests (artists, curators) reproduce

in their subsequent exhibitions the perspective they have been exposed to and/or the already established power relations they have worked within

If we ground our practice on internalized hospitality, the non-abusive situation would imply

1. finding a model to articulate cosmopolitan recognition as the main pre-condition for cosmopolitan rights and universal hospitality
2. stimulating criticality
3. articulating existing ambivalence in a new way—not as a space of desires, but as spaces that accommodate the requirements of internalized hospitality in the curatorial
4. accepting one's own limitations when unable to find a way to deal with ambivalence
5. following accurate requests for rearrangements
6. acting in the space of real needs; acting on what is unstructured

1 Immanuel Kant, "Perpetual Peace: A Philosophical Sketch," in *Kant's Political Writings*, ed. Hans Reiss (Cambridge: Cambridge University Press, 1970), 93–130. Jacques Derrida, *Of Hospitality: Anne Dufourmantelle Invites Jacques Derrida to Respond*, trans. Rachel Bowlby (Stanford, CA: Stanford University Press, 2000). For Derrida, in order to be hospitable, it is first necessary that one have the power to host, that is, have some kind of control over the people being hosted, which means that the guests will be under control: subject to closed boundaries, to nationalism, and even to the exclusion of particular groups. In Derrida's possible conception of hospitality our well-intentioned conceptions of hospitality render the others. See the Internet *Encyclopedia of Philosophy*, "Possible and Impossible Aporias: b. Hospitality," accessed December 2, 2014, http://www.iep.utm.edu/derrida/#SH7b.

2 See Deste Foundation for Contemporary Art, "A Guest + A Host = A Ghost," accessed October 2, 2012, http://deste.gr/exhibition/guest-ghost-host/.

3 Jörg Heiser, Erden Kosova, Jan Verwoert, "9th Istanbul Biennial: City Report," *frieze*, no. 95 (November–December 2005), accessed October 3, 2012, http://www.frieze.com/issue/article/istanbul_city_report/.

4 Charles Esche, "Practicing Hospitality," a panel discussion at "Symposium: Of Hospitality," SMART Museum of Art, The University of Chicago, May 5, 2012, see Vimeo, accessed December 2, 2014, http://vimeo.com/42269151.

5 Ibid.

6 Alex Farquharson, "Institutional Mores," a paper given at the conference "Institutional Attitudes," Brussels, April, 2010, see Vimeo, accessed May 23, 2012, http://vimeo.com/12206073.

7 Paul O'Neill, *The Culture of Curating and the Curating of Culture(s)* (Cambridge, MA: MIT Press, 2012), 54–72.

8 See the Gwangju Biennale website, accessed October 15, 2012, http://www.gwangjubiennale.org/eng/gb/past/intro/?no=1&mode=view&BN _IDX=50&p=1.

9 Angela Harutyunyan, "On the Stage of The Event: The Cairo Seminar in Alexandria; dOCUMENTA (13)," *Contemporary Visual Culture in North Africa and the Middle East* (August 2012), http://www.ibraaz.org/news/32.

10 Ibid.

11 Kant, "Perpetual Peace."

12 Ibid.

13 Dambisa Moyo identifies "the axis of the unloved," in other words, the regions around the world that have been bereft of investment, particularly from Western economies. This means Africa, and also countries in South America, such as Chile and Brazil, and in Eastern Europe, such as Russia and Kazakhstan. See "Dambisa Moyo says China is ahead of the curve in the race for the world's resources," *Africa at LSE* (blog), accessed December 2, 2014, http://blogs.lse.ac.uk/africaatlse/2012/07/03/dambisa-moyo-says-china-is-ahead-of-the-curve-in-the-race-for-the-worlds-resources/.

14 Farquharson, "Institutional Mores."

15 Irit Rogoff, "From Criticism to Critique to Criticality," *eipcp.net. European Institute for Progressive Cultural Policies* (January 2003), http://eipcp.net/transversal/0806/rogoff1/en.

16 "Cosmopolitan right shall be limited to conditions of universal hospitality." Kant, "Perpetual Peace," 329.

Contributors

Beatrice von Bismarck is a professor of art history and visual studies at the Hochschule für Grafik und Buchkunst (HGB) / Academy of Fine Arts Leipzig. She is the initiator and one of the founding members of the postgraduate MA program "Cultures of the Curatorial," which was inaugurated in 2009.

Nanne Buurman is a Leipzig-based art mediator and scholar currently working on her PhD on curatorial authorship at the Freie Universität Berlin, where she was a member of the International Research Training Group "Interart Studies," which is funded by the DFG (German Research Foundation), from 2012 to 2015.

Maja Ćirić is an independent curator and art critic. She is a citizen of Belgrade, Serbia, and the United Transnational Republics (http://transnationalrepublic.org). She received a PhD in art and media theory from the University of Arts in Belgrade, with a dissertation titled "Institutional Critique and Curating."

Alice Creischer and Andreas Siekmann are both artists based in Berlin. Their work focuses mainly on economic and political issues. They work collaboratively and individually as artists, curators, lecturers, and writers and have contributed to many publications, magazines, and fanzines, including, *springerin*, *ANYP*, and *Texte zur Kunst*.

Andrea Fraser is an artist associated with performance and institutional critique. She is Professor of New Genres in the Department of Art, University of California Los Angeles, and is a member of the visiting faculty at the Whitney Independent Study Program, New York.

Lorenzo Fusi is Visiting Academic Curator at the Illingworth Kerr Gallery (Alberta College of Art + Design) in Calgary and Artistic Director of the 46th International Contemporary Art Prize (PIAC 2016), Fondation Prince Pierre de Monaco. He was previously Director of Open Eye Gallery in Liverpool, where he twice curated the Liverpool Biennial (2010 and 2012).

Wiebke Gronemeyer is a curator and researcher based in Hamburg, Germany. In 2015 she graduated with a PhD from Goldsmiths, University of London, with a thesis titled "The Curatorial Complex: Social Dimensions of Knowledge Production." She is a research associate at Jacobs University, Bremen. Information about her research and curatorial practice can be found at www.wiebkegronemeyer.de.

Erik Hagoort is an artist and researcher. He is a tutor on the Master of Fine Art program at St. Joost Academy, Den Bosch/Breda, and teaches "Research Methodologies in the Arts" at the Royal Academy of Fine Arts, Antwerp, where he is currently working on doctoral research in the arts, titled "Resuming Encounters: Sensibility for Asymmetry."

Anthony Huberman has been Director and Chief Curator of CCA Wattis Institute since 2013. He was the founding director of The Artist's Institute in New York.

Thomas Locher is a Berlin-based artist who teaches in Copenhagen. Coming from neo-Conceptualism, he has had a continuous interest in the relationship between subjects and objects, in language and writing, and in textuality and visuality. Over the past couple of years his work has been focused on economic forces through concepts like sharing, gifting, fetishism, and credit.

Benjamin Meyer-Krahmer is a visiting professor of art history and visual studies at the Hochschule für Grafik und Buchkunst (HGB) / Academy of Fine Arts Leipzig. He co-runs the postgraduate MA program "Cultures of the Curatorial" currently with Barbara Steiner.

Dieter Roelstraete is currently a member of the curatorial team for documenta 14 and was formerly the Manilow Senior Curator at the Museum of Contemporary Art Chicago.

Stefan Römer is an artist and art theoretician who lives and works in Berlin. Among other posts he was Professor for Practice and Theory of New Media at the Academy of Fine Arts, Munich (2003–09); Visiting Professor for Creative Writing and Visiting Professor for Design Theory at the Berlin University of the Arts (2010–14).

Jörn Schafaff is an art historian who researches, teaches, and writes about twentieth- and twenty-first-century art. He is a founding member of the postgraduate MA program "Cultures of the Curatorial," inaugurated in 2009 at the Hochschule für Grafik und Buchkunst (HGB) / Academy of Fine Arts Leipzig.

Ruth Sonderegger is Professor of Philosophy and Aesthetic Theory at the Department of Art and Cultural Studies at the Academy of Fine Arts Vienna. From 2007 to 2009 she was Professor of Metaphysics and Its History at the University of Amsterdam.

Image Credits

p. 29: Pierre Huyghe, *Untilled*, 2011–12. Alive entities and inanimate things, made and not made. Dimensions and duration variable. Courtesy of the artist; Marian Goodman Gallery, New York and Paris; Esther Schipper, Berlin. Commissioned and produced by dOCUMENTA (13) with the support of Colección CIAC AC, Mexico; Fondation Louis Vuitton, Paris; Ishikawa Collection, Okayama, Japan.

p. 31: Pierre Huyghe, *Untilled*, 2011–12 (detail). Alive entities and inanimate things, made and not made. Dimensions and duration variable. Courtesy of the artist; Marian Goodman Gallery, New York and Paris; Esther Schipper, Berlin. Commissioned and produced by dOCUMENTA (13) with the support of Colección CIAC AC, Mexico; Fondation Louis Vuitton, Paris; Ishikawa Collection, Okayama, Japan.

p. 81: A seminar with Diedrich Diederichsen, October 29, 2006. Opening weekend: "Histories of Productive Failures: From French Revolution to Manifesta 6," unitednationsplaza, Berlin, October 27-29, 2006. © e-flux.

p. 81: Discussion with Martha Rosler, June 19, 2007. Martha Rosler Library lecture program, unitednationsplaza, Berlin, June 2–August 31, 2007. © e-flux.

p. 82: unitednationsplaza bar: Salon Aleman. A project by Ethan Breckenridge, Julieta Aranda, Eduardo Sarabia, Danna Wajda, Willi Brisco. unitednationsplaza, Berlin, October 27-29, 2006. © e-flux.

p. 83: UNP by day. unitednationsplaza, Berlin, 2006. © e-flux.

p. 83: UNP by night. unitednationsplaza, Berlin, 2006. © e-flux.

pp. 84, 85: A seminar with Liam Gillick, "Five Short Texts on the Possibility of Creating an Economy of Equivalence," May 7–11, 2007. unitednationsplaza, Berlin, 2007. © e-flux.

p. 87: A seminar with Tirdad Zolghadr, "That's Why You Always Find Me in the Kitchen at Parties," March 12-23, 2007. unitednationsplaza, Berlin, 2007. © e-flux.

pp. 90, 91: Interior of UNP by Nikolaus Hirsch and Michel Müller. unitednationsplaza, Berlin, 2006. © e-flux.

p. 102: Louise Lawler, *This Card*, 2000. Invitation to the closing of the exhibition "The Work shown in this space is a response to the existing conditions and/or work previously shown within the space 3," neugerriemschneider, Berlin, 2000. Courtesy of neugerriemschneider, Berlin. © neugerriemschneider, Berlin.

p. 107: Douglas Huebler, *Douglas Huebler: November 1968*, 1968. Advertisement in *Artforum*.

p. 109: Bruce Nauman, *Please/Pay/Attention/Please*, 1973. Collage and letraset, 69.8 × 69.8 cm.

p. 110: Christopher d'Arcangelo, Invitation card to "30 Days Work," 84 West Broadway, New York, 1978-79.

p. 113: "The Work shown in this space is a response to the existing conditions and/or work previously shown within the space 3," neugerriemschneider, Berlin, 2000. Installation views at neugerriemschneider, Berlin, 2000. Courtesy of neugerriemschneider, Berlin.

p. 126: Frontispiece to the first edition of Gertrude Stein's *The Autobiography of Alice B. Toklas* (New York: Harcourt, 1933).

p. 129: Cover of Harald Szeemann, *Museum of Obsessions: by/about/on/with Harald Szeemann*, ed. Peter Gente and Heidi Paris (Berlin: Merve, 1981).

p. 129: Cover of Harald Szeemann, the first edition of Gertrude Stein's *The Autobiography of Alice B. Toklas* (New York: Harcourt, 1933).

p. 134: Man Ray, Gertrude Stein and Alice Toklas in the atelier at 27 rue de Fleurus, Paris, 1922. © Man Ray Trust, Paris / VG Bild-Kunst, Bonn 2016.

p. 135: Diego Velázquez, *Las Meninas*, 1656. Oil on canvas, 318 cm × 276 cm. Prado, Madrid.

p. 138: Pablo Picasso, *Gertrude Stein*, 1906. Oil on canvas, 100 × 81.3 cm. Metropolitan Museum of Art, New York. © Succession Picasso / VG Bild-Kunst, Bonn 2016.

p. 139: Harald Szeemann on the last day of documenta 5, 1972. Photo: Baltasar Burkhard. Source: Szeemann, *Museum of Obsessions*, 174.

p. 152: Rirkrit Tiravanija, *untitled 1994 (meet tim & burkhard)*, 1994. Living room set. Installation view at neugerriemschneider, Berlin, 1994. © neugerriemschneider / Rirkrit Tiravanija Archive Berlin.

p. 156: Rirkrit Tiravanija, still from the video *meet tim & burkhard, 1994*. Installation view at neugerriemschneider, Berlin, 1994. © neugerriemschneider / Rirkrit Tiravanija Archive Berlin.

p. 161: Rirkrit Tiravanija, *untitled 1994 (meet tim & burkhard)*, 1994. Installation view at neugerriemschneider, Berlin, 1994. © neugerriemschneider / Rirkrit Tiravanija Archive Berlin.

p. 193: Stefan Römer, *Mise en Scène*, 2009. Installation view of "Conceptual Paradise: The Studio of Interest," Kunstraum der Leuphana Universität, Lüneburg, December 10, 2009–January 28, 2010. © Stefan Römer.

p. 193: Stefan Römer, installation view of "Conceptual Paradise: The Studio of Interest," Kunstraum der Leuphana Universität, Lüneburg, December 10, 2009–January 28, 2010. © Stefan Römer.

p. 194: Stefan Römer, *Banner 4*, 2009. Installation view of "Conceptual Paradise: The Studio of Interest," Kunstraum der Leuphana Universität, Lüneburg, December 10, 2009–January 28, 2010. © Stefan Römer.

p. 207: Slavs and Tatars, *Hymns of No Resistance*, 2009. Installation view of "The Power to Host," ISCP, Brooklyn, New York, 2011. Photo: Aleksandar Maćašev. Courtesy Aleksandar Maćašev.

p. 210: Installation view of "The Power to Host," ISCP, Brooklyn, New York, 2011. Photo: Aleksandar Maćašev. Courtesy Aleksandar Maćašev.

Cultures of the Curatorial

Hospitality—Hosting Relations in Exhibitions

This book is based on the international conference "Hospitality—Hosting Relations in Exhibitions" held at the Hochschule für Grafik und Buchkunst (HGB) / Academy of Fine Arts Leipzig, December 13–14, 2012.

Published by Sternberg Press and "Cultures of the Curatorial" at the Hochschule für Grafik und Buchkunst (HGB) / Academy of Fine Arts Leipzig.

Editors

Beatrice von Bismarck,
Benjamin Meyer-Krahmer

Managing Editor

Stefan Aue

Copyediting

Joy Beecroft

Translation

Jennifer Bornstein (Creischer / Siekmann), Steven Lindberg (von Bismarck, von Bismarck/Locher, Römer, Schafaff), Amy Patton (Introduction)

Design

Victor Kassis, Surface, Frankfurt am Main / Berlin

Cover

Markus Weisbeck, *Gravitationsmaschine*, 2012. Courtesy of Krome Gallery, Berlin; Kai Middendorff Galerie, Frankfurt am Main. Photo: Das Schmott

Printing

BUD Potsdam

Published with the financial support of the Michael-und-Susanne-Liebelt-Stiftung.

ISBN 978-3-95679-089-8

Kulturen des Kuratorischen an der Hochschule für Grafik und Buchkunst Leipzig
Wächterstraße 11
D-04107 Leipzig
www.kdk-leipzig.de

Sternberg Press
Caroline Schneider
Karl-Marx-Allee 78
D-10243 Berlin
www.sternberg-press.com